US Securities Regulation

A Guidebook for International Companies

Eduardo Vidal and **Jan J H Joosten**

Authors
Eduardo Vidal and Jan JH Joosten

Publisher
Sian O'Neill

Editor
Carolyn Boyle

Marketing manager
Alan Mowat

Production
John Meikle, Russell Anderson

Publishing directors
Guy Davis, Tony Harriss, Mark Lamb

US Securities Regulation: A Guidebook for International Companies
is published by
Globe Law and Business
Globe Business Publishing Ltd
New Hibernia House
Winchester Walk
London SE1 9AG
United Kingdom
Tel +44 20 7234 0606
Fax +44 20 7234 0808
Web www.globelawandbusiness.com

Printed by Antony Rowe Ltd

ISBN 978-1-905783-49-6

Table of contents

Acknowledgements

This book was a collaborative effort by lawyers at our firm, Hughes Hubbard & Reed LLP in New York. First and foremost, the authors of this book must thank our retired partner, Thomas Gilroy, who produced prior versions of this book as a paperback manual over many years. His work provided the foundation for this book. In addition, we thank John Hoyns, co-chairman of the corporate department at our law firm, who unswervingly supported this project from the start, and our colleagues Ellen Friedenberg, Kenneth Katz, William Maguire and Gloria Nusbacher, who reviewed various portions of our manuscript and provided invaluable comments. Finally, we relied on the able assistance of two corporate associates, Jose Bermudez and Kim Natividad, as well as visiting associate Christine Lamsvelt and numerous other associates, for the basic research and writing required to update and supplement the existing work. All errors and omissions, of course, should be attributed solely to the authors.

This book is for informational purposes only and is not intended to be relied upon as legal advice. For more information on the matters discussed in this book, please contact the authors.

1. Introduction

1.1 Background

The US capital markets are the largest and most liquid in the world, and accordingly they attract companies from around the world seeking capital. Those international companies are referred to in the language of the US securities laws as 'foreign private issuers' – that is, non-US issuers of securities from the private sector. Although they are attracted by the abundance and variety of capital available in these markets, they must be prepared to bear the costs of accessing them. These costs include complying with the requirements of US securities laws. While these requirements may seem daunting, they are not insurmountable.

As of mid-2010, approximately 950 foreign private issuers from more than 50 countries were registered with the US Securities and Exchange Commission (SEC). During the period from 2006 to mid-2010, they raised approximately $97.5 billion in the US capital markets through registered public offerings of securities.[1] In addition, during that same period, approximately $1.8 trillion was raised by foreign private issuers through private, unregistered placements of securities in the US capital markets.[2] In the following pages, we set out a guide to the regulation of foreign private issuers in the United States.

The following recent developments in US securities regulations should spark the interest of such issuers:

- amendments to Exchange Act Rule 12g3-2(b), which exempts the securities of qualifying issuers from registration with the SEC, allowing issuers to post the relevant information to their own websites instead of submitting it to the SEC;
- the elimination of the requirement to reconcile financial statements prepared in accordance with International Financial Reporting Standards (IFRS) with generally accepted accounting principles (GAAP) in the United States; and
- the simplification of the rules for deregistering securities from the Exchange Act reporting system and for delisting from a US national securities exchange.

In this book we also explore such controversial new developments as:

- an economic cost-benefit analysis of the Sarbanes-Oxley Act – especially

1 SEC Division of Corporation Finance, International Registered and Reporting Companies Market Summary (December 31 2009); Committee on Capital Markets Regulation, Update Competitiveness Measures Q2 2010 "Relative Size of the Private Rule 144A and Public Equity Markets" (September 22 2010).

2 *US Private Placements Quarterly Review*, Thomson Reuters Deals Intelligence (2006–2010).

Section 404, which mandates internal controls over financial reports;
- the likely consequences of the Dodd-Frank Act, with its estimated 243 rule-making mandates and expansive delegation of authority by Congress to federal regulatory agencies; and
- more aggressive securities law enforcement by the SEC, especially the Foreign Corrupt Practices Act and such proceedings as *SEC v Goldman Sachs*.

This book covers the three types of securities – equity, debt and hybrid – issued in the United States by foreign private issuers that may be either:
- publicly offered after registration with the SEC; or
- privately placed without such registration.

(a) US securities law framework

The SEC is a regulatory agency of the federal government that administers a number of statutes of US securities laws.[3] The two major statutes regulating securities are:
- the Securities Act of 1933, which principally governs capital-raising transactions involving the offer or sale of securities by issuers or underwriters; and
- the Securities Exchange Act of 1934, which principally addresses trading and markets, as well as reporting and other ongoing activities of publicly traded companies and broker/dealers.

On several occasions the US Congress has amended the statutes that comprise the federal securities laws to address perceived problems. Examples of amendatory legislation that are covered in some detail in this book include:
- the Private Securities Litigation Reform Act of 1995;
- the Sarbanes-Oxley Act of 2002; and
- the Dodd-Frank Act of 2010.

In this book we discuss recent developments in US securities laws in the context of a general review of the effects of SEC regulation and practice, with a particular focus on foreign private issuers (as defined below).

US securities laws define 'security' as:

any note, stock, treasury stock, security future, bond, debenture, evidence of indebtedness, certificate of interest or participation in any profit-sharing agreement ..., or any put, call, straddle, option, or privilege entered into on a national securities exchange relating to foreign currency, or, in general, any interest or instrument commonly known as a 'security,' or any certificate of interest or participation in, temporary or interim certificate for, receipt for, guarantee of, or warrant or right to subscribe to or purchase, any of the foregoing.[4]

The US Supreme Court has stated that the definition is "quite broad" and is

---

3 The SEC's website can be found at www.sec.gov. The website contains current and basic materials, including EDGAR filings.

4 Securities Act §2(a)(1).

intended to include "the many types of instruments that in our commercial world fall within the ordinary concept of a security", including "stocks and bonds, along with the countless and variable schemes devised by those that seek the use of the money of others on the promise of profits".[5] Thus, the US securities laws define 'security' in both specific terms (eg, stock, bond, note, debenture) and general terms (eg, any investment contract or "instrument commonly known as a 'security'").

1.2 Regulation of foreign private issuers

(a) Definition

The Securities Act and the Exchange Act use the term 'issuer' to describe any corporation or other person that issues or proposes to issue a security.[6] The regulations under both acts use the term 'foreign private issuer' to describe an issuer that is a citizen of a foreign country or a corporation or other organisation incorporated or organised under the laws of a foreign country (other than the foreign government itself and its political subdivisions).[7]

There is an exception to this definition for any company for which more than 50% of its outstanding voting securities are held by US residents and that either:

- has more than 50% of its assets located in the United States;
- is primarily governed by US officers or directors; or
- is principally administered in the United States.

In any of those cases, such a company is treated as a US domestic issuer. In calculating US resident holdings, shares of record held by brokers and other nominees but owned beneficially by a US resident are counted as owned by a US resident.[8] New SEC rules allow foreign private issuers to assess their status as such once per year on the last business day of their second fiscal quarter.[9]

(b) Advantages of qualifying as a foreign private issuer

There is no general exemption from the US securities laws for foreign private issuers. If their securities are offered or traded in the United States, foreign private issuers need to concern themselves with the relevant laws.

The globalisation of the securities markets has led the SEC to accommodate foreign private issuers in several ways. For example:

- the SEC distinguishes between offshore securities offerings and those that are likely to have an impact on the US securities markets; under Regulation S, offshore offerings are generally exempt from Securities Act registration;
- if a foreign private issuer does not have securities listed on a US national securities exchange and has not registered an offering under the Securities

---

5 *Marine Bank v Weaver*, 455 US 551, 555–556 (1982).
6 Securities Act §2(a)(4); Exchange Act §3(a)(8).
7 Securities Act Rule 405; Exchange Act Rule 3b-4(c).
8 See Securities Act Rule 405 and Exchange Act Rule 3b-4(c) (both referring to Exchange Act Rule 12g3-2(a) for the method of calculating ownership).
9 See SEC Release Nos 33-8959 and 34-58620, "Foreign Issuer Reporting Enhancements" (September 23 2008).

Act, the issuer may be able to avoid entering into the Exchange Act reporting system by making available home-country information on its website under exemptive Rule 12g3-2(b);

- if a foreign private issuer does enter into the Exchange Act reporting system, it may prepare its financial statements in accordance with US GAAP; principles that are generally accepted in its home country, subject to reconciliation to US principles; or IFRS as promulgated by the International Accounting Standards Board. In the latter case, so long as the accompanying auditor's report states that the financial statements are in compliance with IFRS, there is no need for reconciliation to US principles;[10]
- a foreign private issuer has a longer period of time to file its Exchange Act annual reports than its US counterparts;[11]
- a foreign private issuer is exempt from a number of Exchange Act requirements applicable to US reporting companies, including:
  - those contained in the proxy rules;
  - the provisions of Section 16 for reports by officers and directors of their securities transactions and short-swing profit recovery; and
  - current and quarterly interim reporting obligations;[12]
- the SEC provides exemptions from Securities Act registration and the tender offer rules of the Exchange Act for business combinations, acquisitions and other transactions that are essentially foreign – that is, that involve foreign private issuers with limited numbers of US security holders;[13]
- the SEC has revised its foreign private issuer disclosure requirements under the Securities Act and the Exchange Act to conform to the international standards endorsed by the International Organisation of Securities Commissions;[14]
- the SEC has tailored some of its rules to the special circumstances of foreign private issuers and indicated that it would continue to review their situation in its rule-making following the adoption of the Sarbanes-Oxley Act, even though this act did not exempt foreign private issuers from its requirements;
- many provisions for securities disclosure in the newly adopted Dodd-Frank Act expressly exempt or do not apply to foreign private issuers; and

---

10 Form 20-F, Item 17(c). Note, however, that in 2008 the SEC modified Item 17 of Form 20-F to eliminate the option for certain foreign private issuers to omit segment data from their US financial statements (effective for fiscal years ending on or after December 15 2009) and provide a limited reconciliation option with US GAAP (effective for fiscal years ending on or after December 15 2011).
See note 9 above.

11 In 2008, the filing deadline for foreign private issuers was accelerated from six months to four months after fiscal year-end (effective for fiscal years ending on or after December 15 2011). See note 9 and General Instruction A(b) to Form 20-F. For accelerated and large accelerated domestic filers, the deadline is 75 days after fiscal year-end; for non-accelerated domestic filers, it is 90 days. See General Instruction A to Form 10-K.

12 Exchange Act Rule 3a12-3(b) (Proxy statements and Section 16 provisions) (upheld in *Schiller v Tower Semiconductor Ltd*, 449 F3d 286 (2d Circuit June 1 2006)); Exchange Act Rule 13a-11(b) (Current reporting obligations); Exchange Act Rule 13a-13(b) (Interim reporting obligations).

13 SEC Release No 33-7759, "Cross-Border Tender and Exchange Offers, Business Combinations and Rights Offerings" (October 22 1999); SEC Release No 33-8759, "Commission Guidance and Revisions to the Cross-Border Tender Offer, Exchange Offer, Rights Offerings, and Combination Rules and Beneficial Ownership Reporting Rules for Certain Foreign Institutions" (September 19 2008).

14 SEC Release No 33-7745, "International Disclosure Standards" (September 28 1999).

- the SEC recognises that foreign private issuers may make new and different disclosures when they enter the US markets. They are invited to discuss compliance questions with the SEC's Office of International Corporate Finance if they plan to offer securities in the United States or plan to list on a US national securities exchange.[15]

1.3 Becoming subject to US securities regulation

A foreign private issuer may become subject to the same ongoing reporting requirements of the US federal securities laws as a US company:

- It may engage (or its existing security holders may engage) in a public offering of securities in the United States that requires registration under the Securities Act.
- It may have its securities listed on a US national securities exchange and, as a consequence, have to register the securities under the Exchange Act.
- It may have to register under the Exchange Act if its equity securities become owned by a sufficient number of US investors and its assets exceed a certain threshold, unless it invokes the special foreign private issuer exemption of Rule 12g3-2(b).

Following any such Securities Act or Exchange Act registration, the issuer will enter into and remain indefinitely in the Exchange Act's periodic reporting system until suspension or deregistration.[16]

(a) Securities Act of 1933

As mentioned above, the Securities Act[17] regulates the offer and sale of securities in public transactions. Speaking broadly, an issuer's offer or sale of its securities to the public in the United States requires:

- the filing of a registration statement (which includes a prospectus) with the SEC under the Securities Act;
- clearance of the registration statement by the staff of the SEC (unless review is dispensed with by the staff or by SEC rule); and
- distribution of a prospectus that contains extensive business and financial information regarding the issuer.

SEC rules specifically prescribe the contents of the registration statement and prospectus.[18]

Registration of a public offering under the Securities Act subjects the issuer to the periodic reporting requirements of the Exchange Act, thus essentially continuing the type of public disclosure required in a Securities Act registration statement and prospectus.[19]

---

15 SEC, Division of Corporation Finance: International Reporting and Disclosure Issues, III-B (May 1 2001).
16 See the section on deregistration and delisting in "Periodic reporting requirements".
17 15 USC §77a *et seq.*
18 See "Public offerings".
19 Exchange Act §15(d). See "Public offerings" and "Periodic reporting requirements".

There are a number of exemptions from the requirement to register US securities offerings under the Securities Act. Some apply to certain types of securities (eg, commercial paper that meets certain standards)[20] and others apply to certain types of transactions, listed here:

- Private placements – a major transactional exemption for issuers is the so-called 'private offering' or 'private placement' exemption, which accounts for a large portion of US securities transactions. In such a transaction, a group of sophisticated investors (eg, insurance companies, investment funds, banks and other institutions) may be treated as private (ie, non-public) investors that do not need the protection of the Securities Act; and an offering confined to such a group – if not accompanied by any general solicitation or general advertising – need not be registered.[21]
- Rule 144A – offerings through securities firms, acting as initial purchasers, that are directed at 'qualified institutional buyers' are specifically exempted from Securities Act registration by the SEC's Rule 144A.[22]
- Offers to employees – the offer and sale of securities to employees by an issuer is not subject to the reporting requirements of the Exchange Act.[23]

An issuer making an exempt offering does not automatically become subject to the periodic reporting provisions of the Exchange Act, as would be the case with an issuer making a registered public offering.

The acquisition of a publicly held company made, in whole or in part, through shares of a foreign private issuer constitutes an offering to any US shareholders of the acquired company and, depending on the number of US shareholders, may require registration under the Securities Act.[24] As discussed in "International offerings with US participants", certain M&A transactions involving foreign private issuers whose US shareholders do not hold more than 10% of the subject class (as calculated in accordance with the SEC's rules) are exempt from Securities Act registration. The acquisition of a closely held US company for shares of a foreign private issuer may also constitute an offer to the public and require registration under the Securities Act. However, these transactions can frequently be structured as a private offering. The observations made above about becoming subject to the Exchange Act reporting requirements apply here too.

There are two circumstances under which a sale to the public by an existing holder of an issuer's securities (a so-called 'secondary offering') may require registration under the Securities Act, similarly to a 'primary' public offering. Unless exempted under the conditions discussed in "Private placements" below:

- registration will be required where such public sale is made by an affiliate of the issuer – that is, a person who "controls, or is controlled by, or is under common control with" the issuer;[25] and

20 Securities Act §3(a)(3).
21 See "Private placements".
22 See "Private placements".
23 See "American depositary receipts".
24 Securities Act Rule 145 Preliminary Notes.

- the sale must be registered if the holder acquired the securities in an unregistered transaction from the issuer (or an affiliate) with a view to their distribution to the public – even if the selling security holder is not an affiliate of the issuer – thus making the seller an underwriter within the broad definition of that term in the Securities Act.

Any such registration would involve an issuer registration statement identical, with regard to issuer business and financial disclosure, to a registration statement for an issuer public offering, and would similarly subject a non-reporting issuer to the Exchange Act reporting system.

(b) Securities Exchange Act of 1934

As mentioned above, the Exchange Act[26] governs the secondary trading of securities after their initial issuance and offering. Issuers become subject to the reporting requirements of the act in three principal ways:

- through a registered public offering under the Securities Act;
- by listing a class of securities on a national securities exchange; or
- by exceeding a certain threshold number of equity security holders and total assets.

Securities Act registration: Registration of a public offering of securities under the Securities Act requires the issuer to enter the Exchange Act reporting system by also registering under that act.

Listing on national securities exchanges: An issuer wishing to list a class of its securities on a US national securities exchange, such as the New York Stock Exchange or NASDAQ Stock Market, must register the security under the Exchange Act by filing the appropriate registration statement with the SEC.[27] Although an Exchange Act registration statement is not the same as the registration statement required by the Securities Act in connection with an issuer's public offering and is not distributed in the fashion of an offering prospectus, it contains comparable business and financial information, is subject to SEC staff review and is publicly available. If filed at or about the time of a public offering under the Securities Act, it is often simplified by the incorporation of required business and financial information by reference to the Securities Act registration statement.

An Exchange Act registration will subject the issuer to the ongoing periodic reporting requirements of that act,[28] if it has not already become subject to such requirements through Securities Act registration. In addition, listing will bring the issuer under various requirements of the exchange on which it lists.

The conditions to a foreign private issuer listing on a US national securities

---

25 See "Securities litigation risks" below for a brief discussion of control in the context of securities litigation.
26 15 USC §78a *et seq.*
27 Exchange Act §12(b); Exchange Act Regulation 12B (Rules 12b-1 – 12b-37).
28 Exchange Act §13(a).

exchange will depend upon meeting the eligibility requirements of the particular exchange. Typically, these will include having a minimum number of publicly held shares and meeting specified financial criteria.[29]

Exceeding the threshold number of equity security holders: Even if an issuer has never registered an offering under the Securities Act and has not listed its securities on a US national securities exchange, it may have accumulated a number of shareholders that is sizeable enough to require Exchange Act registration under a separate provision of that act.

The Exchange Act requires the registration of an equity security of a foreign private issuer if:

- the class of security is held by at least 500 persons, of whom at least 300 are resident in the United States;[30] and
- the issuer has more than $10 million in total assets.[31]

The application to register must be filed within 120 days of the end of the first fiscal year in which the issuer reaches the threshold.[32] In calculating whether there are 300 or more US holders, a foreign private issuer must include US resident beneficial owners of shares held of record by nominees.[33] Unregistered resales of equity securities that are originally issued outside the United States or are in private or other exempt offerings within the United States may in time result in a foreign private issuer reaching this 300-holder level, especially where significant US market interest in the issuer develops.

A foreign private issuer may invoke exemptive Exchange Act Rule 12g3-2(b)[34] to avoid such registration and subsequent Exchange Act reporting obligations. Under this exemption, the issuer is required to make public electronically an English language version of its home country reports in lieu of filing periodic Exchange Act reports with the SEC.

If a foreign private issuer does not resort to Rule 12g3-2(b), Exchange Act registration and subsequent periodic reporting requirements will be the same as where a class of security is issued in a registered public offering or listed on a US national securities exchange.

(c) Sarbanes-Oxley Act of 2002

In late 2001 Enron Corp – a US issuer that ranked among the largest of all companies

---

29 See "Public offerings" for more information.

30 The relevant type of ownership for purposes of this requirement is shareholder of record ownership. The SEC defines 'of record' to mean securities held by each person who is identified as the owner of such securities on records of security holders maintained by or on behalf of the issuer. In most companies shares are held by brokers for the benefit of their clients, which means that only the brokers are considered shareholders of record. However, note that the definition of 'record holder' also states that if the company knows or has reason to know that the form of holding securities of record is used primarily to circumvent the provisions of the Securities Act, the beneficial owners of such securities shall be deemed to be the record owners thereof. Securities Act Rule 12g5-1.

31 Exchange Act §12(g); Exchange Act Rules 12g-1 and 12g3-2.

32 Exchange Act §12(g).

33 Exchange Act Rules 12g3-2(a) and 12g5-1.

34 See "Periodic reporting requirements" for more discussion of this rule.

in terms of market capitalisation – announced that it was restating its previously published financial statements to make a number of major corrections, including:

- the consolidation of affiliated entities whose accounts had (erroneously) not previously been consolidated with those of Enron;
- the consequent recognition on Enron's consolidated balance sheet of the indebtedness of these affiliated entities; and
- a reduction in the amounts of previously reported Enron earnings and stockholders' equity.[35]

Following a precipitous decline in the company's stock price and a downgrading in the ratings of its debt securities, Enron declared bankruptcy in December 2001.

Enron's bankruptcy was followed by further major corporate collapses that were attributed to improper accounting and failure to discharge financial reporting responsibilities. In June 2002 WorldCom, Inc announced a restatement of its financial statements, transforming reported profits into losses and ultimately involving $76 billion in adjustments. The company filed for bankruptcy the next month.[36] Arthur Andersen, then one of the world's major public accounting firms, which had audited both Enron and WorldCom, disintegrated in the face of aggressive prosecution following these collapses and was criminally convicted in 2002.[37] This conviction was eventually overturned by the US Supreme Court in 2005.[38]

In the ensuing investigations of these and other disclosure shortcomings, the accounting profession and the SEC came in for criticism, along with financial analysts, lawyers, rating agencies, independent or 'outside' directors of corporations and others who are commonly thought to ensure reliable corporate reporting.

The US Congress responded to the Enron and WorldCom accounting scandals by adopting the Sarbanes-Oxley Act in 2002.[39] In recent years this act has come under much criticism for imposing excessive disclosure requirements, especially Section 404, which concerns internal controls over financial reporting.

Applicability to foreign private issuers: The Sarbanes-Oxley Act covers the following areas:

- Enhanced disclosures – specific requirements for textual disclosure by reporting companies have been added or strengthened.
- Auditor independence – audit firms are prohibited from performing specified non-audit services for an audit client and are required to rotate partners and expand the scope of their dealings with the issuer's audit committee.
- Audit committee responsibilities – audit committees of issuers listed on a national securities exchange have to meet heightened committee

35 Enron Corp (SEC File No 1-13159): 8-K Report (November 8 2001); 10-Q Report (for the period ended September 30 2001).

36 *In re WorldCom Inc Securities Litigation*, 346 F Supp 2d 628 (SDNY 2004).

37 See "Indicting Corporations Revisited: Lessons of the Arthur Andersen Prosecution", American College of Trial Lawyers (February 7 2006).

38 *Arthur Andersen LLP v United States*, 544 US 696 (2005).

39 Public Law 107-204, 116 Stat. 745 (2002).

independence standards, directly supervise the auditor and adopt certain prescribed procedures.[40]

- Management responsibility for internal controls – management is required to submit an annual report that affirms its responsibility for internal control over financial reporting and evaluates the effectiveness of its internal controls. The issuer's auditor must issue an attestation report regarding management's evaluation.
- Individual responsibilities – the chief executive officer and chief financial officer of issuers must sign personal certifications as to the truth of the periodic Exchange Act reports; these then become part of that report. Legal personnel are subject to internal reporting obligations with respect to certain violations of law and breaches of fiduciary duties.
- Prohibited activities – certain types of activities that were criticised in connection with Enron and other corporate collapses, such as maintaining contingent obligations off balance sheet, are prohibited or penalised.
- Whistleblower protection – employees who provide information to, or assist in a fraud investigation by, their supervisor, a federal regulatory agency or a member of Congress are protected from retaliation, such as being discharged, suspended, threatened or harassed.

The Sarbanes-Oxley Act applies to the following two groups of issuers:

- those that have entered into the Exchange Act reporting system; and
- those that are registering a public offering under the Securities Act.

Sarbanes-Oxley makes no distinction between US and foreign private issuers.[41] The SEC's rules in these areas are therefore applicable to foreign private issuers that are both Exchange Act reporting companies or are registering a US securities offering. However, the SEC has refined the rules in several respects to accommodate the special concerns of foreign private issuers and maintain the competitiveness of the US capital markets.[42]

Notwithstanding, since 2002 the SEC has also passed new amendments aimed at bringing disclosure requirements for foreign private issuers closer to those required for domestic issuers. For example, the SEC approved new disclosure requirements for the annual Exchange Act reports of foreign private issuers on Form 20-F,[43] including those regarding:

- significant differences in corporate governance practices from those applicable to US companies under stock exchange rules;
- changes in the issuer's certifying accountants;
- fees and charges paid by holders of American depositary receipts (ADRs) to depositaries, and any payments made by depositaries to foreign private issuers; and
- segment data in financial statements.[44]

---

40 See also the section on listing on national securities exchanges in "Public offerings".
41 Sarbanes-Oxley Act §2(a)(7).
42 For more see the section on the Sarbanes-Oxley Act in "Periodic reporting requirements" below.
43 SEC Release Nos 33-8959 and 34-58620, "Foreign Issuer Reporting Enhancements" (September 23 2008).

Additionally, Form 20-F requires financial statements to be audited using US standards, which include auditor independence.[45]

Considering the continuing reach of globalisation and the increased interest of US investors in foreign securities, it would not be surprising to see the SEC continue to level the disclosure requirements for both foreign and domestic issuers.

The Public Company Accounting Oversight Board: The Sarbanes-Oxley Act established a new Public Company Accounting Oversight Board to oversee the audit of public companies that are subject to the US federal securities laws:[46] The SEC was given oversight and enforcement authority over the oversight board, including the power to appoint its members and to approve the board's rules.[47] The constitutionality of this power was challenged. In June 2010 the Supreme Court ruled that the appointments provision of the Sarbanes-Oxley Act was constitutional, but that the board's members could be removed by the SEC for any reason, not just for good cause.[48]

One of the board's principal responsibilities was to establish a system for the registration of all public accounting firms – both US and foreign – that audit issuers which report under the Exchange Act or register a public offering under the Securities Act.[49] The board is authorised to adopt auditing standards that must be met by registered public accounting firms and quality control standards with respect to the issuance of audit reports.[50]

In July 2010 the board proposed amending the current auditing standards, written in the early 1990s, to update the process of obtaining confirmation in the auditing process.[51] The new standards would explicitly incorporate the risk of material misstatement due to error or fraud into the design of confirmation procedures.

The International Organisation of Securities Commissioners and other foreign regulators reacted to Enron-like accounting scandals by establishing, in February 2005, an international board to oversee the setting of auditing standards by the accounting profession. This Public Interest Oversight Board does not have the Public Company Accounting Oversight Board's powers of direct supervision and enforcement over auditing firms, but oversees and evaluates the work of several boards of the International Federation of Accountants.[52]

(d) Dodd-Frank Act of 2010

The Dodd-Frank Act[53] was promulgated by Congress in response to the global credit

44 See Items 16G, 16F, 12.D.3, and 17 of Exchange Act Form 20-F.
45 Form 20-F, General Instruction E(c)(3).
46 Sarbanes-Oxley Act §101.
47 Sarbanes-Oxley Act §107.
48 *Free Enterprise Fund v Public Company Accounting Oversight Board*, 130 S Ct 3138 (2010).
49 Sarbanes-Oxley Act §102.
50 Sarbanes-Oxley Act §103.
51 Press Release, Public Company Account Oversight Board, "PCAOB Proposes New Auditing Standard on Confirmation" (July 13 2010).
52 See Public Interest Oversight Board, "PIOB Mandate", available at www.ipiob.org.
53 Public Law 111-203, 124 Stat 1376 (2010).

crisis that began in 2007. It was signed into law by President Obama on July 21 2010. Its provisions are all-encompassing and affect many, if not all, aspects of the regulation of the financial services industry in the United States.

While the act contains a general framework for financial services industry regulation, most authority over the content, details and implementation of the law has been delegated by Congress to US federal regulatory agencies, including some agencies newly formed by the act.

Estimates indicate that the Dodd-Frank Act will require 243 rule-makings and 67 studies by 10 different federal regulatory agencies, as well as by the US Department of the Treasury.[54] This means that there will be continuing uncertainty about the implications of the act as it is phased in. Furthermore, banks and other financial institutions have launched a lobbying offensive in an attempt to influence the content of the final rules, and there will be heightened concern about unintended consequences given the complexity of the law and its implementation.[55]

While the Dodd-Frank Act focuses on regulating US companies and financial institutions, foreign private issuers are subject to certain of its provisions and expressly exempt from others and may be subject to certain other provisions if the SEC so provides in future rule-makings. Furthermore, foreign financial institutions that do business in the United States through branches, agencies or bank subsidiaries are generally subject to the same rules as comparable US bank holding companies.[56] The following is a summary of some noteworthy provisions included in the act.

Extraterritorial application: The Dodd-Frank Act does not contain a clear description of its jurisdictional reach. Some provisions acknowledge the possibility of extraterritorial application, while others are US-focused or silent on the jurisdictional question. However, the act requires that in the case of a foreign financial institution or foreign non-bank financial institution predominantly engaged in financial activities in the United States,[57] regulators must take into account:

- the principle of national treatment in allowing equality of competitive opportunity; and
- the extent to which a foreign entity is subject to regulation at home.

In practice, this may mean that US regulators will consult with a foreign country's regulatory authorities before imposing any standards on their financial institutions under Dodd-Frank. In addition, the act provides that the new US

54 "The Uncertainty Principle", *The Wall Street Journal* (July 14 2010).

55 "Lobbying Picks Up as Finance Rules Are Written", *The Wall Street Journal* (September 2 2010).

56 Section 211.21(o) of the Federal Reserve Board's Regulation K defines a 'foreign banking organisation' as a foreign bank that:
- operates a branch, agency or commercial lending subsidiary in the United States;
- controls a bank in the United States; or
- controls a corporation under the Edge Act amendment to the Federal Reserve Act of 1913, which is acquired after March 5 1987.

Any company of which the foreign bank is a subsidiary is also included under this definition.

57 A non-bank financial institution is considered to be predominantly engaged in financial activities if 85% or more of the consolidated assets or revenues are derived from financial activities defined in Section 4(k) of the Bank Holding Company Act of 1956.

Financial Stability Oversight Council and the US Federal Reserve Board will generally regulate only the US activities and subsidiaries of foreign financial institutions.

The extent to which the act will affect foreign financial institutions therefore remains unclear. The landscape is further complicated by the *Morrison v National Australia Bank Ltd*[58] decision handed down by the US Supreme Court a month before Dodd-Frank was signed into law. In the *Morrison* case, the court emphasised the importance of the canon of statutory interpretation. This states that, in the absence of clear congressional intent, a US statute will be interpreted to apply only within the jurisdiction of the United States. However, Dodd-Frank overturns *Morrison* to the extent that it applies to the SEC, and allows the SEC to have jurisdiction over a matter brought under the anti-fraud provisions of the Exchange Act and Investment Advisers Act of 1940 if the matter involves:

- conduct within the United States that constitutes significant steps in furtherance of the violation, even if the securities transaction occurs outside the United States and involves only foreign investors; or
- conduct outside the Unites States that has a foreseeable substantial effect within the United States.[59]

Financial Stability and Oversight Council: A major cornerstone of the Dodd-Frank Act is the overhaul of the role of US federal regulatory agencies in the supervision and regulation of financial institutions. The act creates a new regulatory agency, the Financial Stability and Oversight Council, to:

- identify risks to US financial stability that may arise from:
  - the material financial distress or failure, or the ongoing activities, of large, interconnected bank holding companies or non-bank financial institutions; or
  - risks that arise outside the financial services marketplace;
- promote market discipline by eliminating stockholder, creditor and counterparty expectations that the US federal government will shield them from losses in the event of the failure of a bank holding company or non-bank financial institution; and
- respond to emerging threats to the stability of the US financial system.

The council will consist of 15 members, 10 of whom will have voting rights. All will be appointed by the US president. The 10 voting members will consist of the US treasury secretary, who will act as the chairman of the council, the heads of eight US regulatory agencies (including the SEC and the Federal Reserve) and an independent member with insurance expertise.

The council is authorised to determine which domestic or foreign non-bank financial institutions, which financial activities of domestic or foreign non-financial institutions and which financial market utilities and payment, clearance and settlement activities are systemically important. It is also authorised to require the

58 *Morrison v National Australia Bank*, 130 S Ct 2869 (2010).
59 Dodd-Frank Act §929P(b).

supervision and regulation of these systemically significant financial institutions and their activities by the Federal Reserve. The council may also make recommendations to the Federal Reserve concerning the establishment and refinement of more stringent prudential standards for both systemically and non-systemically significant financial institutions, taking into consideration their capital structures, riskiness, complexity, financial activities, size and any other risk-related factors the council deems appropriate.

The council may also request a variety of reports, including:

- periodic or other reports from any non-bank financial institution or bank holding company. These may be used for the purpose of assessing the extent to which a company, or the financial activity or market in which it participates, poses a threat to US financial stability; and
- certified reports from significant financial institutions and their subsidiaries. These may concern the financial condition of the institution, the systems for monitoring and controlling risks, transactions with any subsidiaries of depositary institutions, or the extent to which the institution's or its subsidiaries' activities and operations, under adverse circumstances, have the potential to disrupt financial markets or affect the overall financial stability of the United States.

Financial Stability and Oversight Council and foreign institutions: The Financial Stability and Oversight Council's recommendations and activities apply to foreign institutions, but the Dodd-Frank Act provides that, in making recommendations that affect foreign institutions, the council must:

- give due regard to the principle of national treatment and equality of competitive opportunity; and
- take into account the extent to which the foreign financial institution is subject, on a consolidated basis, to home country standards that are comparable to the standards applied to US financial institutions.

Systemically significant financial institutions: The Dodd-Frank Act subjects 'systemically significant' financial institutions to enhanced regulation by the Federal Reserve, aimed at enhancing the supervision and regulation of these institutions and reducing the risk they present. The act's definition of a 'systemically significant financial institution' includes foreign financial institutions that have operations in the United States or that own US entities under the following circumstances:

- Foreign bank holding companies – the foreign financial institution owns a US bank or is deemed to be a bank holding company under the International Banking Act of 1978 if it operates a branch, agency or commercial lending subsidiary in the United States with total consolidated assets of at least $50 billion. Foreign financial institutions that fall under this category are automatically subject to the enhanced supervision of the Federal Reserve.
- Foreign non-bank financial institutions – the Federal Reserve may also designate a foreign financial institution as systemically significant subject to its supervision if the institution is predominately engaged in financial

activities and the Financial Stability and Oversight Council recommends to the Federal Reserve that, due to its nature, size, scope, scale or concentration, or interconnectedness or mix of activities, it should be designated as systemically significant.

Bank capital requirements: Under the Dodd-Frank Act, US banking agencies must set minimum leverage capital and risk-based capital requirements for insured depositary institutions, depositary institution holding companies, thrift holding companies, some US intermediate bank or thrift holding companies of foreign banking institutions and non-bank systemically significant financial institutions.

The Volcker Rule: The Dodd-Frank Act prohibits certain banking entities, and their affiliates and subsidiaries, from engaging in proprietary trading and from acquiring or retaining any ownership interest in, or sponsoring, a hedge fund or private equity fund. This is known as the 'Volcker Rule'. Included in the definition of 'banking entities' are foreign banks that have a branch, agency or commercial lending subsidiary in the United States. Under the Volcker Rule, foreign banks may engage in proprietary trading, but only if it occurs solely outside the United States. The Volcker Rule may scale back the powers traditionally granted to foreign banks to engage in US activities, such as proprietary trading, that are incidental to the foreign bank's business outside the United States.[60]

Other regulatory agencies: Under the Dodd-Frank Act, the authority of the Federal Reserve is expanded so that it now has regulatory authority over entities previously outside of its reach, including systemically significant financial institutions. In consultation with the Financial Stability and Oversight Council, the Federal Reserve now has authority to establish prudential standards for systemically significant financial institutions that are more stringent than those applied to other financial institutions.

The act also creates several new regulatory agencies in addition to the Financial Stability and Oversight Council:

- The Financial Insurance Office, within the US Treasury, will monitor all aspects of the insurance industry, which is currently regulated by the states.
- The Office of Financial Research, also within the US Treasury, will collect data, perform research and develop risk measurement and monitoring tools, and will also have the right to subpoena affected institutions (ie, systemically significant financial institutions and any other institutions designated by the Federal Reserve) to produce data and information.
- The Bureau of Consumer Financial Protection, within the Federal Reserve, will be dedicated to monitoring and enforcing consumer protection laws and ensuring that US consumers have access to clear and reliable information when selecting financial products such as mortgages, credit cards and so on.

---

60 Dodd-Frank Act §619.

Securities litigation and enforcement: The Dodd-Frank Act provides both the SEC and private litigants with a greater ability to pursue perceived securities law violations. The act expands the categories of actors and actions potentially subject to liability, and adds penalties for securities law violations, such as for aiding and abetting violations of the Securities Act, the Investment Company Act of 1940 and the Investment Advisers Act. The SEC may now bring enforcement actions based on a 'recklessness' standard, rather than the higher 'knowledge' standard previously in place.

The Dodd-Frank Act also strengthens incentives and protections for whistleblowers. Protections are expanded to employees of consolidated subsidiaries and affiliates of publicly listed companies, and the new incentives include payment to whistleblowers who voluntarily bring original information of securities law violations to the SEC that leads to a successful enforcement action and a monetary sanction in excess of $1 million, in an amount of 10% to 30% of the monetary penalty recovered by the regulators.[61] This bounty programme applies not only to financial institutions, but also to all companies that are subject to US securities laws, including foreign private issuers. The SEC has received a vast number of comment letters that are critical of this proposed programme. A main concern is that this programme creates an incentive for employees to bypass their companies' internal compliance programmes by turning directly to the SEC, with hopes of walking away with a handsome reward.[62]

Additionally, as discussed above, the act extends the extraterritorial reach of actions by the United States or the SEC under anti-fraud provisions of federal securities laws. US courts have jurisdiction where an action involves either:

- conduct within the United States that constitutes significant steps in furtherance of a violation, even where the securities transaction occurs abroad or involves only foreign investors; or
- conduct outside the United States that has a substantial effect within the country.

As discussed above, the recent US Supreme Court decision in *Morrison v National Australia Bank Ltd* narrowed the SEC's ability to bring actions under Section 10(b) of the Exchange Act by confirming that this section and Rule 10b-5 do not apply extraterritorially. However, the Dodd-Frank Act explicitly states that enforcement actions by the SEC are not subject to the restrictive *Morrison* test, which focused solely on whether the security purchased or sold was a US security, or whether the purchase or sale occurred in the United States.[63]

Additionally, the Dodd-Frank Act contains two major criminal provisions relating to enforcement:

- a provision suggesting that the US Sentencing Commission recommend increased sentences in the context of securities and mortgage fraud convictions; and

61 See, for example, Dodd-Frank Act §§922-924.
62 Dodd-Frank Act §922.
63 Dodd-Frank Act §929.

- a provision increasing the statute of limitations for securities fraud prosecutions from five to six years.[64]

Swaps and derivatives: The Dodd-Frank Act provides for new federal regulation of the swaps market and gives the US Commodities Futures Trading Commission and the SEC broad authority to regulate the swaps market and its principal participants. A key component of this expanded regulation is that it allows the continued existence of an over-the-counter market in non-standardised swaps, but subjects it to margin, capital and reporting requirements.

The provisions of the act that deal with the derivatives trading activities of foreign entities do not specifically provide for an exemption for these types of entities. Those foreign entities that qualify as swap dealers and major swap participants will be subject to the Dodd-Frank Act. However, the extent to which the swap and derivatives trading activities of foreign entities conducted outside the US with foreign counterparties will be subject to regulation has yet to be determined by federal regulators.

Revisions to the Exchange Act relating to security-based swaps do not apply to "any person transact[ing] a business in security-based swaps without the jurisdiction of the United States, unless such person transacts such business in contravention of such rules and regulations as the [SEC] may prescribe as necessary or appropriate to prevent the evasion of any [Exchange Act] provision" added by the Dodd-Frank Act.[65]

Further, the Dodd-Frank Act provisions relating to non-security-based swaps do not apply to activities outside the United States, unless those activities:

- have a direct and significant connection with activities in, or effect on, commerce in the United States; or
- contravene such rules or regulations as the Commodities Futures Trading Commission may prescribe or promulgate as are necessary or appropriate to prevent the evasion of any provision of the Commodities Exchange Act added by the Dodd-Frank Act.

Additionally, if either the SEC or the Commodities Futures Trading Commission determines that the regulation of swaps in a foreign country undermines the stability of the US financial system, the federal agency may prohibit foreign institutions based in that country from participating in any swap activity in the United States.

Private equity and hedge funds: The Dodd-Frank Act removes the 'private investment adviser' exemption from the Investment Advisers Act, requiring that investment advisers to certain US and foreign private funds register with the SEC. As a result, a substantial number of foreign advisers with US investor clients are now subject to regulation under the Investment Advisers Act and will be required to register with the SEC.

64 Dodd-Frank Act §1079A(a)-(b).
65 Dodd-Frank Act §772(b).

Corporate governance and executive compensation: The Dodd-Frank Act contains a number of provisions related to corporate governance and executive compensation. The most significant of them are as follows:

- Proxy rules – the Dodd-Frank Act requires shareholder advisory votes on executive compensation[66] and imposes new disclosure requirements in company proxy statements.[67] The act also authorises the SEC to adopt 'proxy access' rules that make the company's proxy solicitation materials available for shareholder nominations of directors.[68] All of these provisions were adopted as amendments to the proxy rules, from which foreign private issuers are exempt, and as such they will not apply to foreign private issuers. However, there is one executive compensation disclosure that, as a technical matter, is not limited to proxy statements and could thus be applied to foreign private issuers unless the SEC uses its exemption authority to exclude them.[69]
- Compensation committees – the Dodd-Frank Act requires that all members of any publicly listed company's compensation committee be independent, under a definition of 'independence' determined by its national securities exchange. Foreign private issuers are expressly exempted from this requirement, so long as they provide annual disclosure about why they do not have an independent compensation committee.[70]
- Compensation consultants – the Dodd-Frank Act requires national securities exchanges to adopt listing standards providing that compensation committees are authorised to retain compensation consultants, independent legal counsel and other advisers. The act also requires the SEC to define independence standards for such consultants, counsel and advisers, and requires compensation committees to take these standards into account before retaining consultants or advisers. However, the act does not prohibit the retention of non-independent consultants or advisers. Foreign private issuers listed in the United States are not expressly exempted from these requirements, but the SEC and national securities exchanges are given broad power to exempt institutions. The New York Stock Exchange and NASDAQ have exempted foreign private issuers from most, but not all, of their corporate governance listing standards adopted in the Sarbanes-Oxley era to the extent that the listing standards differ from the company's home country standards, if those differences are disclosed in the company's annual report on Form 20-F.[71]
- Clawbacks – the Dodd-Frank Act requires national securities exchanges to adopt listing standards requiring listed companies to adopt and implement a clawback policy under which the company would recover incentive-based

---

66 Dodd-Frank Act §951.
67 Dodd-Frank Act §§953(a), 955, and 972.
68 Dodd-Frank Act §971.
69 This is the requirement to disclose the ratio of the median compensation of all employees to that of the chief executive officer, as provided in Section 953(b) of the Dodd-Frank Act.
70 Dodd-Frank Act §952.
71 NYSE Listed Company Manual, §303A.00; NASDAQ Stock Market Listing Rules, §5615(a)(3) and IM-5615-3.

compensation received by current or former executive officers if the company was required to prepare an accounting restatement.[72] The amount to be recovered would be the amount of any incentive-based compensation received by the officer in the three years before the restatement, to the extent that it exceeds the amount that would have been payable under the financial statements as restated. Listed companies are also required to disclose their policies regarding incentive-based compensation based on financial information. Foreign private issuers listed in the United States are not expressly exempted from these requirements, but the SEC and national securities exchanges have the power to exempt them.

- Discretionary voting by brokers – the Dodd-Frank Act requires that all US stock exchanges prohibit voting of shares held in street name without instructions from the beneficial owner in any vote with respect to the election of directors or executive compensation. The act also authorises the SEC or an individual national securities exchange to extend the scope of this prohibition to other matters.[73] Given that this provision is directed at the conduct of brokers who are members of a US stock exchange, it will affect all companies that have securities registered under the Exchange Act that have some of their shares held in street name by a US broker, regardless of whether the company is itself listed on a US exchange. It is not yet clear what applicability and effect this provision will have with respect to foreign private issuers.

Other provisions: Other provisions of the Dodd-Frank Act that are worth mentioning are as follows:

- Securitisation – the Dodd-Frank Act requires federal regulators to issue rules requiring issuers and sponsors of certain asset-backed securities transactions and collateralised loan obligations to retain at least 5% of the credit risk of the assets transferred in connection with the securitisation. Until federal regulators issue these new securitisation rules, the extent to which they will apply to foreign issuers is unclear. However, it is anticipated that they are intended to apply to any issuance of asset-backed securities available to US investors.
- Taxpayer bailouts – the Dodd-Frank Act provides that taxpayers will not be called upon to aid ailing financial institutions or pay for their liquidation in the event of failure. Likewise, other provisions of the act seek to provide for the monitoring of the size of financial institutions, in an attempt to avoid a situation where financial institutions grow too big to fail.
- Additional disclosure – the Dodd-Frank Act imposes new Exchange Act disclosure obligations relating to the extraction and use of natural resources. Mining companies are required to provide information regarding violations of mine safety requirements.[74] Companies engaged in the commercial

---

72 Dodd-Frank Act §954.
73 Dodd-Frank Act §957.
74 Dodd-Frank Act §1503.

development of oil, natural gas or minerals are required to disclose information with respect to payments made to various governments in connection with such development.[75] The act requires additional disclosures if certain minerals (defined as 'conflict minerals') are "necessary to the functionality or production" of products manufactured by that issuer. The issuer must disclose whether the specified minerals used in its products originated in the Democratic Republic of the Congo or an adjoining country and, if so, must provide information (which must be audited in accordance with standards to be established by regulation) regarding the source and chain of custody of the minerals, including whether they directly or indirectly finance armed groups in those countries.[76] All of these disclosure provisions appear to apply to all issuers that file Exchange Act reports, including foreign private issuers.

International policy coordination: The Dodd-Frank Act provides that the Financial Stability Oversight Council, the Federal Reserve and the US Treasury must consult with foreign governments, foreign regulatory authorities and other international organisations in setting policy. It also gives the US president discretionary authority to coordinate domestic law with international policy. These provisions provide a mechanism through which international input may play a role in setting US regulatory policy.

Conclusion: Considering that the global credit crisis that began in 2007 was primarily caused by US public policies of easy money, subprime lending and moral hazard, the Dodd-Frank Act constitutes a curious regulatory response. Regulators, including the SEC and the Federal Reserve, failed to see the consequences of their regulations. Yet the Federal Reserve – which, with its easy money policy, was the principal contributor to the crisis – was rewarded with increased regulatory authority. Similarly, the subprime lending promoted by Fannie Mae, Freddie Mac and related institutions and policies is not addressed at all by this act. Finally, the moral hazard of further bailouts remains a distinct possibility, especially by regulators eager to alleviate prior misjudgements. For example, since 2008 the Federal Reserve has continued a policy of near-zero interest rates on federal funds, and by November 2010 Fannie and Freddie had already cost US taxpayers nearly $134 billion; the total cost to rescue and then overhaul them could reach $685 billion.[77]

The Dodd-Frank Act represents an extraordinary delegation of rule-making authority by Congress to federal regulatory agencies, including the SEC and the Federal Reserve. The Dodd-Frank Act may prove to be a regulatory quagmire, but for the most part it should not affect foreign private issuers, unless they are financial institutions.

---

75 Dodd-Frank Act §1504.
76 Dodd-Frank Act §1502.
77 "S&P: Fannie, Freddie Overhaul Could Cost $685 Billion", *The Wall Street Journal* (November 4 2010).

(e) *Other laws*

There are other US securities laws besides the Securities Act, the Exchange Act, the Sarbanes-Oxley Act and the newly enacted Dodd-Frank Act; these are touched upon only tangentially in this book.

Investment Company Act of 1940: The Investment Company Act of 1940 is the most significant of the other US federal securities laws.[78] It provides a comprehensive system of federal regulation of 'investment companies', such as mutual funds. Issuers may be characterised as investment companies either:

- because they are primarily engaged in the business of investing, reinvesting or trading in securities; or
- because they own 'investment securities' with a value in excess of 40% of the issuer's total assets – exclusive of US government securities and cash – on an unconsolidated basis. The act's definition of investment securities excludes US government securities and securities issued by majority-owned subsidiaries that are not investment companies.[79]

The Investment Company Act places extensive and cumbersome restrictions on the activities of investment companies. An issuer that is not in the securities business but falls under this act's coverage because of its ownership of investment securities (often referred to as an 'inadvertent investment company') will likely find that restrictions designed to control the activities of mutual funds and other traditional investment firms are wholly inappropriate to its manner of conducting business.

Foreign private issuers that come within the definition of 'investment company' may be precluded from making a public offering in the United States. Such issuers will need to exercise care in making private placements in the United States or other sales to US persons, to ensure that the number of beneficial owners of their securities in the United States does not exceed certain limits established by the SEC's interpretations of the act. Although the SEC has adopted rules that provide exemptions for certain non-US banks and insurance companies, it has not established a general exemption for foreign private issuers. If such issuers fit the definition of 'investment company', they may need exemptive or other relief from the SEC in connection with capital-raising transactions.

Investment Advisers Act of 1940: The Investment Advisers Act[80] regulates the registration, conduct and reporting requirements of investment advisers. 'Investment advisers' are generally defined as entities that are in the business of, and compensated for, giving advice regarding securities (eg, stocks and bonds), either directly or using publications.[81] 'Advice' means directly providing advice on securities (eg, specific recommendations) and also providing analysis or reports on securities.

Unless otherwise exempted, investment advisers are required to register with the

78 15 USC §80a-1 *et seq.*
79 Investment Company Act §3(a).
80 15 USC §80b-1 *et seq.*
81 Investment Advisers Act §202(a)(11).

SEC.[82] Once registered, such investment advisers must, among other things:

- maintain books and records in accordance with SEC rules;
- disclose certain information to clients and potential clients;
- comply with various conduct restrictions; and
- submit to inspection by the SEC.[83]

The registration provision of the Investment Advisers Act makes it unlawful for any investment adviser to engage in interstate commerce in connection with the investment advisory business without registering with the SEC.[84]

Investment advisers located outside the United States are also covered by the registration requirements of the act. Given that the SEC has interpreted this act narrowly with respect to foreign investment advisers, it generally applies to foreign advisers that deal with investor clients residing in the United States and not to foreign advisers when they deal with clients outside of the United States, even if they direct their foreign client's transactions to a US broker-dealer. Note, however, that foreign investment advisers with more than 14 US clients must register under this act regardless of their assets under management. Under the Dodd-Frank Act, a foreign private adviser is exempt from the Investment Advisers Act registration requirements if it meets the following qualifications:

- has no place of business in the United States;
- has fewer than 15 US clients and investors in private funds advised by the adviser;
- has less than $25 million (or such higher amount as the SEC may determine in a rule-making process) of aggregate assets under management attributable to US clients and investors in private funds by the adviser;
- does not hold itself out as an investment adviser in the United States; and
- does not advise any registered investment company or business development company.[85]

The Investment Advisers Act also gives the SEC authority to promulgate anti-fraud rules for all investment advisers (whether they are registered or unregistered),[86] and sets out an enforcement mechanism for violations of any provision of the act and its rules.

State securities laws: US laws regulating the issuance and trading of securities exist at both the federal and state levels. The former are far more significant than the so-called 'blue-sky' laws of the 50 states, although a particular state's securities law requirements have to be considered by issuers and underwriters when a securities

82 Investment Advisers Act §203.
83 Investment Advisers Act §201 *et seq.*
84 Investment Advisers Act §203(a).
85 Dodd-Frank Act §523.
86 See, for example, SEC Release No IA-2628, "Prohibition of Fraud by Advisers to Certain Pooled Investment Vehicles" (August 3 2007), which "prohibits advisers to pooled investment vehicles from making false or misleading statements to, or otherwise defrauding, investors or prospective investors in those pooled vehicles".

offering is made in that state. Historically, state regulators have had the power to reject an offering that they found objectionable under their standards (eg, due to excessive financial benefits to underwriters or promoters). This was known as 'merit' review of securities being offered, as opposed to the mere disclosure requirements of the SEC.

The National Securities Markets Improvement Act of 1996[87] amended the Securities Act to strip the states of most of this power.[88] State regulators may now require registration or qualification of securities offerings only in very limited circumstances. The states have been left only with the authority to require filings of notices for certain types of offerings and the jurisdiction to bring enforcement proceedings for fraud or other misconduct.

State securities and corporation laws may impose limited financial reporting requirements,[89] but they are far less extensive than the ongoing reporting obligations that are found in the Exchange Act.

There are state as well as federal civil liability laws that permit private lawsuits for damages where there has been fraud or other misconduct in the sale of securities. However, the Securities Litigation Uniform Standards Act of 1998 was intended to reduce the risks of such state litigation.[90]

1.4 Securities and Exchange Commission

(a) Origin

The SEC is an independent agency created by the US Congress in 1934 to enforce the US securities laws and regulate the securities industry. It was established in response to the stock market crash of 1929 and the Great Depression that followed, as Congress sought to restore confidence among the investing public by introducing federal regulatory review of securities transactions.

Section 4 of the Exchange Act establishes the organisational structure of the agency.[91] It is comprised of five commissioners appointed by the US president who serve staggered five-year terms. The US president designates one commissioner as the agency's chief executive, commonly referred to as the chairman of the SEC. To ensure non-partisanship, no more than three commissioners may be from the same political party. The agency is organised into five divisions and 16 offices with approximately 3,500 employees. Generally, the SEC administers various securities laws, including the Securities Act, the Exchange Act, the Investment Company Act and the Investment Advisers Act. Applicable provisions of the Sarbanes-Oxley Act and the Dodd-Frank Act have been incorporated as amendments to one or more of these statutes.

(b) Rule-making authority

The federal securities statutes provide the general framework of US securities law.

---

87 15 USC §78a *et seq.*
88 Securities Act §18.
89 See, for example, California Corporations Code §2117.
90 See the section on state law in "Securities litigation risks".
91 Exchange Act §4(a).

Congress has given the SEC the authority to supplement the statutes with its own rules and regulations. In certain instances, this power is broadly granted, while in others it is more specifically tailored. For example, Section 19(a) of the Securities Act loosely states, "the Commission shall have the authority from time to time to make ... such rules and regulations as may be necessary to carry out the provisions of the title."[92] In contrast, other sections of the Securities Act, such as Section 2(a)(15), narrowly restrict the SEC's rule-making power to defining particular terms: "The term 'accredited investor' shall mean:... (ii) any person who, on the basis of [a number of financial factors] qualifies as an accredited investor under rules and regulations which the Commission shall proscribe."[93] It is important to note that the penalty provisions of both the Securities Act and the Exchange Act make it clear that Congress intended the SEC's final rules to carry the force of law regardless of how extensive the rule-making power is in a particular situation.[94]

In addition to formal rule-making, the SEC makes many pronouncements in the form of non-binding SEC releases, which, although not equivalent to laws, are important sources of information as they represent the SEC's interpretation of various issues. Other types of non-binding SEC communications include comment letters (letters to public companies raising questions and requesting comments) and no-action letters (letters indicating that the SEC will not take enforcement action if a company engages in a particular action). All of these various communications are published and made available on the SEC's website (www.sec.gov), with Exchange Act and Securities Act filings available on the SEC's online database EDGAR (Electronic Data Gathering, Analysis and Retrieval).[95] The SEC website also contains Compliance and Disclosure Interpretations that reflect the informal views of the SEC staff on interpretive questions of general applicability arising under the securities laws.

(c) *Enforcement*

The SEC's enforcement powers include its ability to conduct investigations into possible violations of US securities laws and its prosecution of civil suits in federal courts and in SEC administrative proceedings. Often, SEC investigations and civil suits result in settlements with the companies or individuals at issue. The SEC has come under intense criticism during the last few years because of its failure to discern, or at least warn against, the global credit crisis that started in June 2007, and especially its failure to detect the Ponzi scheme conducted by Bernard Madoff that became public in 2009. In the latter case, the SEC had received repeated tips over the prior decade and had specifically investigated the situation without finding a problem. This case in particular demonstrates the limits of relying on government regulation and enforcement to protect the public from investment fraud.

Along the same lines, in an enforcement case filed in April 2010 and arising from

92 Securities Act §19(a).
93 Securities Act §2(a)(15).
94 See Securities Act §24; Exchange Act §21A.
95 See the EDGAR website at www.sec.gov/edgar.shtml. See also the section on other disclosure issues in "Periodic reporting requirements".

the global credit crisis, the SEC accused Goldman Sachs of securities fraud in connection with the packaging of mortgage-backed securities selected, in part, by hedge fund investor John Paulson. In July 2010 the SEC settled this case, withdrawing the fraud claim, for a fine of $550 million. This is an exceptionally high amount compared to other SEC fines, although it was considered small by the defendant and the investment community. Both the filing of this case and its settlement were approved by majorities of only three to two of the commissioners, highlighting the political nature of this prosecution.[96] There has generally been a tradition of judicial deference to settlements reached by the SEC, although the law grants US federal judges authority to reject settlements that they believe do not serve the public interest.[97] However, in a series of cases arising from the global credit crisis, federal courts have been increasingly reluctant to rubber stamp such settlements and have expressed concern that the SEC may be claiming victory without holding companies properly accountable:

- In September 2009 a federal judge in New York initially rejected a $33 million settlement by the SEC with Bank of America over bonuses paid to Merrill Lynch executives just before the bank took over Merrill Lynch. In February 2010 the judge required the SEC to impose on Bank of America a $150 million fine, allocating the penalty in such a way that aggrieved shareholders would not bear the cost of it or of the adoption of remedial actions.[98]
- In September 2010 the Justice Department dropped charges against one of the former Merrill Lynch officials – just days before a scheduled retrial involving the only criminal case against a member of the financial community for alleged misdeeds relating to Enron. This follows the unravelling of other related cases at the appellate court level. The Justice Department's lack of preparation for the case has led to criticisms that the commissioners were using the lawsuit for the mere purpose of harassment.[99]
- In August 2010 a federal judge in Washington, DC refused to approve a $75 million settlement by the SEC with Citibank over the bank's misstatements about its exposure to subprime mortgages.[100] Among other things, the SEC alleged that Citibank understated its exposure to subprime mortgages by nearly $40 billion. The SEC had calculated that Citibank realised a benefit of up to $123 million from such misrepresentations. The judge requested additional legal briefs from the parties and, in September 2010, indicated that she would accept such settlement conditioned upon:
    - the SEC's certifying that the remedies Citibank claimed to have put in

96 *SEC v Goldman, Sachs & Co, Consent of Defendant Goldman, Sachs & Co*, Case No 10-CV-3229 (SDNY July 20 2010).

97 Binyamin Appelbaum, "U.S. Judges Sound Off on Bank Settlements", *The New York Times* (August 23 2010).

98 *Securities and Exchange Commission v Bank of America Corporation*, Civil Action Nos 09-6829, 10-0215 (SDNY February 22 2010).

99 John R Emshwiller, "U.S. Won't Seek Retrial of Former Merrill Lynch Official", *The Wall Street Journal* (September 16 2010).

100 SEC Litigation Release No 21605, "SEC Charges Citigroup Inc in Connection with Misleading Disclosures Regarding Its Exposure to Sub-Prime Assets" (July 29 2010).

place to prevent a similar situation were adequate and would remain so for a given period of time; and

- rewording the settlement agreement to clarify that the $75 million would be used to compensate the shareholders that suffered losses because of Citibank's misstatements.[101]

The increased attention by federal judges over SEC settlements points to the delicate balance that the SEC must strike as it pursues cases stemming from the global credit crisis – holding senior executives accountable and creating a deterrent for corporate wrongdoing, while avoiding excessive collateral damage for shareholders that had already been victimised.[102]

Although these recent examples may indicate that regulators need to do a better job explaining to the courts why judges should approve a proposed settlement, and that the regulators should seek more punitive settlements to satisfy the courts that must approve those settlements, such a possibility may prove short-lived. A new provision of the Dodd-Frank Act[103] allows the SEC to impose civil monetary penalties in an administrative proceeding against anyone that violates a provision of US securities laws – and thereby avoid requiring court approval of any settlement. Such an administrative proceeding is instead instituted before the SEC commissioners, who may approve the filing and settlement without further judicial review.[104]

101 Wyatt Edwards, "Judge Accepts Citigroup's Settlement With SEC", *The New York Times* (September 24 2010).

102 Kara Scannell, "Citi's Pact With SEC Is Held Up By Judge", *The Wall Street Journal* (August 17 2010).

103 Dodd-Frank Act §929p.

104 Peter J Henning, *Can the SEC Avoid Scrutiny of Its Settlements?*, DealBook Blog, NYTimes.com (August 17 2010).

2. Public offerings

2.1 Background

A foreign private issuer considering entry into the US capital markets may broadly do so by means of a public offering of its securities to US investors (or, on a restricted basis, through a private offering, as outlined in the next chapter). An issuer contemplating a public offering will most likely be looking at a contemporaneous listing on a US national securities exchange.

Either a public offering or a listing will bring the foreign private issuer into the reporting system of the Exchange Act, where it will remain indefinitely subject to suspension or withdrawal possibilities.[105]

The mechanics of registering public offerings of securities in the US under the Securities Act are basically the same for foreign private issuers and for US issuers. While the content of the disclosure in a registration statement follows the same general pattern for both types of issuers, there are some significant differences:

- Financial statements of foreign private issuers need not be presented in accordance with US generally accepted accounting principles (GAAP) if:
  - the financial statements are accompanied by a reconciliation to US GAAP; or
  - the financial statements are prepared in accordance with International Financial Reporting Standards (IFRS) as issued by the International Accounting Standards Board;[106]
- the SEC has aligned its textual disclosure requirements for foreign private issuers with international standards and has modified some burdensome US issuer disclosures.[107]

2.2 Registration under the Securities Act

US securities laws, such as the registration requirements of the Securities Act and the anti-fraud provisions of both the Securities Act and the Exchange Act, apply to both US and foreign private issuers seeking to raise capital through a public offering of securities in the United States. Foreign private issuers that make a registered public offering also become subject to the reporting requirements of the Exchange Act, unless an exemption is available. Issuers that list their securities on a national exchange must

105 These are outlined in outlined in the section on delisting and deregistering in "Periodic reporting requirements".
106 For more on international disclosure standards, see "Periodic reporting requirements".
107 See "Periodic reporting requirements".

register their securities and file the necessary reports under the Exchange Act.

Generally, to comply with the Securities Act, a US public offering must be registered with the SEC and a prospectus, which is part of the registration statement, must be delivered to investors. Before a public offering begins, a Securities Act registration statement is prepared and filed with the SEC, after which the preliminary prospectus is distributed to offerees. The registration statement describes the issuer's business, its financial condition, the securities and the offering's terms. However, the securities may not be sold until the registration statement is declared effective by the SEC. A final prospectus must then be sent or delivered to the investors before or at the same time as their purchases occur.

The information concerning the issuer, the securities and terms is provided to the investors, which are to make their own determinations of whether to purchase the securities. The SEC does not weigh in on the offering's merits.

(a) Offering Reform Rules

After years of complaints that its public offering rules unduly impeded the capital-raising process[108] – and following ineffective attempts to deal with the situation[109] – the SEC extensively revised the public offering regulatory structure under the Securities Act in 2005.[110] These Offering Reform Rules became effective on December 1 2005 and apply to both US and foreign private issuers.

The Offering Reform Rules were predicated on two major developments over recent years:

- the growth of electronic dissemination of information (including use of the Internet); and
- the enhancement of Exchange Act reporting.[111]

Because an issuer that has entered the Exchange Act reporting system regularly provides significant business and financial information, its reports already give the investment community much of the material information that is required in offering documents under the Securities Act. The Offering Reform Rules recognise different categories of issuers – ranging from companies that have not entered the Exchange Act reporting system (eg, those contemplating initial public offerings) to sizeable companies already reporting under the Exchange Act (also known as 'well-known seasoned issuers'[112]) – and accordingly scale down various of the SEC's offering restrictions.

2.3 General procedures and disclosure obligations

Unless a type of security is exempted by Section 3 of the Securities Act, or a transaction in a non-exempt security is exempted by Section 3 or 4, Section 5 of this act requires that:

---

108 See, for example, SEC, "Report of the Advisory Committee on the Capital Formation and Regulatory Processes" (July 24 1996); American Bar Association Committee on the Federal Regulation of Securities, Letter to the SEC's Division of Corporation Finance (August 22 2001).

109 See SEC Release No 33-7606A (November 13 1998), colloquially known as the 'Aircraft Carrier' release.

110 SEC Release No 33-8591, "Securities Offering Reform" (July 19 2005).

111 See "Periodic reporting requirements".

112 See the section on simplified registration procedures in this chapter.

- no offers to sell a security be made prior to the filing of a 'registration statement' with the SEC;
- a registration statement be 'in effect' as to a security before it is sold; and
- a prospectus meeting the informational requirements of Section 10 of this act be delivered to investors with or prior to the sale of the security.

The prospectus is part of the registration statement. While the entire registration statement is available to the public and is subject to SEC review once it is filed with the SEC, the prospectus is the part that contains most of the meaningful business and financial information regarding the security and its issuer.

The minimum content of the registration statement is dictated by rules and forms promulgated by the SEC. Basic foreign private issuer registration Form F-1 and other foreign private issuer registration forms (Forms F-3 and F-4) make extensive reference to Form 20-F (for annual reports), which calls for various textual descriptions and issuer financial statements, and to Regulation S-K, which prescribes additional information and exhibits. (Form 40-F, calling for comparable information, is available to certain Canadian foreign private issuers.) The issuer is required by rule and by the instructions to Form 20-F to provide "such further material information" as is necessary to make the registration statement and the prospectus "not misleading"[113] – mirroring the philosophy of the civil liability provisions of Sections 11 and 12 of the Securities Act and the anti-fraud provisions of Rule 10b-5 under the Exchange Act.

A Form F-1 registration statement contains two parts:

- Part I contains business information and the issuer's financial condition. The prospectus constitutes this Part I of the registration statement, minus the Form F-1 cover page, and is written in narrative form and not necessarily in the order in which the items are set forth on Form F-1. The front and back cover pages of the prospectus must have certain information, such as the issuer's name and English translation thereof, if applicable, the number and type of securities being offered, the offering price, the national securities exchange where the securities will be listed, the SEC legend, the underwriters' names, a prominent cross-reference to the risk factors section and a detailed table of contents.[114]
- Part II contains other information that is not required to be in the prospectus, such as information about indemnification and recent sales, exhibits (including material agreements) and financial statement schedules and undertakings. Part II need not be delivered to investors but is available to them through the SEC's website.

The SEC registration process may be divided into three periods:

- the pre-filing period;
- the period between filing and effectiveness, or 'waiting period'; and
- the period after effectiveness.

113 Securities Act Rule 408; General Instruction C(c) of Form 20-F.
114 Regulation S-K Items 501-502.

(a) Pre-filing period

During the pre-filing period, the Securities Act prohibits any sale of securities and any offer to sell or offer to buy, whether written or oral.[115] Marketing activity is prohibited during this period. During this period the registration statement is prepared for filing with the SEC.

The registration statement for a public offering of securities is:

- prepared by the issuer and its counsel, with the assistance of its underwriters and their counsel if the offering is to be underwritten;
- signed by the issuer, by the issuer's principal executive, accounting and financial officers, and by a majority of the issuer's board of directors.[116] Where a foreign private issuer has two governing boards, it is signed by the members of whichever board acts most like a US board; and
- filed electronically with the SEC in Washington, DC,[117] at which point it becomes publicly available through the SEC's website. The registration statement is filed before the SEC reviews it. This holds true for 'secondary' public offerings of outstanding securities that are required to be registered, as well as for offerings of new securities by the issuer. Once the registration statement is filed, the securities covered thereby may be offered, but not sold.

The SEC's Division of Corporation Finance will make an initial determination whether the registration statement should be reviewed by its staff. Registration statements filed by foreign private issuers that have not entered the Exchange Act reporting system are virtually certain to be reviewed. Registration statements of seasoned companies that have a substantial history of public filings with the SEC may well not be reviewed. Registrations statements of well-known seasoned issuers using automatic effectiveness procedures will not be reviewed.[118]

(b) Waiting period

The waiting period commences when the registration statement is filed with the SEC and ends when it is declared effective. The securities covered by the registration may be offered but not sold once the registration statement is filed. Oral communications are permitted during this time. These communications are necessary to market the offering and may include road shows. Written offers to sell may not be made, except by means of a preliminary prospectus, also known as a 'red herring prospectus', or a summary prospectus. (This is discussed further below.) Oral offers to sell are permitted, provided that they are not materially false or misleading, since this may result in liability under Act Section 12(a)(2) of the Securities Act and Exchange Act Rule 10b-5. Accordingly, market practice is to script carefully what is to be said at road shows and otherwise. Oral offers to buy are permitted without any restrictions. Sales transactions cannot be finalised until the SEC has declared the registration statement effective.

---

115 Securities Act §5(a)(1); §5(c).
116 Securities Act §6(a).
117 See the section on other disclosure issues in "Periodic reporting requirements".
118 For an explanation of these, see the section on simplified registration procedures in this chapter.

(c) *Effectiveness*

Under Section 5(a) of the Securities Act, a registration statement must be declared effective before the registered security can be sold. US and foreign private issuers that qualify as well-known seasoned issuers can control the timing of an offering by using automatic effectiveness procedures that cause the registration statement to become effective upon filing, without SEC action.

Other issuers need an SEC order declaring the registration effective in order to sell the offered securities in compliance with Section 5(a). Despite provisions in the Securities Act for the automatic effectiveness of a registration statement 20 days after its filing,[119] as a practical matter it will not become effective until the SEC staff issues an order declaring it effective on a specified date requested by the issuer. Such staff action will not take place until after the staff has concluded either:

- that it will not review the registration statement; or
- following review, that all suggested corrections and amplifications have been made and all requested supplemental information has been received.

Effectiveness can be earlier than the expiration of 20 days following filing, but in most cases will be substantially later than the end of this period.

(d) *Prospectus delivery*

Once the registration statement is effective, Section 5(b) of the Securities Act imposes the further requirement that the prospectus part of the registration statement be delivered to investors at or prior to the sale of the registered security. The prospectus is prepared and delivered as a separate document. It may be delivered electronically, so long as the issuer is assured of its actual delivery.

However, during the waiting period (ie, the period between filing and effectiveness of the registration statement), Section 5(b) permits any oral offer, as well as written offers to potential investors that are made by means of a preliminary prospectus that meets the requirements of Section 10 of the Securities Act, except for price and other last-minute offering information (a 'Section 10' or 'statutory' prospectus).[120] This is often distributed to potential investors to give them the opportunity to appraise the merits of the offering, and is sometimes referred to as a 'red herring prospectus' due to the disclosure statement historically printed in red ink on its cover, which explicitly states that the issuing company is not attempting to sell its shares because the registration statement is not yet effective.

This preliminary prospectus is often distributed as part of the process of putting together the underwriting syndicate, discussed below. However, the preliminary prospectus should not be distributed as soon as it is, or in the form that it was, filed as part of the registration statement, because there is a chance that the SEC may regard the registration statement as deficient in some way. Most issuers wait to circulate the preliminary prospectus until after they have received and amended the registration statement in response to SEC staff comments.

---

119 Securities Act §8.
120 Securities Act §10; Securities Act Rule 430(a).

Free-writing prospectuses: Securities Act Rules 163 and 433, adopted as part of the Offering Reform Rules, introduced the concept of the 'free-writing prospectus',[121] in effect saying that any form of written offer during the waiting period (including offers by any form of electronic medium, including audiotape, CD-Rom, email or website) comports with Section 10 of the Securites Act and is permissible. Rule 433 contains a number of conditions to the use of free-writing prospectuses:

- Well-known seasoned issuers may make written or oral offers at any time. If they make written offers before they file a registration statement that becomes automatically effective upon filing, those written offers are treated as free-writing prospectuses.[122]
- Other issuers – both companies that have not entered the Exchange Act reporting system (eg, foreign private issuers contemplating an initial public offering) and Exchange Act reporting companies that do not meet the public float threshold required of a well-known seasoned issuer – will find that use of free-writing prospectuses will add a substantial measure of flexibility to offering activity during the waiting period.

In offerings made by these non-reporting or unseasoned issuers, including initial public offerings, the free-writing prospectus may not be disseminated unless it is accompanied or preceded by delivery of the red herring prospectus. As a result, these issuers may effect delivery of a free-writing prospectus only in an electronic form that contains an active link to the prospectus.[123] Whether used by a non-reporting, unseasoned issuer or a well-known seasoned issuer, a free-writing prospectus must contain a legend indicating where a prospectus and registration statement are available and recommend that investors read the prospectus.

After effectiveness and pricing, a final prospectus is prepared that includes the pricing and syndicate information, and this final prospectus is filed with the SEC. However, under the Offering Reform Rules, material information such as price must be conveyed to investors at the time of sale,[124] which is likely to be prior to preparation of the final prospectus. Alternatively, the issuer may amend its registration statement just before it becomes effective to include a final prospectus containing the pricing information.

2.4 Publicity

(a) Pre-filing publicity

If an offering is to be registered with the SEC, Section 5(c) of the Securities Act prohibits any written or oral offer of the securities to the public prior to the filing of the registration statement – hence the reference to this period as the 'quiet period'. It is not uncommon for offerings in Europe, for example, to be preceded by television and press advertising campaigns, but US laws concerning pre-filing publicity are

121 Securities Act Rule 405.
122 Securities Act Rule 163.
123 Securities Act Rule 433.
124 SEC Release No 33-8591, "Securities Offering Reform" (August 2 2005).

much more conservative than those in other countries:

- The Offering Reform Rules exclude well-known seasoned issuers from the prohibitions concerning written or oral offers, provided that, in the case of written offers, they observe certain legend and filing requirements.[125]
- All other US and foreign private issuers must concern themselves with the strictures against pre-filing offers.

The SEC considers that Section 5(c) extends not only to specific pre-filing offers by means of a prospectus-type document, but also to less formal activities that will likely condition the market for the securities that will be covered by the registration statement. Bullish pre-offering publicity about the issuer and its earnings prospects is likely to raise serious questions with the SEC staff as to whether such a campaign is tantamount to a prohibited offer to sell prior to the filing of the registration statement.

Market-conditioning activity that violates the rules governing public offerings is often referred to as 'gun-jumping'. As is the case with many other aspects of the registration process, gun-jumping has become an often complex judgmental area where the advice of counsel is necessary.

The SEC's sanctions for what it regards as an illegal offer prior to the filing of the registration statement include a refusal to permit the effectiveness of the registration statement (and hence the commencement of sales) until a substantial additional period of time has elapsed to allow the impact of the violation to diminish.

Foreign private issuers, unfamiliar with such nuances of US securities law, should not assume that pre-filing publicity is permissible even if it is permissible under its home country regulations. If a foreign private issuer that is not a well-known seasoned issuer engages in financial advertising and promotion to acquaint the US market with the investment qualities of its securities, it runs a substantial risk of SEC delay of the registration process and the consequent loss of a favourable public market.

Rules adopted in October 1999 permit pre-filing communications in the context of business combination and exchange offer transactions where securities of the acquirer will be issued.126 These rules also exempt certain offerings by foreign private issuers from registration.127

For example, during the period immediately leading up to the initial public offering by Google, Inc in 2004, the two founders were interviewed on the company's prospects by Playboy magazine. This interview caused a substantial delay in the offering process, which the SEC considered necessary to give the capital markets a chance to cool off from the effects of the inopportune disclosure.

---

125 Securities Act Rule 163.

126 SEC Release No 33-7760, "Regulation of Takeovers and Security Holder Communications" (October 22 1999).

127 SEC Release No 33-7759, "Cross-Border Tender and Exchange Offers, Business Combinations and Rights Offerings" (October 22 1999); SEC Release No 33-8957 "Commission Guidance and Revision to the Cross-Border Tender Offer, Exchange Offer, Rights Offering, and Business Combination Rules and Beneficial Ownership Reporting Rules for Certain Foreign Institutions" (September 19 2008). See "International offerings with US participants".

The SEC has issued guidelines to help issuers respond to information requests while not opening themselves to liability for gun-jumping.[128] Issuers should, if in the ordinary course in accordance with past practice:

- continue to advertise their products and services, send out their periodic reports to stockholders, and publish their proxy statements and dividend notices;
- announce factual business and financial developments, such as receiving a contract or opening a new facility; and
- answer unsolicited inquires from financial professionals concerning factual information.

However, issuers should avoid the following until the US offering has been completed:

- meetings with US securities analysts and similar groups, because it would be difficult to avoid questions about the offering;
- any public relations activities that differ from its customary practices;
- optimistic predictions in any publicity about the issuer in the United States; and
- press conferences, unless there are other developments affecting the issuer.

(b) Privatisations

The prospect of a public sale of securities of a government-owned business entity – privatisation – typically becomes the subject of speculation in the investment community and media well in advance of the time that an actual financing begins. It is often difficult, if not impossible, to avoid advance public discussion of the business and finances of such a company.

The SEC staff has shown a willingness to apply Section 5(c) of the Securities Act in a way that recognises this practical difficulty and permits a reasonable amount of pre-filing discussion. It has approved carefully crafted guidelines for contacts with the media, security analysts and potential investors inside and outside the United States.[129] The SEC is likely to show further flexibility in future privatisation transactions, especially because many will likely involve dispositions by the US government of bailed-out companies back to the private sector.

(c) 'Safe harbour' protections

The Offering Reform Rules created 'safe harbour' protections that issuers may follow to minimise the risk of their communications being treated as offers that violate Section 5(c):

- All communications more than 30 days prior to filing a registration statement will not be considered offers, so long as they do not reference the impending registered offering and the issuer takes reasonable steps to prevent further publications within the 30-day pre-filing period.[130]

---

128 SEC Release No 33-8591, "Securities Offering Reform" (July 19 2005).
129 Deutsche Telekom AG, SEC No-Action Letter (June 13 1995).

- Communication of regularly released factual business information and 'forward-looking information'[131] by Exchange Act reporting companies and by non-reporting foreign private issuers that meet certain size and trading tests similarly will not be treated as offers for Section 5 purposes.[132] Generally, the regular release of factual business information to customers, suppliers and the like will not be deemed to constitute offers.[133]

The SEC previously established a safe harbour addressing the uncertainties created when an issuer commences a private offering,[134] abandons it before selling the privately offered securities and files a Securities Act registration statement. If the private and public offerings are integrated into a single transaction, the private offering can be found to have violated Section 5(c).

Noting that conditions in the capital markets may shift quickly, in 2001 the SEC adopted Rule 155 under the Securities Act to create a safe harbour for issuers wishing to convert to a different type of offering.[135] By waiting 30 days after the termination of all offering activity in a private offering in which no securities have been sold and observing the other conditions of Rule 155, an issuer may avoid integration and proceed to register a public offering of securities. When publishing its Offering Reform Rules in 2005, the SEC said that issuers could continue to rely on this safe harbour.[136]

Conversely, the public character of a registered offering raises a question about the exempt status of a private offering undertaken following withdrawal of the registration statement. If the issuer waits 30 days after withdrawal of the registration and observes other Rule 155 conditions, integration of the two offerings may similarly be avoided if the issuer proceeds with a private placement.

Other SEC safe harbours include three that particularly affect foreign private issuers:

- the non-integration of Regulation S offshore offerings with domestic US offerings;[137]
- offerings by foreign private issuers to minority US holders that are exempted by Rules 801 and 802 (which require, among other conditions, that US holders hold no more than 10% of the securities subject to the offering);[138] and
- the treatment of offers and sales under employee benefit plans pursuant to Rule 701 as discrete offerings.[139]

---

130 Securities Act Rule 163A.
131 See "Periodic reporting requirements".
132 Securities Act Rule 168.
133 Securities Act Rule 169.
134 See "Private placements".
135 SEC Release No 33-7943, "Integration of Abandoned Offerings" (January 26 2001).
136 SEC Release No 33-8591, "Securities Offering Reform" (July 19 2005).
137 Regulation S offshore transactions are discussed further in "Private placements".
138 See "International offerings with US participants" for more detail.
139 The compensation of US employees is discussed further in "American depositary receipts".

(d) *Waiting period publicity*

As discussed above, the preliminary prospectus and free-writing prospectuses are used to market the offering during the waiting period between filing and effectiveness of the registration statement. Oral communications may also be used during this time, though the content of the communications must be limited to the information included in the preliminary prospectus. Additionally, any proposed publicity surrounding the issuer or its senior management should be discussed and vetted by the issuer's counsel. Similarly, any information on the issuer's website is considered a written communication and, as with the pre-filing period, the website should be carefully reviewed to ensure that it does not contain information that could constitute an offer or sale during the waiting period.

Road shows have long been the centrepiece of the publicity process during the waiting period. 'Road shows' are defined by Rule 433 as "presentation[s] regarding an offering by one or more members of the issuer's management" and often involve members of the issuer's management and its managing underwriters travelling for meetings with potential investors, analysts, brokers and potential underwriting syndicate members in the weeks immediately preceding the effectiveness and pricing of the offering.[140] These conventional in-person road shows are considered oral communications, even when slides or visual aids are presented, so long as they are not printed and given to the participants. As such, in-person road shows are not subject to the requirements that apply to written communications. Additionally, in-person road shows that are transmitted live via the Internet or telephone are considered oral communications as well.

Internet road shows that are recorded and not presented live are considered written communications. Historically, they were not permitted prior to the effectiveness of the registration statement. However, under the Offering Reform Rules, these internet road shows are considered to be free-writing prospectuses and must comply with the applicable free-writing prospectus rules. If the offering is of equity or convertible securities by a non-reporting issuer (as of the time that the registration statement is filed), then no filing is required, so long as the "issuer makes at least one version of a *bona fide* electronic road show presentation available without restriction to any person" who seeks access to it.[141] Additionally, the internet road show audience need not be limited in any way; nor must the presentation simply be a recording of a live presentation. Internet road shows may also be downloaded by viewers and there may be multiple versions of the road show.

2.5 SEC review

The SEC's Division of Corporation Finance reviews registration statements only to determine whether their informational content meets the disclosure standards prescribed by the SEC's rules and regulations. The Securities Act does not require substantive approval by the SEC of the investment merits of the offered security.

---

140 Securities Act Rule 433(h)(4).
141 Securities Act Rule 433(d)(8).

If the SEC believes that disclosure is inadequate or misleading, however, it has the practical power either to prevent the offering from becoming effective or to take action against the issuer and other participants in the registration process following effectiveness of the defective registration statement. As discussed in "Securities litigation risks" below, these regulatory powers are supplemented by a civil liability structure that enables investors to assert a variety of claims based on misstatements or omissions in registration statements and prospectuses. Neither review nor non-review by the SEC precludes private litigants from maintaining such civil actions.

The Division of Corporation Finance has a staff of lawyers, accountants and investment analysts who review registration statements as well as other documents (eg, quarterly, annual and other reports) filed by issuers with the SEC. Filings are typically examined by staff personnel who handle the filings of companies engaged in the same principal business as the registrant. The review process will normally include a comparison of other companies' business and financial disclosures to those of the registrant.

Generally, SEC review of the registration statement for an initial public offering will follow these steps:

- The staff will contact the issuer to advise whether the registration statement will be reviewed.
- If reviewed, the issuer can expect to wait approximately 30 days after filing of the registration statement to receive the comments of the staff – these comments may be voluminous and will probably be communicated by letter.
- At the same time, the issuer's underwriters may distribute an initial prospectus in preliminary or red herring form and may conduct road shows to stimulate investor interest – however, it may be beneficial to wait if major comments are expected.
- The issuer will respond to the staff's comments by making amendments to the registration statement. It should be noted that this response is public. The amendment process involves revising the registration statement, including the prospectus, with appropriate changes in textual material and financial statement presentation, and refiling the amended registration statement with the SEC.
- If the changes are significant, the amended preliminary prospectus will have to be recirculated to the original recipients, which is a reason why issuers and underwriters often defer wide circulation until after the SEC's initial review.
- The amended material will again be reviewed and may cause further staff comments and a repetition of the amendment process.
- Once the staff has no further comments, upon request of the issuer and underwriters the SEC will declare the registration statement effective and the prospectus will be printed and distributed in final form with offering price information.

(a) Review of draft submissions

The Division of Corporation Finance recognises that a foreign private issuer may have special problems that it would like to resolve with the SEC before its filing of a registration statement makes business and financial information public. The division has an informal process of reviewing a draft of a foreign private issuer's first Securities Act registration statement before filing, if the issuer requests it. Staff review and comment on such a draft are made on a confidential basis.[142] One of the advantages to a foreign private issuer of this procedure is that changes can be made to reflect SEC comments without the public disclosure that accompanies an amendment to a filed registration statement. However, once the foreign private issuer registers a transaction under the Securities Act or a class of securities under the Exchange Act, the SEC will not accept additional draft submissions or review or screen a registration statement until it is publicly filed.

To take advantage of staff review of a pre-filing draft of a registration statement, the foreign private issuer should be prepared to submit a draft that is complete in all material respects, including audited financial statements that are accompanied by a signed report of the auditing firm. The timing and scope of staff review of a pre-filing draft are generally the same as for publicly filed registration statements.

(b) Preparation and due diligence

Most companies prepare material describing their businesses – to promote their products and services, to broaden their contacts with the financial community and to inform their shareholders. Many foreign private issuers publish comprehensive reports that include extensive business information and detailed financial statements, particularly if they are listed on a stock exchange in their home country.[143] But rarely can such reports be converted into a Securities Act prospectus simply by altering their form and making minor changes.

Due diligence basics: The disclosure and financial statement instructions of Form 20-F and Regulation S-K require a great deal of investigatory work. Underwriters and counsel for the underwriters and for the issuer will engage in a pre-offering investigation of the issuer's affairs, a process known as 'due diligence'. The due diligence process is carried out to enable the underwriters and others to fulfil their gatekeeping responsibilities in the offering process and to assert defences against claims of civil liability.

This process is particularly geared to the provisions of Section 11 of the Securities Act which allows a person that, directly from the issuer or in the secondary market, purchased securities covered by a registration statement to assert a claim of civil liability by proving that it bought securities registered pursuant to a registration statement which contained a misstatement or omission of material fact. This claim can be brought against various parties, including the issuer – its directors, chief executive officer, chief financial officer and auditors – and the underwriters.

---

142 SEC Division of Corporation Finance, "International Reporting and Disclosure Issues", III-B (May 1 2001).

143 Such reports may be used as a substitute for the reports otherwise mandated by the Exchange Act in situations where a foreign private issuer invokes Exchange Act Rule 12g3-2(b) in order to avoid registration and reporting under that act. See the section on determination of US ownership in "International offerings with US participants".

Adequate due diligence permits offering participants (other than the issuer) to use the defence of 'reasonable investigation'.[144]

SEC rules do not specifically say what a due diligence investigation should cover or how it should be conducted. Over the years, securities professionals have developed techniques designed to enable offering participants (other than the issuer) to meet the standard of 'reasonableness'; but whether a particular investigation measures up to that standard may ultimately be decided only in litigation. The December 2004 and March 2005 opinions of the court supervising the *WorldCom* civil litigation contain comprehensive recent judicial analyses of the due diligence defence. They emphasise the need to question implausible financial reports and to do more than simply take the statements of issuer personnel at face value.[145]

Reputational concerns and the fear of civil liability cause underwriters, auditors, lawyers and other securities professionals to expend efforts that foreign private issuers unfamiliar with the US registration process may regard as excessive. One positive result, however, is that the registration process results in a publicly available body of information about the issuer that can give US investors a greater sense of reliability and can enhance the marketability of its securities. Also, the effort invested in an initial public offering becomes the foundation for compliance with the Exchange Act ongoing reporting system and for future financings.[146]

Typically, the due diligence investigation is conducted by the issuer's counsel, by the managing underwriter on behalf of the underwriting syndicate and by the underwriter's counsel. Its scope is greatest in initial public offerings – which can involve meetings with the issuer's senior management, site visits and interviews of key customers or suppliers. Letters provided by counsel and auditors are used to support the underwriters' claim of having made a reasonable investigation that did not reveal any material misstatements or omissions in the registration statement.

***WorldCom*:** In 2004 a US federal court in New York had to decide the standard of diligence that had to be shown by WorldCom's underwriters – who were relying on the due diligence defence – in relation to the financial statements, where the annual financial statements were covered by an audit report and the interim financial statements were covered by a comfort letter. The court held that the underwriters could not blindly rely on audited financial statements, and that the underwriters had a duty of further investigation in light of the 'red flags' that were present in the financial statements.[147]

Comfort letters: The comfort letter is a part of the due diligence investigation and is delivered by an audit firm to the underwriters and the issuer's board of directors. It primarily concerns the unaudited financial information that appears in a prospectus.

---

144 Civil liability risks are discussed further in "Securities litigation risks".

145 *In re WorldCom, Inc Securities Litigation*, 346 F Supp 2d 628 (SDNY December 15 2004) (underwriters), *In re WorldCom, Inc Securities Litigation*, 2005 WL 638268 (SDNY March 21 2005) (directors). See also Report of Task Force on Sellers' Due Diligence, *The Business Lawyer*, Vol 48 no 3 (May 1993).

146 Appendix C contains a sample checklist for due diligence review in international securities offerings.

147 See *In re WorldCom, Inc Securities Litigation*, 346 F Supp 2d 628 (SDNY December 15 2004).

While not specifically called for under US securities law, it is universally requested by underwriters as part of their due diligence and for ensuring the accuracy of the prospectus. The following conditions apply:

- Letters prepared in accordance with the Statement on Auditing Standards 72 of the American Institute of Certified Public Accountants are the basis of the comfort letter. In an unregistered transaction, Statement 72 requires the underwriters to state that they are conducting a substantially consistent due diligence review as would be done in a registered offering,
- In accordance with Statement 72, accountants can comment only on unaudited interim financial statements for which they have performed a limited review using 'negative assurance'. After 135 days from the date of the latest audited financial statements, auditors cannot deliver negative assurances and must instead use a 'procedures' letter. In this case the auditors take the same steps as in a comfort letter, but with the conclusion that "the officers of the [c]ompany stated that" rather than using negative assurance. The auditors use the procedures letter to pass-through the management's statements rather than a statement by the auditing firm, as is done in a negative assurance.

(c) ***Cost and timing***

The principal cost associated with a registered public offering – the underwriters' discounts and commissions – must be set forth in the prospectus.[148] The prospectus must also estimate other expenses of the offering.[149] These are broken down in the registration statement, which will typically show the following as the largest items:

- auditor's costs;
- printing costs;
- fees and expenses of the issuer's lawyers; and
- transfer agent fees.

Other costs of a registered offering include:

- the SEC registration fee;
- listing fees (if the offered securities are to be listed on a US national securities exchange);
- US federal and state taxes and fees, if any;
- director and officer liability insurance premiums; and
- charges of indenture trustees and rating agencies (in offerings of debt securities), or of the depositary bank (in offerings of ADRs).

Apart from SEC registration and stock exchange listing fees, costs are not proportional to the size of the offering. There is an irreducible amount of work to be done whether the securities issue is large or small. Wide differences in costs often result from issuers' particular problems – for example, the need for special audit work

148 Form F-1, Item 4 (referencing the information required by Form 20-F, Item 9-F-1).
149 Form F-1, Item 4 (referencing the information required by Form 20-F, Item 9-F-2).

or for comprehensive investigation of matters such as tax, environmental or intellectual property uncertainties.

Cost differences are frequently cited as a prime reason for selecting the unregistered private offering process rather than going the route of a registered public offering. Very often, on analysis, the difference is not as great as commonly thought. A properly crafted private offering memorandum may need nearly as much due diligence, legal, auditing and printing work as a registration statement.[150]

The time needed for a registered public offering under the Securities Act is not measured solely by the period from filing with the SEC to effectiveness of the registration statement. The project begins much earlier. For an initial public offering of a foreign private issuer, it is reasonable to add at least two months for pre-filing work.

A registered public offering requires a foreign private issuer to provide:

- audited balance sheets for its two most recently completed fiscal years; and
- audited income and cash-flow statements for its three most recently completed fiscal years.[151]

Separate audited financial statements may be needed for significant companies that the issuer has recently acquired or is likely to acquire. Completion of the necessary audits is a crucial element of timing, as is the preparation of the reconciliation to US GAAP that is required if home country accounting principles rather than IFRS are followed.[152]

Where there is a likelihood of SEC review – as in an initial public offering – a foreign private issuer may often choose to make an unregistered private offering rather than register a public offering in order to eliminate the review period. Practically speaking, the preparation period is likely to be about the same, and placement agents or initial purchasers (which fulfil the role of underwriters in a private offering) may well urge the distribution of a preliminary offering memorandum, in much the same fashion as a preliminary or red herring prospectus – and potential institutional investors may insist on it. But the private offering does not have to wait for possible SEC staff comments and, as a result, there may be a better opportunity to catch favourable market conditions.

A detailed timetable and allocation of responsibilities should be prepared prior to starting work on the registration statement. It should allow time for pre-filing review, if the foreign private issuer elects to submit a draft to the SEC staff.[153]

2.6 Preparation for initial public offerings

(a) Underwriting

The first step in preparing for a registered public offering of securities is to find an underwriter to manage the issuance and distribution process. An underwriter, usually an investment bank or other financial institution, is an entity that agrees to help an

150 This is discussed further in "Private placements".
151 Form 20-F, Item 8.
152 See the section on international disclosure standards in "Periodic reporting requirements".
153 Appendix E presents a sample timeline for international securities offerings.

issuer sell securities to the public.

Generally, the issuer will select one firm to act as the 'managing underwriter'. It will lead the offering process and form a syndicate, or group of underwriters, to share in the underwriting responsibilities for the total offering. In selecting the managing underwriter, some things that a foreign private issuer should consider include:

- the underwriter's experience in public offerings in the issuer's country and industry, to see how well the underwriter understands the issuer, its industry, its country and the factors on which investors will focus when deciding whether to invest;
- whether the underwriter has strong distribution capabilities with retail and institutional investors, the effectiveness of its retail or institutional sales force and the scope of the underwriter's international reach;
- the strength of the individual investment bankers and overall team assigned to work on the offering, to increase the likelihood of a smooth, professional offering and interest from investors on the road show;
- the underwriter's record of after-market price performance; and
- whether the underwriter has a well-known country or industry analyst willing to provide post-offering coverage.

The four basic types of underwriting are as follows:

- Firm commitment underwriting – the underwriters purchase all of the securities from the issuer at a discounted price and then attempt to resell them to investors. This is the most common form of underwriting, in which the underwriters bear all of the risk. In practice, however, the underwriters do not enter into the underwriting agreement until they have placed all of the securities with investors during a road show process – that is, at pricing; thus, the real risk lasts only approximately three business days until the securities trade is settled.
- Best efforts underwriting – the underwriters agree to use their best efforts in selling the issuer's securities to the public. By acting as an agent, and not directly purchasing any securities, the underwriters' risk is reduced. However, the risk to the company is increased.
- Standby underwriting – the issuer offers its existing shareholders the right to purchase securities at a set price and the underwriters agree to buy any securities that remain unpurchased by the shareholders. This form is commonly used in rights offerings.
- Dutch auction underwriting – the underwriters conduct an auction in which all investors submit bids based on the price and number of securities they wish to purchase. The sale or 'clearing' price is the lowest bid price that would allow all of the securities to be sold.

A form of underwriting agreement is negotiated between the issuer and the prospective managing underwriter (acting for all of the underwriters) covering these and other aspects of the transaction as further mentioned below.

The following agreements are usually entered into in connection with an underwritten offering of securities:

- Underwriting agreement – the issuer will make representations with respect to certain matters, such as the accuracy of the registration statement and the validity of the securities. This agreement also lays out closing conditions, such as the delivery of legal opinions, counsel's letters, officers' certificates and comfort letters.
- Agreement among underwriters – this establishes the underwriting syndicate for the proposed public offering and governs the relationship between underwriters. US underwriters generally use a master agreement that has been signed in advance and is simply implemented by a set procedure every time the underwriter desires to be the manager of an offering syndicate.
- Selected dealers agreement – this provides for non-syndicate dealers to join the selling group at a discounted price.
- Intersyndicate agreement – in a global public offering, this establishes an international underwriting syndicate if securities are to be sold outside the United States. It allows separate syndicates handling the domestic offering and the international offering to coordinate their respective offerings in separate capital markets.

While these agreements may be negotiated and informally agreed upon early in the process, they are not executed until much later. For example, as noted above, the underwriting agreement is typically not finalised until the offering is priced – at the time the registration statement becomes effective.

The issuer and underwriter typically negotiate the following when structuring the offering:

- the type of security to be sold;
- the offering size;
- the approximate number of shares;
- the price range per share;
- whether any stockholders will also be selling; and
- any 'lock-up' periods during which the stockholders cannot sell their shares in the public markets. In a lock-up agreement, the stockholders agree not to sell their shares in the public market for a pre-determined amount of time. This helps to prevent stockholders from depressing the market during the offering and afterwards, until the market has stabilised.

Marketing process post-filing: After the registration statement has been filed, the managing underwriter undertakes a marketing effort using the preliminary or red herring prospectus. The underwriters offer the securities during the marketing period by soliciting indications of interest during road shows, as discussed above. The marketing is complete when the issuer asks the SEC to declare the registration effective and the SEC notifies the issuer that it is ready to declare it effective. In a successful case, the offering is sold out immediately after pricing.

Regulation M: Issuers should also be aware of the applicability of Regulation M,[154] which limits certain activities – such as passive market making and stabilisation – by distribution participants and other parties. This is intended to prevent manipulative conduct by those with an interest in the outcome of the securities distribution. Securities that are the subject of a distribution, as well as any securities into which they may be converted, exchanged or exercised, or that may determine their value, are subject to Regulation M. Underwriters should ensure that market activities undertaken with respect to the rights and new shares are conducted in compliance with Regulation M.

(b) Corporate governance and best practices

In preparation of an initial public offering, issuers will want to engage – with the advice of their counsel and prospective underwriters – in a programme of 'corporate clean-up'. First-time registrants should review their corporate governance structures and internal procedures to bring them into line with those of public companies.

Disclosure controls and procedures: The certification rules adopted by the SEC in accordance with Section 302 of the Sarbanes-Oxley Act introduced the concept of 'disclosure controls and procedures' to the preparation of periodic Exchange Act reports. Broadly speaking, these are controls and procedures that ensure timely collection and evaluation of information that is potentially subject to Exchange Act reporting.[155] Disclosure controls and procedures should be established before an initial public offering or an initial stock exchange listing, both in connection with the exercise of due diligence and in preparation for entering the Exchange Act reporting regime. Periodic review of such controls and procedures is important not only to meet any Exchange Act requirements, but also to assure that reports incorporated into Form F-3 and Form F-4 registrations meet the Securities Act requirements.

Other practices required by the Sarbanes-Oxley Act: Along with the establishment of disclosure controls and procedures, a foreign private issuer should review its internal control over financial reporting for material weaknesses, as contemplated by Section 404 of the Sarbanes-Oxley Act.[156] Assurance of adequate internal controls will be vital to auditors and underwriters of an initial public offering. Other pre-offering steps may include:

- adding outside (independent) directors to the board of directors;
- creating or enhancing an audit committee;
- restructuring relationships with auditors;
- establishing procedures to assure compliance with other provisions of the Sarbanes-Oxley Act;[157]

---

154 See SEC Release No 34-38067, "Antimanipulation Rules Concerning Securities Offerings" (December 20 1996); 17 CFR §§242.100-105.

155 For more on the Sarbanes-Oxley Act see "Periodic reporting requirements".

156 See more in "Periodic reporting requirements".

157 These are discussed further in the section on the Sarbanes-Oxley Act in "Periodic reporting requirements".

- reviewing procurement practices to ensure that these transactions are conducted at arm's length;
- reviewing related-party transactions by the issuer with its management and owners; and
- eliminating any issuer loans to executive officers and directors that violate the Sarbanes-Oxley Act.

2.7 Simplified registration procedures

For some time, both US issuers and foreign private issuers have had the ability to reduce Securities Act registration burdens by following certain simplified 'short-form' and 'shelf' registration procedures. These procedures are available if the issuer meets a certain size requirement (as described below) and has filed at least one annual report under the Exchange Act. (A foreign report made available under the provisions of Rule 12g3-2(b) does not suffice for these purposes.[158])

However, foreign private issuers will likely find that their first registered public offering will be made in accordance with regular Securities Act procedures because they will not previously have filed an Exchange Act annual report. But this initial registration will trigger the reporting requirements of the Exchange Act and thereafter regular annual reports will have to be filed with the SEC. Assuming that the issuer meets the size requirement described below, subsequent registered public offerings will thus be able to take advantage of short-form and shelf registration procedures.

A foreign private issuer might file an Exchange Act annual report independently of a plan to engage in public financing in the United States. In this case the simplified registration procedures may be available for its initial registered offering:

- A foreign private issuer might apply for listing on a US national securities exchange, which would require Exchange Act registration and reporting; or
- It might find itself facing registration under the Exchange Act because it develops a sizeable US shareholder base and does not meet the conditions of Rule 12g3-2(b).

The basics of simplified registration described below – providing disclosure by incorporating other documents and supplementing prospectuses to reflect individual takedowns – will be familiar to foreign private issuers operating under EU rules that contain comparable features.[159]

(a) Short-form registration

The essential financial and business disclosures in a Securities Act registration statement and in an Exchange Act annual report are similar. Rather than repeat the information that is already publicly available in Exchange Act reports, issuers that qualify for special short-form Securities Act registration can simply 'incorporate by reference' their Exchange Act reports and achieve considerable cost and time savings.

---

158 Rule 12g3-2(b) is discussed further in "Periodic reporting requirements".
159 EU Directive 2003/71/EC 2004 OJ (L 345).

The principal short-form registration form for US issuers is Form S-3. Foreign private issuers have the benefit of a comparable simplified registration form – Form F-3. Both require the issuer to state that it is incorporating in the prospectus not only existing Exchange Act reports, but also reports to be filed in the future prior to termination of the offering. In the case of foreign private issuers, this entails mandatory incorporation of Form 20-F annual reports and optional incorporation of Form 6-K reports.[160] The incorporation of future reports is a basic ingredient of the shelf registration process, described below.

Form F-3 is available as follows:

- for those foreign private issuers with a 'public float' (ie, the market value of outstanding shares in the hands of public investors as opposed to company officers, directors or controlling shareholders) of $75 million and an Exchange Act reporting history that includes at least one Exchange Act annual report.[161] It is also available for smaller companies if they meet the form's other requirements, are not shell companies, sell no more than one-third of their public float over a 12-month period and have a class of equity securities listed on a national securities exchange;[162]
- to register the offering of investment-grade non-convertible securities of a foreign private issuer or its majority-owned subsidiaries, without regard to the size of the public float. Again, this mirrors the treatment of US issuers; and
- without any public float requirement,[163] for:
  - secondary offerings by shareholders;
  - certain rights offers and dividend or interest reinvestment plans of foreign private issuers; and
  - conversions of convertible securities and exercise of warrants.

The Offering Reform Rules have also given issuers that do not qualify for Form S-3 or Form F-3 greater latitude to incorporate information from their Exchange Act filings. In a non-shelf offering, a foreign private issuer that has filed at least one Form 20-F annual report may satisfy the bulk of the prospectus informational requirements of Form F-1 by reference to its existing Exchange Act materials. This comes with the proviso that it make such reports readily available on its website.[164]

Securities Act registration Form S-4 (for US issuers) and Form F-4 (for foreign private issuers) apply to exchange offers and business combination transactions that involve the public offering of the issuer's securities. They normally call for business and financial information about both the acquiring company and the company it seeks to acquire. In instances where either of these companies is an Exchange Act

160 Form 6-K contains interim information which the issuer otherwise files or makes public pursuant to home country regulatory or stock exchange requirements or distributes to its security holders.

161 Form F-3, General Instructions I-A, I-B-1.

162 SEC Release No 33-8878, "Revisions to the Eligibility Requirements for Primary Securities Offerings on Forms S-3 and F-3" (December 19 2007).

163 Under Securities Act Rule 406, the public float is calculated based on the number of shares outstanding prior to the offering and the estimated public offering price of the securities.

164 SEC Release No 33-8591, "Securities Offering Reform", V-B-3 (July 19 2005).

reporting company, business and financial information may be incorporated from existing Exchange Act reports.[165]

A special type of short-form registration, on Form S-8, is available to Exchange Act reporting companies (including foreign private issuers) for stock-based compensation of employees.[166]

(b) Shelf registration

Historically, there has been a tension between:

- the desire to register securities not only for an immediate transaction, but also for contemplated future transactions; and
- the need for current disclosure of business and financial information at the time of the particular offering.

The SEC has struck a balance by permitting so-called 'shelf' registration. This allows issuers that are current in meeting their Exchange Act reporting obligations to file Securities Act registration statements for securities planned to be issued not only immediately, but also in the foreseeable future.[167] The procedure is as follows:

- Broadly speaking, following the filing and effectiveness of a registration statement – containing a general description of an issuer's securities and incorporating by reference its existing and prospective Exchange Act reports – a prospectus supplement is distributed with respect to each particular issue of securities. The supplement will contain information as to that issue and any material information concerning the issuer that has not been made public in the interim through periodic Exchange Act reports.
- Prospectus supplements are normally distributed, without prior review by the staff of the SEC, within a few days after the terms of the particular offering are fixed.
- The SEC permits an issuer to use a single registration statement – known as a 'universal shelf registration statement' – to register the offering of debt, equity and other securities. The amount of each class of securities to be offered is not specified until the prospectus supplement for a particular offering is distributed.[168]

US issuers can take advantage of these shelf registration procedures where they satisfy the conditions (described above) that entitle them to use Form S-3. Similarly, foreign private issuers can use shelf registration procedures when eligible to use Form F-3.

(c) Well-known seasoned issuers

The Offering Reform Rules identify a well-known seasoned issuer (often abbreviated as 'WKSI') as an issuer (either a US or a foreign private issuer) that:

---

165 Form F-4, Part I-B – I-C (Items 10-17).

166 For more details on the compensation of US employees see "American depositary receipts".

167 Securities Act Rule 415.

168 SEC Release No 33-8591, "Securities Offering Reform", V-B-2 (July 19 2005).

- has entered the Exchange Act reporting system;
- has filed at least one Form 10-K or Form 20-F annual report; and
- either has a public float of at least $700 million as of a recent determination date or has registered at least $1 billion in non-convertible, non-equity securities over the past three years.[169]

A foreign private issuer cannot become a well-known seasoned issuer until it enters the Exchange Act reporting system. But once it does become a reporting company and files a 20-F annual report and meets the $700 million size threshold, it can realise the following benefits when registering public offerings under the Securities Act:

- It can offer its securities in advance of filing the required Securities Act registration statement;
- It will not be limited to use of a statutory prospectus in making written offers before or after filing the registration statement; and
- It can avoid SEC review and be able to time the effectiveness of the registration statement.

If a foreign private issuer continues to maintain its status as a well-known seasoned issuer, it will also find it easier than other foreign private issuers to exit the reporting system of the Securities Act under Exchange Act Rule 12h-6.[170]

A well-known seasoned issuer may use an 'automatic shelf registration' statement to register any offering of securities, other than an offering for a business combination transaction.[171] Automatic shelf registration offers much greater flexibility in registering securities:

- Automatic shelf registration statements (and post-effective amendments thereto) become effective immediately upon filing;[172]
- Issuers may register unspecified amounts of different specified types of securities on Form S-3 or Form F-3, as applicable;
- Automatic shelf registration statements may add additional classes of securities after effectiveness and may accommodate both primary and secondary (selling stockholder) offerings;
- An automatic shelf registration statement may be used for three years without a new filing; and
- Collateral benefits to foreign private issuers include the ability to extend rights offers to US holders, which in the past have been routinely excluded from participating in rights offerings.[173]

(d) Investigation and liability

Exchange Act reports that are incorporated into Securities Act registration statements

---

169 Securities Act Rule 405.
170 See the section on delisting and deregulation in "Periodic reporting requirements".
171 SEC Release No 33-8591, "Securities Offering Reform", V-B-2 (July 19 2005).
172 Securities Act Rules 462(e), (f).
173 SEC Release No 33-8591, "Securities Offering Reform" (July 19 2005), fn 508.

not only are subject to the civil liability provisions of the Exchange Act, but also become subject to those of the Securities Act.[174] A material misstatement or omission in the incorporated document would be actionable under Sections 11 and 12 of the Securities Act, as well as Rule 10b-5 under the Exchange Act Rule.[175]

Realistically, prospectus supplements under a conventional shelf registration statement and post-effective amendments of an automatic shelf registration statement will not be prepared under the same extensive due diligence procedures employed in preparing an initial public offering. Any investigatory focus therefore shifts to the issuer's Exchange Act reports. This should be recognised at the time that Form 10-K or Form 20-F annual reports are drafted.

2.8 Listing on national securities exchanges

US federal securities laws do not require an issuer to maintain a market for the trading of its securities in the United States. Instead, they regulate trading in whatever market develops. The Exchange Act provides an extensive system of continuous issuer reporting and broker/dealer supervision, as well as rules designed to prohibit fraudulent or manipulative conduct. The SEC has regulatory oversight of the US national securities exchanges.[176] Rules that the exchanges propose to adopt or amend – including those discussed below relating to listing standards and corporate governance – must be submitted to the SEC for approval.[177]

(a) NYSE and NASDAQ

In 2006 the two principal US capital markets – the New York Stock Exchange (NYSE) and the NASDAQ Stock Market – underwent major structural changes that were approved by the SEC. Both institutions are now for-profit entities and compete for listings.

In 2005 the NYSE acquired Archipelago Holdings, Inc (including the Pacific Stock Exchange) and the three markets continued as separate entities under the holding company NYSE Group, Inc.[178] In 2006 NYSE Group, Inc and Euronext NV – a cross-border exchange organisation that operates major stock exchanges and derivatives trading facilities in Europe – merged into a new group named NYSE Euronext. The SEC continues to regulate the US markets of NYSE Euronext, while its European markets continue to be regulated by their existing regulators.[179]

In contrast, NASDAQ historically operated as a US national securities association, under the supervision and control of the National Association of Securities Dealers. From the perspective of an issuer, it functioned much like an exchange, with admission requirements, corporate governance rules and other special rules

---

174 Form F-3, Item 10 (Regulation S-K, Item 512).
175 For more, see "Securities litigation risks".
176 Exchange Act §§5, 6.
177 Exchange Act §19.
178 SEC Release No 34-53382, "Self-Regulatory Organizations; New York Stock Exchange, Inc; Order Granting Approval of Proposed Rule Change and Amendment Nos. 1, 3, and 5 Thereto and Notice of Filing and Order Granting Accelerated Approval to Amendment Nos. 6 and 8 Relating to the NYSE's Business Combination with Archipelago Holdings, Inc" (February 27 2006).
179 Press Release, New York Stock Exchange, "NYSE Group and Euronext N.V. Agree to a Merger of Equals" (June 2 2006).

comparable to those of the NYSE. NASDAQ became a US national securities exchange (like the NYSE) on January 13 2006, when the SEC approved its application to become a registered national securities exchange.[180]

Exchange listings: If an issuer chooses to list its equity or debt securities on a US national securities exchange, it must not only apply to the exchange for listing, but also arrange for the class of securities to become registered under the Exchange Act (if such registration has not already taken place).[181]

The SEC and the applicable US national securities exchange will coordinate the approval of the registration of the securities under the Exchange Act, as well as their admission to trading on the exchange. It is appropriate that both entities be kept informed of the Exchange Act registration process and of the exchange listing application.

The listing application is a document prepared in accordance with the rules and requirements of the particular US national securities exchange. The form of listing application will vary depending upon the particular exchange to which application is made, but will tend to repeat much of the information already contained in the Exchange Act registration statement.

The listing process is generally as follows:

- The issuer requests a preliminary eligibility opinion from the exchange or otherwise verifies with the exchange that it meets the eligibility requirements;
- The issuer then files the listing application and supporting documents with the exchange and files its Exchange Act registration statement with the SEC;
- The exchange certifies to the SEC that it has approved the securities for listing and registration; and
- The SEC then declares the registration statement effective and trading begins on a date selected by the issuer and the exchange.

A foreign private issuer making a registered public offering under the Securities Act, or facing Exchange Act registration because its US shareholder base has reached the 300-holder level is not required to list its securities on a US national securities exchange, because listing is voluntary. The decision of whether to list will depend on the issuer's and its financial advisers' evaluation of the benefits of having such a market and whether the issuer can meet the applicable admission requirements.

NYSE listing standards: Each US national securities exchange has size criteria – which may relate to assets, earnings, market capitalisation or number of shareholders – that must be satisfied as a condition to listing.[182]

A foreign private issuer may elect to qualify for NYSE listing under the NYSE's worldwide or domestic standards.[183] Both standards include:

---

180 SEC Litigation Release No 34-53128, "In the Matter of the Application of The Nasdaq Stock Market LLC for Registration as a National Securities Exchange" (January 13 2006).

181 Exchange Act §12(b).

182 Appendix I contains a chart listing the requirements of the NYSE in greater detail.

183 NYSE Listed Company Manual §103.01.

- distribution and size criteria (minimum numbers of publicly held shares and round-lot holders, and minimum market value of publicly held shares); and
- minimum financial criteria (in terms of pre-tax earnings, cash flow or market capitalisation and revenue).

NASDAQ listing standards: NASDAQ has four market tiers:

- the Global Select Market, with the highest of NASDAQ's financial listing standards. In order to qualify for the Global Market, the standards that a foreign private issuer must meet include:[184]
  - a minimum bid price of at least $4 per share;
  - at least 1.25 million publicly held shares;
  - at least 450 round-lot holders; and
  - additional requirements with respect to income, market value, cash flows and market capitalisation;[185]
- the Global Market, formerly the NASDAQ National Market;
- the Capital Market, formerly the NASDAQ Small Cap Market; and
- the PORTAL Market for Rule 144A securities.

In addition, both exchanges impose a variety of substantive requirements, some of which – in particular, the corporate governance requirements discussed later in this chapter – may present problems for foreign private issuers. NYSE rules include:

- requirements to solicit proxies for shareholder meetings (even if no dispensation is granted to a foreign private issuer by the NYSE, the SEC's proxy rules would not apply);
- quorum requirements for shareholder meetings and minimum voting requirements on certain matters; and
- limitations on creating classes of stock with disparate voting rights.

It is usually important for a foreign private issuer to use the NYSE's confidential review procedures in order to determine which waivers or special interpretations of particular NYSE rules may be necessary and whether such waivers or interpretations can be obtained.[186]

Disclosure requirements: With respect to disclosure, some exchange requirements overlap provisions of the Exchange Act. For example:

- there are NYSE rules that require listed companies to make prompt public disclosure of material corporate developments. These reflect to some extent the philosophy of Rule 10b-5 and Regulation FD under the Exchange Act. The NYSE will often ask companies to give public explanations of reasons for unusual trading activity in their listed securities; and[187]

---

184 NASDAQ Listing Rule 5400.
185 Appendix I contains a chart listing the requirements of NASDAQ's Global Select Market in greater detail.
186 NYSE Listed Company Manual §101.00.
187 NYSE Listed Company Manual §202.03-05

- the NYSE generally requires its listed companies to disseminate quarterly earnings information and to publish an annual report to shareholders within three months of the end of the fiscal year.[188] Unless waivers are obtained, this imposes an additional burden on foreign private issuers, which are called upon by the Exchange Act only to file as interim reports on Form 6-K whatever is publicly disclosed in their home countries. In addition, they are given six months (four months for fiscal years ending on or after December 15 2011) after the end of the fiscal year to file an annual report on Form 20-F. The NYSE will generally grant appropriate relief from this additional reporting burden.

(b) Corporate governance rules

Well before the Sarbanes-Oxley Act, the NYSE and NASDAQ had rules that addressed the relative powers, responsibilities and rights of directors, management and shareholders. Compliance with these corporate governance rules is a prerequisite to listing.

Both the NYSE and NASDAQ re-examined those features of their corporate governance rules relating to audit committees in 1999 and amended them to enhance audit committee independence and functions, and to require the committees to have charters that described their responsibilities.[189] As indicated in "Periodic reporting requirements" below, the Sarbanes-Oxley Act directed the SEC to require national securities exchanges to expand their audit committee rules further, which the SEC did on April 9 2003.[190]

The NYSE and NASDAQ adopted further rule amendments – both in the audit committee areas covered by Sarbanes-Oxley and in other areas of corporate governance – that were approved by the SEC on November 4 2003 and November 3 2004, respectively.[191] Principal features that apply to listed US issuers include those described below.

Audit and other committees: In addition to an audit committee, the NYSE requires that the nominating, corporate governance and compensation committees of listed companies be composed solely of independent directors. The principal functions of these committees are, respectively, as follows:

- nominating committee – to select or recommend nominees for the board of directors;
- corporate governance committee – to develop a set of corporate governance principles applicable to the company; and
- compensation commitee – to set the chief executive officer's compensation and make recommendations with respect to non-CEO compensation, incentive compensation plans and equity-based plans.

---

188 NYSE Listed Company Manual §901.01, II-1, II-4 and §901.02, II-1, II-4.
189 SEC Release No 34-42233 (December 14 1999) (NYSE rules); SEC Release No 34-42231 (December 14 1999) (NASDAQ rules).
190 SEC Release No 33-8220, "Standards Relating to Listed Company Audit Committees" (April 9 2003).
191 SEC Release No 34-48745 (November 4 2003); SEC Release No 34-50625 (November 3 2004).

Each committee is required to have a charter that sets forth its responsibilities and requires it to undergo an annual performance evaluation.

The NASDAQ Stock Market Listing Rules require such functions to be performed either by committees consisting solely of independent directors or by a majority of the company's independent directors operating in executive session.[192]

Independence: A majority of the directors – and all directors who are members of the audit committee – must be independent. The NYSE Listed Company Manual and the NASDAQ Stock Market Listing Rules spell out a number of present or past relationships that are deemed to impair independence, and also require the issuer's board of directors to affirmatively determine that there are no other relationships that would impair independence.[193] The same requirement also applies to all members of the nominating, corporate governance and compensation committees of NYSE companies and – with a limited exception for 'controlled companies',[194] and 'exceptional and limited circumstances'[195] – the members of the comparable committees of NASDAQ companies.

In addition, audit committee members must meet two tests of independence prescribed by Section 301 of the Sarbanes-Oxley Act:

- They must accept no payment from the issuer other than for board or committee service; and
- They must not be an 'affiliate' of the issuer.

Under SEC rules, an 'affiliate' of an issuer is a person that controls, is controlled by or is under common control with the issuer. For purposes of the Section 301 test, the SEC adopted a safe harbour provision, under which a person who is neither an executive officer nor an owner of 10% or more of a class of voting equity securities of the issuer (and who is not an executive officer, inside director, general partner or managing member of an affiliate) is not an affiliate.

The Dodd-Frank Act requires US national securities exchanges to adopt independence standards for compensation committee members that are similar to those that currently apply to audit committee members.[196] However, whereas a director who fails to meet these standards is automatically disqualified from serving on the audit committee, the new provision requires the exchanges to create a definition of 'independence' for compensation committee members. This definition must consider the source of compensation of the committee member (including any fees paid by the company), the affiliate status of the member and other relevant factors. Foreign private issuers are expressly exempted from this requirement, so long as they provide annual disclosure about why they do not have an independent compensation committee.

---

192 NYSE Listed Company Manual, §§303A.04-0.5; NASDAQ Stock Manual Listing Rules, §5605(d)-(e).
193 NYSE Listed Company Manual, §303A.02; NASDAQ Stock Market Listing Rule 5605(a)(2).
194 NASDAQ Stock Market Listing Rule 5615(c).
195 NASDAQ Stock Market Listing Rule 5605(d)(3)(e).
196 Dodd-Frank Act §952.

Audit committee functions: A number of Sarbanes-Oxley Act provisions have affected audit committee procedures:

- Authority over auditor – reflecting the requirements of Section 301 of the Sarbanes-Oxley Act, the rules of the NYSE (Listed Company Manual, Section 303A.06) and NASDAQ (Listing Rule 5605(c)) require that the audit committee be directly responsible for the appointment, compensation and oversight of the work of the auditor, and that the auditor report directly to this committee.
- Complaints, advisers, funding – as further specified by Section 301 of the Sarbanes-Oxley Act, the rules require that:
  - the audit committee establish procedures for treatment of complaints received by the issuer regarding accounting or auditing matters, and for confidential submission by employees of concerns regarding questionable accounting or auditing;
  - the committee have authority to engage independent counsel and other advisers at its discretion; and
  - the issuer provide funding, as determined by the committee, for payment of the auditor and any such advisers.
- Pre-approval of audit and non-audit services – Section 202 of the Sarbanes-Oxley Act specifies that the audit committee shall pre-approve both audit services and non-audit services (eg, tax services) that an auditor is not prohibited from performing for an audit client by Section 201 of the same act.[197] Charters of NYSE and NASDAQ-listed issuers should reflect the pre-approval requirement as a responsibility of the audit committee.

Code of ethics; financial expert: The Sarbanes-Oxley Act and rules adopted by the SEC on January 23 2003 require disclosure of whether the issuer has a 'code of ethics' for its principal executive officer and senior financial officers, and whether the issuer's audit committee has a 'financial expert'.[198] The NYSE and NASDAQ require such a code of ethics for directors, officers and employees. Both organisations require a level of financial competence through the presence of:

- at least one audit committee member with accounting or related financial management expertise (NYSE); or
- at least one member with an accounting or comparable background that results in financial sophistication (NASDAQ).[199]

Shareholder approval of stock plans: Both the NYSE and NASDAQ require shareholder approval of all stock compensation plans or the material revisions of such plans, subject to very limited exceptions.[200]

---

197 See "Periodic reporting requirements".
198 See "Periodic reporting requirements".
199 NYSE Listed Company Manual, Section 303A.10; NASDAQ Stock Market Listing Rule 5610.
200 NYSE Listed Company Manual §303A.08; NASDAQ Stock Market Listing Rule 5635(c).

(c) Application to foreign private issuers

Home country practice: Both the NYSE and NASDAQ recognise that their corporate governance standards may conflict with those of a foreign private issuer's home country corporate laws or the rules of its principal foreign securities market:

- The NYSE states that listed foreign private issuers "are permitted to follow home country practice in lieu of" the provisions of the NYSE's corporate governance rules, except for the audit committee provisions and certain certification requirements.[201]
- NASDAQ allows a foreign private issuer to depart from its corporate governance rules other than the provisions dealing with audit committees, voting rights and notice of non-compliance. These permitted departures are available only if the issuer provides a letter from outside counsel in the issuer's home country certifying "that the issuer's practices are not prohibited" by home country law.[202]

Disclosure of differences: The NYSE requires foreign private issuers to disclose the significant ways in which their actual corporate governance practices (as distinguished from general home country corporate governance practices) differ from those followed by listed US issuers. The NYSE expects a "brief, general summary" of the significant differences. This information must be provided in Form 20-F or, if the issuer does not file such a form, either in the issuer's annual report filed with the SEC or in English on the issuer's website.[203] This disclosure is a required element of Form 20-F.[204]

NASDAQ requires a foreign private issuer to disclose each corporate governance requirement that it does not follow and describe the home country practice that it follows instead. This disclosure is required in Form 20-F. A foreign private issuer that does not file Form 20-F may make this disclosure only on its website. NASDAQ requires similar disclosure at the time that an issuer makes its initial public offering or first listing on NASDAQ, in which case the disclosure must be included in the registration statement or on the issuer's website.[205]

Limited exemptions from Sarbanes-Oxley provisions: In its April 9 2003 release, in which it adopted the audit committee rules required by Section 301 of the Sarbanes-Oxley Act, the SEC observes that this act "makes no distinction between domestic and foreign issuers". But it goes on to recognise that the SEC's responsive rules could "conflict with legal requirements, corporate governance standards and the methods for providing auditor oversight in the home jurisdictions of some foreign issuers", and provides certain limited exemptions for foreign private issuers from the act's standard of audit committee independence and its requirement that the committee have direct responsibility over the auditor.[206] These are as follows:

---

201 NYSE Listed Company Manual §303A.00.
202 NASDAQ Stock Market Listing Rules §5615(3).
203 NYSE Listed Company Manual §303A.11.
204 Form 20-F, Item 16G.
205 NASDAQ Stock Market Listing Rules §5615(3).

- An employee who is not an executive officer is exempt from the Section 301 independence standard if serving pursuant to home country legal, collective bargaining or listing requirements;
- One non-voting committee member who is neither an executive officer nor the committee chair may be exempt from the non-affiliate portion of the Section 301 independence standard if he or she owns (or represents the owner of) more than 50% of the foreign private issuer's voting common equity;
- One committee member who is not an executive officer may be exempt from the non-affiliate portion of such standard if he or she represents a foreign government or foreign governmental entity that is an affiliate of the foreign private issuer; and
- A foreign private issuer will generally be exempt from the audit committee provisions of Section 301 where:
  - it is listed or quoted on a foreign exchange or inter-dealer quotation system; and
  - it is subject to auditor oversight through a board of auditors or statutory auditor that is separate from the issuer's own board and meets various conditions, including performance of the functions required by Section 301.[207]

Foreign private issuers must be aware of these limited exemptions because the NYSE's and NASDAQ's audit committee corporate governance rules incorporate them by direct reference to Exchange Act Rule 10A-3.[208]

---

206 SEC Release No 33-8220, "Standards Relating to Listed Company Audit Committees" (April 9 2003).

207 These conditions are that:
- the board of auditors or statutory auditor is established and selected pursuant to home country legal or listing provisions that either require or permit such a board or auditor and set independence standards for it;
- the board of auditors or statutory auditor is not elected by management, and none of the foreign issuer's executive officers is a member of the board of auditors or statutory auditor; and
- the board of auditors or statutory auditor is responsible for the appointment, retention and oversight of the work performed by any registered public accounting firm hired by the issuer.

208 See NYSE Listed Company Manual §303A.06; NASDAQ Listing Rule 5605(c).

3. Private placements

3.1 Overview

As previously discussed, the Securities Act requires the registration of any offer or sale of securities made in the United States, unless a specific exemption is available. A properly structured 'private' offering makes use of such statutory exemptions as Rule 144A, Regulation D[209] or Section 4(2) of the Securities Act to enable foreign private issuers to enter the US capital markets without undertaking a public registered offering.

A private offering in the United States has several advantages over a public offering:

- Offering documents in an unregistered private offering are not subject to the detailed disclosure requirements applicable to a registered public offering (unless non-accredited investors are involved)[210] and do not have to be filed in advance with, or cleared by, the SEC. They are, however, subject to the anti-fraud provisions of Rule 10b-5 under the Exchange Act.[211]
- When an issuer makes a private offering, it does not automatically come within the periodic reporting provisions of the Exchange Act, although it may become subject to such requirements if it develops a sufficient US shareholder base or elects to list its securities on a US national securities exchange.
- The expenses related to a private offering (eg, accounting, legal and underwriting costs) are generally lower than those for a registered public offering because:
  - the issuer can avoid the registration process under the Securities Act; and
  - the issuer does not have to pay the fees for listing on a US national securities exchange.
- The timing of the offering is not restricted by US registration requirements.
- Because a private offering of securities under Rule 144A may be placed with large and sophisticated US institutional investors known as 'qualified

209 Securities Act Rules 501-508.

210 Securities Act Rule 502(b).

211 See Securities Act Regulation D Preliminary Notes. Exchange Act Rule 10b-5 states "It shall be unlawful for any person, directly or indirectly, by the use of any means..., (a) To employ any device, scheme, or artifice to defraud, (b) To make any untrue statement of a material fact or to omit to state a material fact necessary in order to make the statements made, in the light of the circumstances under which they were made, not misleading, or (c) To engage in any act, practice, or course of business which operates or would operate as a fraud or deceit upon any person, in connection with the purchase or sale of any security."

institutional buyers' and immediately resold in the foreign private issuer's home market, the issuer can access the US capital markets faster than through a US public offering and take advantage of market windows. This advantage, however, is less important for well-known seasoned issuers which can access the US capital markets quickly because of their ability to use automatic shelf registration.

There are, of course, disadvantages to a private offering in the United States over a public offering:

- Issuers must concern themselves with the prohibition against 'general solicitation' in the United States, whereas the SEC has liberalised the communications allowed before and during US public offerings.
- Purchasers of securities from underwriters in a registered public offering may freely resell them without the need for further registration (unless the purchasers are 'affiliates' of the issuer). The same is not true of purchasers of privately placed securities. Securities purchased in a private placement are not freely tradable, unless the resale is exempt from registration, as discussed below. For this reason, these securities are characterised as 'restricted securities'[212] (defined by the SEC as securities acquired from the issuer "in a transaction or chain of transactions not involving any public offering"). Purchasers' receipt of such securities is commonly accompanied by express resale restrictions imposed by the issuer to avoid the risk of an illegal secondary offering.[213]

Due to these disadvantages, a public offering in the United States provides access to a larger market of investors and tends to be better for larger offerings than private placements. US public offerings also ensure ease of future access to the US public markets because of their eligibility for short form and shelf registration.[214]

(a) Securities Act Section 4(1) exemption

Section 4(1) of the Securities Act exempts transactions by persons other than issuers, underwriters or dealers.[215] It is the most commonly used registration exemption for resales of securities in the secondary market and is also called the 'ordinary trading exemption'.

An 'underwriter' is defined broadly to include any person who either purchases securities from an issuer or an affiliate with the goal of distribution, or offers or sells securities in connection with a distribution (public offering).[216] A 'broker-dealer' is any person who engages in securities transactions on behalf of others or who is regularly engaged in the business of buying or selling securities.[217]

The circumstances in which the Section 4(1) exemption applies are spelled out in

212 Securities Act Rule 144(a)(3).
213 Securities Act Rule 502(d).
214 See Appendix B for a further comparison of private placements and public offerings by foreign private issuers.
215 Securities Act §4(1).
216 Securities Act §2(a)(11).

the safe harbours of Rule 144 and Rule 144A discussed below. Precautions must be taken by the issuer so that unregistered resales of restricted securities by the initial purchasers either:

- come within the exemption in Section 4(1) of the act for "transactions by any person other than an issuer, underwriter or dealer";
- are made outside the United States in accordance with Regulation S; or
- are otherwise exempt from registration requirements.

(b) Resales under safe harbour Rule 144

Rule 144 is one of two 'safe harbour' rules of the SEC that spell out circumstances in which the Section 4(1) exemption from registration can apply to resales of restricted securities in the United States. The SEC deems a person reselling in accordance with Rule 144 "not to be engaged in a distribution of such securities and therefore not an underwriter", with the result that the resale would be entitled to a Section 4(1) exemption.[218] Non-affiliates selling restricted securities of non-reporting issuers (or of issuers that have been reporting under the Exchange Act for less than 90 days) may resell the securities without registration after the passage of one year from the time of original acquisition of the securities from the issuer (or, if later, from an affiliate of the issuer).[219] For sales of restricted securities of Exchange Act reporting issuers that have been reporting for at least 90 days, the holding period is six months rather than one year; however, resales may be made only if the issuer has met the current public information requirements by having filed all required Exchange Act reports during the past 12 months.[220] The holding period does not begin until the full purchase price is paid.[221] In addition, for securities acquired pursuant to a subscription agreement, the agreement must have been accepted by the issuer or the shares must have been issued before the holding period begins.

New investors may 'tack' or add on the holding period of prior investors that were not affiliates of the issuer.[222] The holding period restarts for any intervening ownership by the issuer or its affiliates. Rule 144(d) sets out specific tacking provisions for different situations, such as stock dividends, pledges, gifts, mergers and option exercises.

Persons that are affiliates of the issuer, or that were affiliates in the 90 days prior to the sale, may also use Rule 144, but their sales are subject to additional limitations with respect to the amount sold, limitations on the manner of sale and a notice requirement.[223]

Limits on amount of securities sold: Sales of securities of the same class by a

---

217 Securities Act §2(a)(12). An ordinary purchaser who uses a broker-dealer to resell his securities may rely on the registration exemption under Section 4(3) of the Securities Act.

218 See Preliminary Note to Securities Act Rule 144; see also, SEC Release No 33-5223, "Notice of Adoption of Rule 144 Relating to the Definition of the Terms 'Underwriter' In Sections 4(1) And 2(11) and 'Brokers' Transactions' in Section 4(4) of the Securities Act of 1933, Adoption of Form 144, and Rescission of Rules 154 and 155 under that Act" (January 11 1972).

219 Securities Act Rules 144(b)(1) and (d).

220 Securities Act Rules 144(b)(1) and (c)(1).

221 Securities Act Rules 144(d)(1)(iii) and (2).

222 See SEC Investor Information, "Rule 144: Selling Restricted and Control Securities" (August 6 2008).

223 Securities Act Rule 144(b)(2).

particular affiliate (and certain aggregated entities) in any three-month period may not exceed the greater of:

- 1% of the issuer's outstanding shares of the same class of securities;
- the average weekly reported trading volume of that class of securities on US national securities exchanges for the four weeks before the sale; or
- the average weekly trading volume reported pursuant to an effective transaction reporting plan or an effective national market system plan for the four weeks before the sale.[224]

Debt securities may not exceed these restrictions; nor may they exceed 10% of the principal amount of the particular tranche or class of securities.[225] These volume restrictions do not apply to sales by non-affiliates of the issuer.

Manner of sale: Sales by affiliates must be transacted through either a Section 4(4) broker transaction, a transaction directly with a market maker or a 'riskless principal transaction'. The latter is a trade in which a broker or dealer buys or sells securities as a principal to satisfy a customer's order, and in which offsetting trades are executed at the same price (other than an explicit markup, markdown, commission or fee). A Section 4(4) 'broker's transaction' means that the broker must:

- execute the orders as agent and receive no more than the usual customary commission;
- not solicit or arrange for the solicitation of orders to buy in anticipation of or in connection with the sale; and
- not be aware, after reasonable inquiry, of circumstances that indicate the person for whose account the securities are sold is an underwriter of the securities, or that the transaction is part of a distribution of those securities.[226]

The seller may not:

- solicit or arrange for the solicitation of orders to buy in anticipation of or in connection with the sale; or
- make any payment in connection with the offer or sale to anyone other than the broker executing the order.[227]

Notice of sale: If Rule 144 sales by an affiliate involve more than 5,000 shares or have an aggregate sale price of more than $50,000 in any three-month period, the seller must file notice of the sale with the SEC on Form 144.[228] The notice of sale requirement does not apply to sales by non-affiliates.

(c) Securities Act Section 4(2) private placements

Section 4(2) of the Securities Act provides a private placement exemption for any

---

224 Securities Act Rule 144(e)(1).
225 Securities Act Rule 144(e)(2).
226 Securities Act Rule 144(f)-(g).
227 Securities Act Rule 144(f).
228 Securities Act Rule 144(h).

transaction by an issuer that does not involve a public offering. It does not exempt the securities from registration indefinitely, and resales must either be registered or fall under an available registration exemption.

Such private placements are most commonly made directly to institutional investors by issuers, without the participation of an underwriter. An investment bank will likely act as financial adviser to the issuer, and the purchasers will mainly be insurance companies, pension funds and other institutional investors with sophisticated knowledge of the capital markets.

These investors almost always intend to hold the securities to maturity, subject to their potential need to restructure their portfolio. In such cases these investors usually rely on the exemption provided by Section '4(1½)' described below to dispose of such securities. As a result, they invest mostly in self-liquidating debt securities and mandatorily redeemable preferred stock, and also in private equity securities with registration rights or puts.

In order to clarify what constitutes a 'private' rather than a 'public' offering, in 1982 the SEC adopted Regulation D, which provides 'safe harbour' guidelines.

(d) 'Safe harbour' Regulation D

Regulation D[229] under the Securities Act is a collection of rules that govern the limited offer and sale of securities without Securities Act registration. Issuers often follow Regulation D guidelines to assure the availability of an exemption from registration. Regulation D is non-exclusive. Therefore, even if an offering does not comply with the regulation's requirements, an exemption under Section 4(2) may still be available.

Regulation D contains three alternative safe harbours from registration requirements:

- Rule 504 permits offerings of up to $1 million per year by non-reporting companies (including foreign private issuers that provide information under Rule 12g3-2(b)). There is no limitation on the categories of investors that may purchase securities under Rule 504 and no requirement to provide any particular information (although the offering is subject to anti-fraud rules).
- Rule 505 permits offerings of up to $5 million per year, provided that the number of purchasers is limited to 'accredited investors' plus no more than 35 non-accredited investors, about which specified information must be provided. This rule is not available if the issuer or any of its officers, directors or significant shareholders has engaged in certain 'bad acts'.
- Rule 506 permits an offering of any size to an unlimited number of accredited investors and up to 35 non-accredited investors. As under Rule 505, specified information must be provided if any purchasers in the offering are not accredited investors. In addition, each purchaser that is not an accredited investor must have "such knowledge and experience in financial and business matters that he or she is capable of evaluating the merits and risks

229 Securities Act Rules 501-508, 17 CFR §230.501 *et seq.*

of the prospective investment". This latter requirement may be satisfied with the assistance of a 'purchaser representative' that meets this standard and is neither an affiliate nor an employee of the issuer.[230]

Certain requirements are common to two or more of these rules:

- All three exemptions are subject to a prohibition on general solicitation and general advertising of the offering. There is a limited exception from this prohibition for press conferences held and similar press-related materials released outside the United States (and, in the case only of Rule 504, there are other exceptions for offerings sold under certain types of state law provisions).[231]
- In the case of Rules 504 and 505, the applicable dollar limit is reduced by the amount of offerings under specified exemptions from registration.
- All three rules require the issuer to file with the SEC and regularly update a notice of sale on Form D containing information about the offering, as described below.[232]

Accredited investors: 'Accredited investors' include most categories of institutional investors and other persons who are presumptively sophisticated and financially able to bear investment risks.[233] Rule 501(a) of Regulation D includes the following eight categories in the definition of 'accredited investors', including investors which the issuer reasonably believes qualify in these categories:

- institutional investors, which include US banks, US branches of agencies of foreign banks, registered broker-dealers and registered investment companies,
- business development companies;
- small business investment companies;
- private business development companies;
- corporations, partnerships and tax-exempt organisations with assets of more than $5 million. Limited liability companies with more than $5 million are accredited investors if they meet additional requirements of Rule 501(a)(3);
- the issuer's directors, executive officers and general partners. The definition does not include persons in these capacities at the issuer's subsidiaries;
- individuals with a net worth of more than $1 million (excluding the value of the person's primary residence);[234]
- individuals with an annual income of more than $200,000 or whose joint annual income with their spouse exceeds $300,000;
- trusts with more than $5 million in assets; and
- entities whose equity owners are all accredited investors.

---

230 Securities Act Rule 501(h).
231 Securities Act Rules 502(c) and 504(b)(1).
232 Securities Act Rule 503.
233 Securities Act Rule 501(a).
234 Section 413(a) of the Dodd-Frank Act amends the definition of 'accredited investor' with regard to natural person-accredited investors by excluding the value of the person's primary residence from the calculation of net worth. See also SEC Compliance and Disclosure Interpretation Q. 255.47, interpreting this change.

Under Dodd-Frank, the SEC is required to issue rules in 2011 that will disqualify felons and other 'bad actors' from relying on Rule 506 of Regulation D. These rules will also disqualify an offering or sale by a person that has been convicted of a felony or misdemeanour in connection with a purchase or sale of securities or a false SEC filing, or is subject to a final order that:

- bars them from engaging in securities activities, among others; or
- is the result of violating a law or regulation that prohibits fraudulent, manipulative or deceptive conduct in relation to an offer or sale of securities, within the 10 years prior to the Regulation D offer.[235]

Timing and procedure: All sales that are part of the same Regulation D offering must satisfy all of its terms and conditions. Rule 502(a) of Regulation D provides a six-month integration safe harbour to determine which sales are part of the same Regulation D offering. Offers and sales made more than six months before the start of the offering and more than six months after the end of the offering are not considered part of the same offering.

Regulation D requires an issuer to file a notice with the SEC on Form D, no later than 15 days after the first sale of securities has been made. Companies must file Form D electronically through the SEC's website; the forms are then immediately accessible to the public. Amendments to Form D must be made to correct material errors of fact, when there are changes in information and annually if it is a continuous offering that is still ongoing (on or before the first anniversary of the first filing of the Form D or most recent amendment). Issuers should make sure to check state securities law requirements and submit a copy of Form D to state authorities if required. As already noted in "Public offerings", in 2001 the SEC adopted safe harbour Rule 155 to allow issuers to switch from a public offering to a private placement under certain conditions.

Proposed changes to Regulation D: In August 2007 the SEC proposed changes to Regulation D,[236] including:

- creating a new safe harbour for 'large accredited investors' to allow an issuer to sell an unlimited amount of securities to them in offerings involving a limited amount of advertising. Large accredited investors would be similar to accredited investors, but with higher dollar thresholds. They would include entities with more than $10 million in assets, individuals who either own more than $2.5 million in investments or have an annual income of more than $400,000 ($600,000 if married), and all categories of entities and individuals included in aspects of the definition of 'accredited investor' that do not involve dollar thresholds;
- shortening the timeframe needed between offerings to avoid integration of the offerings from six months to 90 days; and

---

235 Dodd-Frank Act §926.

236 See SEC Release No 33-8828, "Revisions of Limited Offering Exemptions in Regulation D" (August 3 2007).

- liberalisation of private placements during public offerings, making it possible to conduct a concurrent private placement if the issuer can establish that the participants were not solicited through the registration statement.

However, the SEC has not finalised these revisions to Regulation D and continues to take comments upon the proposed changes.

(e) Section '4(1½)' resales

The Section '4(1½)' exemption is not established by any written SEC rule or regulation. Instead, it was developed by securities attorneys to allow resales of unregistered securities among sophisticated investors, on the basis of Section 4(1) and with a Section 4(2) structure: it was thus named Section '4(1½)'.[237] Under Section 4(1½) exemption theory, the holder of securities acquired through a private placement may sell them as long as the resale does not constitute a public offering or other distribution, a structure to which the SEC has not objected. This is the case when a purchaser is sophisticated and has access to all material information regarding the issuer. Section 4(1½) is generally used either for side-by-side offerings to both qualified institutional buyers (as described below) and other institutional investors, or for offerings made only to institutional investors.

Sellers typically follow the rules applicable to Section 4(2) or Regulation D when using Section 4(1½), such as limiting the overall number of buyers and obtaining written certifications as to their investor suitability and intent, in addition to:

- legending the securities;[238]
- notifying purchasers that the securities are unregistered and are not permitted to be resold in the United States without registration or an exemption;
- providing purchasers with information regarding the issuer and the securities;
- providing the issuer with the right to obtain legal opinions from an institutional buyer that is not a qualified institutional buyer that the sale of the securities is not required to be registered;
- notifying buyers of any 'stop transfer' procedures that may apply to the unregistered securities;
- implementing written transfer procedures (eg, transferee certifications); and
- requiring each purchaser to deliver an investor representation letter stating sophisticated financial knowledge.

3.2 Rule 144A offerings

(a) Overview

Rule 144A under the Securities Act provides a specific safe harbour exemption from its registration requirements for resales of privately placed and other 'restricted'

---

237 As discussed above, Section 4(2) may not be directly relied on by investors because it applies only to sales by issuers.

238 See the discussion of Regulation D this chapter; see also Appendix F for a sample legend for Regulation S, Regulation D and Rule 144A offerings.

securities to 'qualified institutional buyers' such as insurance companies, pension funds, mutual funds, hedge funds and commercial and investment banks. As further discussed below, the rule defines qualified institutional buyers by listing categories of institutional and other investors, and by prescribing a qualification test based on the size of the buyer's securities portfolio. As Rule 144A applies only to resales, an issuer cannot utilise this exemption. However, it is important because it allows a financial intermediary to buy unregistered securities from the issuer and resell them. In essence, taken together, Section 4(2) of the Securities Act and Rule 144A enable 'underwritten' private placements.

Transactions that qualify under Rule 144A are not 'distributions', as they do not involve public offerings, and are therefore not subject to registration under the Securities Act.[239] A person or party that sells under this rule is not an underwriter (within its statutory meaning) and therefore has an exemption under Section 4(1) for the sale.[240] A Rule 144A exemption is not available to the issuer, which must instead rely on Section 4(2).

Rule 144A was designed to improve the liquidity of the institutional secondary market for privately placed securities. Personnel in charge of buying for the portfolios of traditional institutional investors tend to regard Rule 144A securities as having a substantial degree of liquidity, in view of the breadth of the market. Although these continue to be 'restricted securities' for purposes of general Securities Act registration,[241] their free transferability among qualified institutional buyers brings them close economically to securities that have been issued in a registered public offering.

The PORTAL market operated by NASDAQ has attempted to provide liquidity for these privately placed securities, with moderate success.[242]

Issuer exemptions: Rule 144A is a resale safe harbour and is not available to the issuer of the securities. For the initial sale to the initial purchaser, issuers must continue to rely on other exemptions from registration, such as the private offering exemptions afforded by Section 4(2) and Regulation D, or the offshore offering provisions of Regulation S of the Securities Act. Immediate resale of restricted securities under Rule 144A will not cause an issuer to lose an otherwise valid exemption.[243]

Foreign private issuers making private placements of securities in the United States directly to institutional investors may confine the offering to accredited investors – the classification of offerees that places the least burden on an issuer seeking to invoke the Regulation D exemption for issuers of private offerings. The definition of 'accredited investor' in Regulation D is not the same as that of 'qualified institutional buyer' in Rule 144A (although most qualified institutional buyers would

239 Securities Act Rule 144A(b)-(c).

240 Securities Act Rule 144A(b).

241 Securities Act Rule 144A Preliminary Note 6; Securities Act Rule 144(a)(3)(iii).

242 Press Release, The NASDAQ Stock Market, Inc, "The PORTAL Market Trading System Will Begin Operating on August 15" (August 1 2007).

243 Securities Act Rule 144A Preliminary Note 7; SEC Release No 33-6862, "Resale of Restricted Securities", II-A (April 23 1990).

also be accredited investors). However, Rule 144A will be available for resales to qualified institutional buyers even if the issuer has sold to persons that would not be qualified institutional buyers.

(b) Placements through initial purchasers

Private placements are typically targeted for the Rule 144A institutional market in a two-stage transactional process, in which:

- an issuer sells the securities to an initial purchaser under the Section 4(2) exemption for issuers of private offerings; and
- the initial purchaser resells such securities pursuant to Rule 144A.

In such a two-stage process, the initial purchaser is acting functionally as if it were an underwriter in a registered public offering. But under Rule 144A, the initial purchaser's resales to qualified institutional buyers will be deemed not to involve a distribution to the public and hence not to be transactions by an 'underwriter' (using that term in the technical sense applied in Section 4(1)).[244]

Alternatively, the issuer may use a securities firm as a placement agent rather than as a dealer. In this configuration, the issuer sells directly to the private investors and the securities firm is compensated on a commission basis.

Although the Rule 144A exemption protects resales only to the qualified institutional buyer market, it is not uncommon for the issuer and the securities firm acting as initial purchaser to structure the transaction so as to permit resale not just under Rule 144A to qualified institutional buyers, but also to persons who – although not coming within the rule's definition of 'qualified institutional buyer' – would be 'accredited investors' under the Regulation D definition discussed above. A private placement permitting resales not only to qualified institutional buyers under Rule 144A, but also to accredited investors will target a larger investor group. But given that this rule protects only resales to qualified institutional buyers, it will be necessary in these instances to follow the more cumbersome procedures of a Section 4(1½) type of transaction. These procedures consist of the delivery of investment letters by the purchasers, and in some cases the delivery of legal opinions, stop-transfer procedures, legended securities and large minimum denominations for the restricted securities.

(c) General structure of Rule 144A

Rule 144A is available for resales by initial purchasers of restricted securities to qualified institutional buyers, subject to two eligibility requirements:

- The securities may not be issued by an open-end investment company that is subject to registration under the Investment Company Act; and
- At the time of their initial issuance, the securities may not be substantially identical or interchangeable with, or of the same class or series as, any security already listed on a US national securities exchange. Eligibility is not affected if the securities are subsequently listed on a US national securities exchange.[245]

---

244 Securities Act Rule 144A(b).

245 For further discussion see the section on "Ineligible securities" in this chapter.

In addition to the foregoing requirements, Rule 144A requires that:

- the seller reasonably believe that the securities are offered or sold only to qualified institutional buyers;
- US issuers that are not reporting under the Exchange Act and foreign private issuers that are neither reporting under the Exchange Act nor providing information under Exchange Act Rule 12g3-2(b) provide 'reasonably current' information concerning the issuer to any holder requesting it, while the security is restricted; and
- the seller notify the purchaser that the seller may rely on the Rule 144A exemption.

Securities that are acquired via Rule 144A are restricted securities within the meaning of Rule 144(a)(3).[246]

In addition, the PORTAL market operated by NASDAQ has attempted to provide liquidity for these privately placed securities.[247]

Rule 144A offering memorandum: The SEC has stated that the contents of a Rule 144A offering memorandum do not expose the parties to such an offering to liability under Section 11 or 12(a)(2) of the Securities Act.[248] Nevertheless, investment banks typically conduct the same type of due diligence as in a public offering.

Rule 144 resales: Restricted securities may be traded indefinitely among qualified institutional buyers in the 144A market without Securities Act registration. To sell outside this market, a prospective seller must either have the issuer register the resale or find another exemption. While restricted securities could be sold privately outside this market on the basis of general Section 4(1) or Section 4(1½) principles, and might be sold publicly under general Section 4(1) principles, in all probability the seller will look to the specific provisions of Rule 144 to make unregistered non-Rule 144A resales in the United States. A resale under Rule 144 will change a restricted security into an unrestricted one that may be freely traded in the US public markets.[249]

Regulation S: Generally, sales of securities in secondary offshore transactions pursuant to the resale safe harbour of Rule 904 of Regulation S are exempt from the registration requirements of the Securities Act so long as they are not accompanied by directed selling efforts in the United States.

Where buyers have acquired securities privately placed in the United States by a foreign private issuer, they may either use the resale exemption of Rule 144A to resell without registration within the qualified institutional buyer market, resell in the

246 Securities Act Rule 144A Preliminary Note 6; Securities Act Rule 144(a)(3).

247 Press Release, The NASDAQ Stock Market, Inc, "The PORTAL Market Trading System Will Begin Operating on August 15" (August 1 2007). For further discussion of the PORTAL market see "PORTAL Rules" in this chapter.

248 See *In re Safety-Kleen Bondholder Litigation*, Brief for Securities and Exchange Commission, as *Amicus Curiae*, No 3 Civ 01145 (DSC 2001).

249 For a more detailed discussion of Rule 144, see previously in this chapter.

United States without registration within the limitations of Rule 144, or effect an unregistered public resale outside the United States by following the provisions of Rule 904 of Regulation S.

In global offerings, foreign private issuers simultaneously:

- place securities in the United States that are targeted for resale under Rule 144A to qualified institutional buyers; and
- use Regulation S to exempt an offering outside the United States from registration.[250]

Anti-fraud provisions: Rule 144A provides an exemption only from the registration requirements of the Securities Act. It does not diminish the applicability of the anti-fraud provisions of Rule 10b-5 under the Exchange Act. Issuers will find that prospective institutional buyers of securities expect substantial business and financial disclosure by the issuer.[251]

Rule 144A has its own limited informational requirement, discussed below, which may or may not apply in a particular case, depending upon the status of the issuer. General disclosure and civil liability considerations, however, will be matters of concern in any private placement.[252]

State laws: The National Securities Markets Improvement Act of 1996 has made most state 'blue-sky' registration and qualification laws inapplicable to Rule 144A-structured offerings. In any event, virtually all such state laws exempt offers and sales to institutional purchasers. While definitions vary from state to state, as a general rule sales to qualified institutional buyers will be exempt under the state's own requirements.

(d) Qualified institutional buyers

For a transaction to come within the resale exemption provided by Rule 144A, the securities must be offered or sold only to specified large institutions and other specified entities (not necessarily institutional in nature) that come within this rule's definition of 'qualified institutional buyers'; or to offerees or purchasers that the seller, or any person acting on the seller's behalf, reasonably believes are qualified institutional buyers.[253]

A 'qualified institutional buyer' (often referred to as a 'QIB') is defined as an entity:

- coming within an extensive list of purchasers set forth in Rule 144A(a)(1), such as banks, savings and loan associations, insurance companies, registered investment companies, certain governmental and private employee benefit plans, and trusts, registered investment advisers, registered dealers, corporations, partnerships and others; and

250 See this chapter below for a more detailed discussion of Regulation S.
251 Issuer disclosure is discussed further in this chapter below.
252 General disclosure and civil liability concerns are discussed in this chapter below, and in "Securities litigation risks".
253 Securities Act Rule 144A(d)(1).

- acting for its own account or the account of other qualified institutional buyers, "that in the aggregate owns and invests on a discretionary basis at least $100 million in securities" of issuers that are not affiliates of the buyer (or, in the case of dealers, $10 million).[254] This includes entities formed for the sole purpose of acquiring restricted securities, provided that they satisfy the $100 million threshold.

Banks and savings and loan associations must also have a net worth of at least $25 million in order to be qualified institutional buyers, although this net worth test does not apply to their affiliates unless these are themselves banks or savings and loan associations. This additional test applies to both foreign and domestic banks and to US branches of foreign banks.

For purposes of calculating the amount of securities owned and invested on a discretionary basis, the following instruments and interests are excluded:

- bank deposit notes and certificates of deposit;
- loan participations;
- repurchase agreements and securities owned but subject to a repurchase agreement; and
- currency, interest rate and commodity swaps.

Securities are generally valued at cost rather than market value. A parent company will normally be permitted to aggregate holdings of its wholly owned and majority-owned subsidiaries.

For purposes of determining whether a prospective purchaser meets the securities ownership and discretionary investment test, sellers in Rule 144A transactions may rely on the following non-exclusive methods of determination:

- on the prospective purchaser's most recent publicly available financial statements, on the most recent information appearing in documents filed with the SEC, other federal or state regulatory agencies or foreign governmental or self-regulatory organisations or on recognised securities manuals such as Moody's and Standard & Poor's, provided in each case that such information is not more than 16 months old (18 months for a foreign purchaser) at the time of the sale;
- on a certification by an executive officer of the prospective purchaser (unless the seller knows that the certification is false);[255] and
- on lists of qualified institutional buyers provided by third parties, as long as such information is not more than 16 months old at the time of the sale.

Generally, securities that are privately placed to only qualified institutional buyers under Rule 144A, or other institutional investors, or offered in offshore transactions under Regulation S, are exempt from Regulation M.[256]

---

254 Securities Act Rule 144A(a)(1).

255 Securities Act Rule 144A(d)(1)(iv).

256 See the section on preparation in "Public offerings" for a discussion of Regulation M.

(e) *Ineligible securities*

Rule 144A does not extend to the offer or sale of securities that, when issued, are of the same class as securities that were listed on a US national securities exchange. These are generally referred to as 'fungible' securities.[257] This 'non-fungibility' limitation is designed to address concerns that the rule could result in undesirable side-by-side public and private markets in the same class of security.[258]

The following is an explanation of when various securities are considered to be fungible (and thus ineligible for resale under Rule 144A):[259]

- Common stock – shares of common stock are of the same 'class' if they are of "substantially similar character and the holders thereof enjoy substantially similar rights and privileges".
- Series preferred or debt – shares of preferred stock and debt securities issued in what are commonly viewed as different series will generally be viewed as "different, non-fungible classes" for Rule 144A purposes. This generally means that preferred stock or debt securities with the same dividend rates, liquidation preferences, voting rights, convertibility or other material similarities will be considered of the same class.
- American depositary receipts (ADRs) – where publicly traded ADRs are listed on a US national securities exchange, the deposited securities underlying them are also considered publicly traded and securities of the same class.[260]
- Convertible securities – a security convertible or exchangeable into a security so listed is treated as a security of the same class as the underlying security unless, at issuance, it is subject to an effective conversion premium of at least 10%.
- Warrants – whether trading as part of a unit with another security or separately, a warrant is treated as a security of the same class as the underlying security, unless it has a life of at least three years and an effective exercise premium of at least 10%.

In the interest of certainty to the seller, eligibility for resale will be determined at the time of issuance. The privately placed restricted securities of non-publicly traded issuers that thereafter create a public trading market in other securities of the same class will still be eligible for sale in reliance on Rule 144A.

Additionally, Rule 144A does not apply to securities issued by a mutual fund, asset investment trust or face-amount certificate company that is required to be registered under the Investment Company Act.[261]

(f) *Solicitation and resale procedures*

Although Rule 144A does not expressly prohibit general solicitation, practitioners

---

257 Securities Act Rule 144A(d)(3)(i); SEC Release No 33-6862, "Resale of Restricted Securities; Changes to the Method of Determining Holding Period of Restricted Securities under Rules 144 and 145" (Rule 144A Adopting Release) (April 23 1990).

258 SEC Release No 33-6839, IV-B (July 19 1989).

259 SEC Release No 33-6862, "Resale of Restricted Securities; Changes to the Method of Determining Holding Period of Restricted Securities under Rules 144 and 145" (Rule 144A Adopting Release) (April 23 1990).

260 See the chapter on "American depositary receipts".

261 Securities Act Rule 144A(d)(3)(ii).

and the SEC have articulated this prohibition in connection with Rule 144A resales. This is consistent with the prohibition against general solicitation in Regulation D and against directed selling efforts in the United States under Regulation S.

In connection with the Offering Reform Rules, the SEC carved out an exception from the Regulation D prohibition of general solicitation (under specified conditions) for research reports relating to the issuer in a Rule 144A offering, where the broker or dealer author is an offering participant.[262] US distribution of these reports must be limited to permitted offerees.

Since qualified institutional buyers are presumably sophisticated in securities matters, Rule 144A does not require the establishment of any specific procedures for making resales to such purchasers. It requires only that the seller and any person acting on the seller's behalf take reasonable steps to ensure that the purchaser is aware that the seller is relying on the registration exemption provided by Rule 144A.[263] The SEC expects qualified institutional buyers to take adequate steps to guard against a subsequent non-exempt distribution of restricted securities sold under this rule without any policing by sellers.

Where the seller takes such reasonable steps to ensure buyer awareness, the seller's transaction will be protected by the safe harbour, notwithstanding any subsequent unregistered, non-exempt offer or sale by a purchaser. Current practice in Rule 144A placements is to include in the offering memorandum a notice that sellers are relying on Rule 144A and a discussion of methods of unregistered resale that would be permissible for privately placed restricted securities.

(g) *Information requirements*

Rule 144A contains no specific informational requirement in connection with the resale of securities of:

- foreign private issuers providing information under Exchange Act Rule 12g3-2(b); and
- issuers that are reporting companies under the Exchange Act.

However, other issuers, in order for their securities to be eligible for resale under Rule 144A, must provide holders and prospective purchasers designated by holders the right to obtain, upon request, a limited amount of basic business and financial information.[264]

Nature of information: In the case of companies reporting under the Exchange Act and foreign private issuers already publishing information under Rule 12g3-2(b) of that act, there is no additional requirement in Rule 144A prescribing information that the issuer must provide to a qualified institutional buyer. Other issuers must provide purchasers with the right to obtain a limited amount of business and financial information concerning the issuer.[265] The specified information must be " reasonably current" and consist of "a very brief statement of the nature of the

262 Securities Act Rules 138(b) and 139(b).
263 Securities Act Rule 144A(d)(2).
264 Securities Act Rule 144A(d)(4).
265 *Id.*

business of the issuer and the products and services it offers", as well as specified financial statements, as discussed in more detail below.[266] The requested information must be received by the purchaser at or prior to the time of the sale.[267] Rule 144A does does not require that the financial information be prepared in accordance with US GAAP. SEC staff will not respond to questions with respect to the adequacy of the information provided pursuant to Rule 144A.

Such information must be "reasonably current in relation to the date of resale" under Rule 144A. This means that:

- the business description must be as of a date within 12 months of the resale date;
- the balance sheet must be as of a date less than 16 months before the sale; and
- the profit, loss, and retained earnings statements must be for the 12 months preceding the date of the balance sheet (with interim statements if the balance sheet is more than six months old).[268]

With regard to foreign private issuers, the required information will be presumed to be reasonably current if it meets the timing requirements of the issuer's home country or principal trading markets.

This informational requirement is a minimum standard. It is meaningful only in determining whether the Rule 144A exemption from Securities Act registration is available. Private offering memoranda targeting the qualified institutional buyer market are generally prepared in accordance with the due diligence and full informational principles discussed below, not only for marketing reasons, but also to avoid misstatements or omissions that could be actionable under Rule 10b-5 under the Exchange Act.

Making information available: Rule 144A does not specify how the right to obtain such information is created. The SEC suggests that the obligation could be imposed, among other ways, in the terms of the security, by contract, by corporate law or by rules of applicable securities exchanges or other self-regulatory organisations.[269] Where the issuer's status requires it to provide information for the purpose of Rule 144A resales, the offering memorandum and related material will presumably reflect the information requirement.

(h) PORTAL rules

In conjunction with the adoption of Rule 144A in 1990, the SEC approved a proposal by the National Association of Securities Dealers (NASD) to establish a special trading system, known as PORTAL, for trading restricted securities eligible for resale under Rule 144A. Only qualified institutional buyers may purchase in the PORTAL system.[270]

---

266 Securities Act Rule 144A(d)(4)(i).
267 Securities Act Rule 144A(d)(4).
268 Securities Act Rule 144A(d)(4)(ii).
269 SEC Release No 33-6862, "Resale of Restricted Securities; Changes to the Method of Determining Holding Period of Restricted Securities under Rules 144 and 145" (Rule 144A Adopting Release) (April 23 1990).
270 SEC Release No 34-27956, II-B-2 (April 27 1990).

The PORTAL system was designed to ensure that any secondary trading in the system would comply with Rule 144A. NASD members are required to report the resale of PORTAL securities:

- into the US public market under Rule 144; and
- from the US private market to an offshore market, or from an offshore market to the US private market; but they need not report wholly-offshore resales of PORTAL securities that were sold under Regulation S.

Foreign private issuers with securities trading on PORTAL will not be prevented from using Rule 12g3-2(b) under the Exchange Act.[271] Quotations on PORTAL will not be deemed 'directed selling efforts' within the meaning of Regulation S.[272] Just as Rule 144A provides a non-exclusive basis for resale of restricted securities without Securities Act registration, so too does PORTAL afford a non-exclusive structure for trading such securities solely in the institutional secondary market.

In November 2007 the NASD and 12 major securities firms announced the formation of the PORTAL Alliance to replace the PORTAL system. The SEC approved a rule change permitting Rule 144A securities to use alternative settlement processes to be quoted on the PORTAL system in order to facilitate the formation of the alliance.[273]

(i) Mechanics of pricing and closing

It is market practice for a Rule 144A offering to be treated much like an underwritten registered offering. The purchase agreement between the issuer and the initial purchasers for a Rule 144A offering typically resembles an underwriting agreement for an SEC-registered offering and typically includes:

- representations and warranties to confirm the accuracy of the offering memorandum;
- terms governing the mechanics of the transaction;
- covenants or agreements regarding disclosure, payments for various expenses and solicitation;
- closing conditions;
- indemnities relating to losses for false information or omissions; and
- terms governing termination of the agreement.

In many cases these transactions also include a registration rights agreement that obligates the issuer to register the offered securities under the Securities Act within a certain period. In these cases the issuer will generally file a registration statement to allow investors to exchange the securities purchased in the Rule 144A offering for SEC-registered securities. The registration rights agreement also sets out procedures and timing for the registration process. It is entered into on the closing date. Additionally, an issuer may make a private placement and then exchange the restricted securities for unrestricted securities. This is known as an A/B exchange offer

---

271 For more on Rule 12g3-2(b) see "Periodic reporting requirements".

272 See below for more on Regulation S transactions.

273 SEC Release No 34-56176, "Order Granting the Nasdaq Stock Market LLC's Application for an Exemption Pursuant to Section 36 of the Securities Exchange Act of 1934" (July 31 2007).

or 'Exxon Capital' exchange offer (after an SEC no-action letter). These securities offered in the exchange have identical terms as the original securities, but are no longer subject to resale restrictions.[274]

3.3 Regulation S offshore transactions

(a) Overview

Regulation S under the Securities Act[275] specifies that "offerings and sales that occur outside the United States" are not required to be registered under the Securities Act. This applies both to:

- public and private offerings by issuers outside the United States meeting the conditions of Rule 903 of Regulation S; and
- resale offerings outside the United States meeting the conditions of Rule 904.

If securities are sold in a secondary offshore transaction that is not accompanied by 'directed selling efforts' in the United States, pursuant to the resale safe harbour of Rule 904, there is no requirement to register the resale under the Securities Act. Thus, where a foreign private issuer places securities privately in the United States with institutional investors, those investors could effect an unregistered resale of the privately placed securities in the foreign private issuer's home country or elsewhere outside the United States by following the provisions of Rule 904. The resale may be public or private, immediate or deferred. There is no need to agonise over the availability of an exemption under Section 4(1).

(b) Conditions to use of Regulation S

Two basic conditions are applicable to any offering or resale under Regulation S. The offer or sale of securities must be:

- made in an offshore transaction; and
- accompanied by no 'directed selling efforts' in the United States.[276]

Offshore transactions: For an offer or sale to constitute an offshore transaction:

- the offer must either be made to a person outside the United States; or
- the transaction must be executed on an offshore capital market.[277]

Rule 902(b) of Regulation S specifies that many of the stock exchanges in the world's financial centres are designated offshore securities markets, including the stock exchanges of Amsterdam, Brussels, Frankfurt, London, Paris, Mexico City and Tokyo.

No directed selling efforts: 'Directed selling efforts' are activities "undertaken for the purpose of, or that could reasonably be expected to have the effect of, conditioning the market" in the United States for the securities.[278] Advertisements and press releases

---

274 For further discussion of registration rights agreements and A/B exchange offers see below.
275 Securities Act Rules 901-905.
276 Securities Act Rules 903 and 904.
277 Securities Act Rule 902(h); Securities Act Rules 138 and 139.

in the United States regarding the imminence of an offshore offering, or the posting of offshore offering materials on websites, may constitute such efforts. The SEC has taken a broad view of what constitutes directed selling efforts and foreign private issuers must be particularly careful in this area and use tools such as website blockers to block access by US residents to their offering materials.[279]

However, certain activities are not considered directed selling efforts:

- The SEC allows foreign private issuers that report under the Exchange Act or use Rule 12g3-2(b) to make limited statements in the United States regarding impending offshore offerings under Regulation S without having such statements treated as directed selling efforts. The statements must include a disclaimer that the securities are not being offered in the US and the issuer must take steps to guard against sales to US persons.
- US journalists are permitted to attend offshore press conferences and meetings with issuer representatives held in conjunction with offshore offerings and global offerings with both international and US components.
- Rule 135e of the Securities Act provides that a foreign private issuer, selling security holder or its representatives are not deemed to offer any security for sale by virtue of providing journalists access to press conferences held outside the United States, to meetings with the issuer or selling security holder representatives that are conducted outside the United States or to press-related materials outside the United States, at which a present or proposed offering of securities is discussed, so long as:
  - the present or proposed offering is not being solely conducted in the United States;
  - access is provided to both US and foreign journalists; and
  - any written press-related materials relating to the US offering contain language indicating that the materials are not an offer of securities for sale in the United States and, if the issuer or selling security holder intends to register any part of the offering in the United States, a statement noting this intention.[280]
- One-on-one interviews with US journalists are covered by the Rule 135e safe harbour. However, if the one-on-one meeting is exclusive to a purely US publication and no other one-on-one interviews are given to other foreign publications, this may signal to the SEC that this is a directed selling effort to channel publicity to the offering in the United States. If an issuer conducts a press conference that complies with Rule 135e either before or after the exclusive one-on-one meeting with a purely domestic publication, the one-on-one interview is covered by the safe harbour.[281]

---

278 Securities Act Rule 902(c).

279 See SEC Release No 33-7516, "Interpretation: Re: Use of Internet Web Sites To Offer Securities, Solicit Securities Transactions, or Advertise Investment Services Offshore" (March 23 1998).

280 SEC Release No 33-7470, "Offshore Press Conferences, Meetings with Company Representatives Conducted Offshore and Press-Related Materials Released Offshore" (October 10 1997); Securities Act Rule 135e (providing a safe harbour for "a foreign private issuer or foreign government issuer, selling security holder, or their representative").

281 *Id.*

- Compliance with the rules permits such attendance without it being viewed:
  - as a directed selling effort for purposes of Regulation S;
  - as an illegal offer to sell securities in the United States in violation of the Securities Act; or
  - as a general solicitation that would impair an otherwise valid private offering exemption from the Securities Act's registration requirements.[282]
- In its 2005 Offering Reform Rules,[283] the SEC confirmed that brokers and dealers participating in Regulation S offerings by foreign private issuers that are reporting companies under the Exchange Act may distribute research reports in the United States regarding the issuers without such reports being deemed directed selling efforts or inconsistent with an offshore transaction if certain conditions are satisfied:
  - The SEC defines a 'research report' as a written communication that includes opinions, recommendations or information regarding the securities of an issuer, or an analysis of an issuer's securities, thereby encompassing a broad category of research reports, whether issuer-specific or industry research that separately identifies the issuer. The research report does not have to provide sufficient information on which to base an investment decision.
  - These research reports are not deemed to constitute directed selling efforts or to be inconsistent with an offshore transaction if:
    - the broker or dealer publishes or distributes research reports in the regular course of its business;
    - the foreign private issuer has been registered with the SEC for at least a year and is up to date on all required reports;
    - the foreign private issuer satisfies certain public float thresholds or is issuing non-convertible investment grade securities; and
    - the foreign private issuer has had its equity securities trading on a designated offshore securities market for at least one year, or has a worldwide market value of its outstanding common equity held by non-affiliates of $700 million or more.[284]
- Advertisements of publicly offered securities that list the underwriters in the offering (known as 'tombstone advertisements') made in compliance with Rule 135 are permitted in any publication with less than 20% of its general circulation in the United States.[285]

Definition of 'US person': Regulation S distinguishes between and provides exemptions based on whether the selling activities are directed to 'US persons'. The regulation defines the 'United States' to include the United States of America, its

---

282 See *id.* For further discussion regarding publicity guidelines to guard against a general solicitation, see Appendix D.

283 SEC Release No 33-8591, "Securities Offering Reform" (July 19 2005). See the section on registration under the securities act in "Public offerings" for further discussion regarding the 2005 Offering Reform Rules.

284 Securities Act Rules 138 and 139; See Securities Act Rule 902(c)(3)(viii).

285 Securities Act Rule 902(c)(3)(iii).

territories and possessions, any state of the United States and the District of Columbia. 'US persons' are any natural persons residing in the US (whether or not they have US citizenship), or any partnership, corporation, agency, trust or discretionary account held by or for the benefit of a US person. The following are not US persons:

- US citizens living outside of the United States;[286]
- an employee benefit plan set up under the law of a country other than the United States;
- foreign branches of US banks or insurance companies; and
- international organisations such as the International Monetary Fund or the United Nations.[287]

(c) *Effect on foreign private issuers*

Regulation S distinguishes between:

- foreign private issuers that have a substantial US market interest in their securities; and
- foreign private issuers that do not have a substantial US market interest in their securities.

Regulation S specifies what is meant by 'substantial US market interest' in terms of the amount of trading on US national securities exchanges (in the case of equity securities), and the number and amount of securities holdings in the United States (in the case of debt securities):[288]

- For equity securities, a substantial US market interest exists if either:
  - US national securities exchanges constituted the largest market interest for the securities during the previous fiscal year; or
  - 20% or more of the trading in the class of securities was conducted on US national exchanges and less than 55% of all such trading was conducted in any single foreign country.
- For debt securities, a substantial US market interest exists if:
  - at least 300 US persons hold the issuer's debt;
  - US persons hold at least $1 billion of the issuer's aggregate debt securities; and
  - US persons hold at least 20% of the issuer's aggregate debt.

If a foreign private issuer has no substantial US market interest in its securities, it may sell them in offshore transactions – so long as they are not accompanied by directed selling efforts in the United States, as discussed above.[289] If substantial US market interest exists, Regulation S prescribes certain additional conditions to be met by a foreign private issuer in order to avoid the need for registration under the Securities Act. These conditions include the imposition on purchasers of so-called 'distribution compliance periods' during which neither the issuer nor any 'distributor' (eg, an

286 Securities Act Rule 902(k)(1).
287 Securities Act Rule 902(k)(2).
288 Securities Act Rule 90(2)(j); SEC Release No 33-7505, "Offshore Offers and Sales" (February 17 1998).
289 Securities Act Rule 903.

underwriter or dealer) may offer or sell the securities to a US person. The distribution compliance period is 40 days for a foreign private issuer's debt securities. For equity securities, the period for reporting issuers is 40 days and for non-reporting foreign private issuers it is one year.[290]

In order to deter perceived abuses of Regulation S by US issuers, the rules for US issuers are more strict. Equity securities sold offshore under Regulation S by any US issuer have a one-year distribution compliance period and purchasers of the equity securities must treat them as restricted securities for purposes of resale into the United States.[291]

(d) *What Regulation S does not exempt from*

Regulation S exempts offerings of securities that occur outside the United States only from the registration requirements of the Securities Act. It does not exempt those offshore transactions from other provisions of the US federal securities laws, such as the anti-fraud provisions of Rule 10b-5 of the Exchange Act.[292] A securities offering outside the United States could properly be made without registration, yet under certain circumstances be subject to enforcement proceedings, penalties or private damage suits under other provisions if the offering was made on the basis of fraud or misleading information.[293]

(e) *Contemporaneous US and international offerings*

A foreign private issuer may invoke Regulation S with respect to a public or private offering of securities that occurs outside the United States, even though the foreign offering accompanies a US registered or private offering.

A private offering in the United States does not lose an otherwise applicable exemption from the registration requirements simply because it is accompanied by an offering outside the United States that meets Regulation S conditions.[294] However, the foreign offering materials should not be used to solicit investors for the US private offering.[295] In the context of a public offering in the United States, the foreign offering materials should not be used to offer a US component to the public before SEC registration.[296] There are special Exchange Act rules that are designed to prevent market manipulation in connection with US securities offerings. Regulation M[297] addresses the propriety of certain offering practices by issuers and their underwriters, such as buying the offeror's securities and stabilising the market price of its securities while the offering is in progress. Where there are contemporaneous US and offshore (Regulation S) offerings by foreign private issuers, the issuers and their securities professionals need to examine whether home country offering practices create

290 Securities Act Rule 903(b)(2), (3).
291 Securities Act Rule 905.
292 Securities Act Regulation S Preliminary Note 3.
293 These circumstances are discussed in more detail in "Securities litigation risks".
294 Securities Act Rules 101(b)(10), 102(b)(7), Regulation M; 17 CFR §242.100.
295 For more see the section on electronic communication and the EDGAR system in "Periodic reporting requirements".
296 See "Public offerings".
297 Exchange Act Rules 100-105.

problems under the US rules.[298] Transactions in securities eligible for resale under Rule 144A are generally excluded from the market manipulation restrictions of Regulation M. The Regulation M stabilising rules include several features designed to accommodate multinational offerings.[299]

3.4 Resale registrations

(a) *Overview*

Purchasers in private placements may request a covenant by the issuer to register their resales under the Securities Act (or possibly condition the private placement closing on the effectiveness of such a registration). These registration rights contractually provide liquidity to investors by establishing a procedure to register the resale of securities acquired in a private offering and oblige the issuer to file a registration statement for the restricted securities.

Many private offerings under Rule 144A include registration covenants to enhance liquidity by giving the prospective institutional investors the comfort of being able to sell outside the qualified institutional buyer market during the rule's holding period following original issuance of the securities. (The Rule 144 holding period is six months for securities issued by Exchange Act reporting companies and one year for other securities.)

Foreign private issuers that are not reporting companies under the Exchange Act prefer not to grant registration rights to purchasers – for the same reasons as these issuers look to avoid Securities Act registration in the first place. As alternatives, foreign private issuers can point not just to Rule 144A, but also to the availability of Rule 904 of Regulation S, which permits unregistered resales outside the United States. Because foreign capital markets are presumably receptive to foreign private issuers' securities, the absence of US registration rights for their securities is less likely to create a significant price differential.

Two principal methods for registering Rule 144A securities after their private placement are:

- A/B exchange offers (also known as Exxon Capital transactions); and
- shelf registrations.

(b) *A/B exchange offers*

A/B exchange offers – commonly called 'Exxon Capital' transactions, after an early case where this technique was used[300] – are generally used when an issuer must raise capital quickly by avoiding the SEC review process before it receives its funds, but the investors still want the benefit and liquidity of registered securities. In these transactions, the issuer initially issues unregistered securities, subsequently registers new securities with substantially similar terms and then exchanges those registered securities for the unregistered securities within a specified period after completion of the unregistered

298 Securities Act Rule 104.
299 Securities Act Rule 105.
300 *Exxon Capital Holdings Corp*, SEC No-Action Letter (May 13 1988).

offering. The initial securities are thus privately placed and then promptly exchanged for similar securities that have been registered under the Securities Act.

The issuer's obligation to file an exchange offer registration statement is contained in a registration rights agreement with the initial purchasers. The issuer is usually subject to a payment of additional interest if it does not complete the exchange offer in a timely fashion.

Subject to certain conditions, upon completion of the exchange offer, the securities issued in the registered public offering may then be freely traded just like securities issued in any other registered public offering. This process may be used for certain debt or preferred stock offerings and for certain initial equity offerings by foreign private issuers. These A/B exchange offer transactions are usually the preferred way of providing holders of Rule 144A securities with freely tradable securities. They also eliminate the need to update shelf registration statements constantly.

A typical A/B exchange offer timeline will require the issuer to:

- file a registration statement to begin the exchange offer within 180 days of the original issuance of the privately placed securities;
- cause the registration statement to be declared effective within 220 days of the original issuance of the securities; and
- complete the exchange offer within 30 business days of the exchange offer registration statement being declared effective. The exchange offer must remain open for at least 20 business days under Exchange Act Rule 14e-1.

Since the Rule 144 holding periods were shortened in 2008, initial purchasers are generally agreeing to forgo registration rights. The issuer pays additional interest if the securities cannot be freely resold after an agreed period, which is usually one year.

Exxon Capital transactions generally cannot be used in connection with Rule 144A offerings of convertible securities. Contingent rights are generally agreed to in offerings of convertible securities. The issuer is required to file an exchange offer registration statement only if any of the registrable securities are not freely tradable on the registration trigger date. The trigger date typically refers to the fifth day after the one-year anniversary of the original issuance of the securities. The registration rights agreement terminates if the securities can be freely resold. If a registration statement is not filed by the trigger date or the securities are not otherwise freely transferable by the first anniversary, then the issuer must pay additional interest to the holders.

(c) Shelf registrations

Shelf registrations, which allow a single registration statement for the issuance of multiple tranches of securities, are available under Rule 415 of the Securities Act. They are used when the issuer determines that an exchange offer registration is not available or an Exxon Capital transaction cannot be used. They permit either delayed

301 Securities Act Rule 415(a)(1)(i).

or continuous offerings of securities "which are to be offered or sold solely by or on behalf of a person or persons other than the registrant".[301] The issuer files a shelf registration statement if:

- the exchange offer registration is not available;
- the exchange offer is not completed within a negotiated period from the closing date; or
- a legal opinion from the holder's counsel states that it must be filed.

Securities held by affiliates of an issuer and 'allotment securities' (securities purchased directly from the issuer and not resold to investors) held by the initial purchasers cannot be exchanged in an Exxon Capital transaction. As a result, most registration rights agreements still include provisions for a resale shelf registration so as to give initial purchasers rights to require the issuer to file a resale registration statement under which they can sell their securities.

The registration statement must be kept continuously effective for at least one year to ensure that the resale exemption continues to apply, and some registration rights agreements may require this indefinitely. Shelf registrations may also include the additional requirement that the holders notify the issuer whenever any resales occur.

(d) Types of registration rights

Registration rights are contractual rights and are typically demanded by investors in Rule 144A and Regulation S offerings, as well as in traditional Section 4(2) private placements. They may be demanded by large investors in Rule 144A offerings that want to sell in underwritten offerings. Registration rights in a traditional Section 4(2) private placement provide a mechanism for restricted securities to be registered under the Securities Act and sold in a public offering, such as when the Rule 144 exemption is not available.

There are three types of registration rights that the issuer may grant:

- 'demand' registration rights;
- 'piggyback' registration rights; and
- 'evergreen' registration rights.

Demand registration rights: Demand registration rights permit the holder of the issuer's securities to require that the issuer use its reasonable best efforts to register all or a portion of the holder's securities with the SEC. As registrations are very time consuming and expensive, and expose the issuer to substantial risks of liability, demand rights are limited in terms of how and when the demand may be made.

The issuer's obligation to register securities may also be conditioned on the receipt of demands from holders of a minimum amount of securities (eg, 25%) or a US dollar threshold to ensure that the issuer is not required to incur the time and expense of registering a small number of shares. Typical demand provisions may include:

- a time period specifying when the registration statement must be filed following a demand (eg, 90 days) and how long the issuer agrees to keep the registration statement effective (eg, 60 to 90 days rather than indefinitely);

- a provision entitling the issuer to postpone the holder's request for a specified amount of time if the issuer or the issuer's underwriter has in good faith determined that the holder's request would materially and adversely affect the issuer's offering. Such a period is known as a 'blackout period';
- a provision limiting the number of demands that may be made and requiring a certain amount of time to have lapsed since the last request was made; and
- the inclusion of an overall expiration date after which no more demands may be made or a date prior to which no demands may be made.

Piggyback registration rights: Piggyback registration rights permit the holder to include its shares in a registration that the issuer may be planning on behalf of itself or for the benefit of other stockholders. Typically, the issuer will provide written notice to all of its security holders with piggyback registration rights of its intention to register securities. The holder may then decide whether to include its shares in the issuer's registration statement. The issuer may limit this piggyback right to cover only those securities of the same class that the issuer is otherwise registering rather than having the piggyback right attach even if the issuer is registering a type of security different from the holder's. If a holder has only piggyback rights and not demand rights, the holder cannot trigger the registration process.

Piggyback rights may cause delays in the registration process being undertaken by the issuer and may complicate pricing and marketing efforts if the holders are permitted to withdraw from a transaction. Typical piggyback provisions may include:

- a requirement for a participating holder to sell in the offering through the same underwriters that the issuer is using. This is to ensure an orderly distribution;
- a requirement for the holder to refrain from making any sales until a specified period of time after completion of the distribution;
- the ability of the issuer to withdraw the registration of its securities up to the point of the registration statement becoming effective, without then having to proceed with registering any of the holder's securities;
- a provision that the holder may not be permitted to include its securities in the registration, or that they may include only a *pro rata* share, if the issuer's underwriter determines that including the piggyback request may have a material and adverse effect on the pricing, timing or distribution of the issuer's securities; and
- a provision providing for priority of the particular holder's right to piggyback on the issuer's registration before any other persons that may receive restricted securities from the issuer, but were not parties to the registration rights agreement itself.

Evergreen registration rights: Evergreen registration rights require the issuer to maintain an 'evergreen' registration statement in effect with the SEC. The issuer must keep its registration statement current until the holders have completed their sales – in other words, the prospectus must be updated and the registration statement amended in order to reflect new developments. Evergreen registration rights are seldom granted.

3.5 Disclosure in private placements

The detailed disclosure requirements that govern the content of a registration statement and prospectus in a public offering registered under the Securities Act are not specifically applicable to an offering memorandum or other offering documents in a private placement exempt from registration. However, many practitioners advise issuers to provide similarly extensive information in order to ensure the accuracy of their private offering memorandum.[302]

A prudent issuer would be well advised to prepare an offering memorandum that is not greatly different in content and appearance from the prospectus that is prepared in the course of a registered public offering. This will thus contain a business description and financial statements comparable to those appearing in a prospectus.

Private placement issuers will find that prospective institutional buyers of securities expect substantial business and financial disclosure by the issuer. It is important both to the issuer and to investment banking firms acting in a dealer or agent capacity for the issuer – from a reputational standpoint, as well as from the standpoint of liability – that there be no misstatement and no omission of information that is material to a proper understanding of the business and financial condition and prospects of the issuer.

Foreign private issuers that report under the Exchange Act, but choose the private offering route rather than registering a particular offering under the Securities Act, may simulate the incorporation by reference techniques used with respect to registered offerings and use their Form 20-F and Form 6-K reports to provide private offering disclosure. Referencing the information in an issuer's unrelated registered offering prospectus should not extend the Securities Act's Section 12 civil liabilities, which are applicable to registered offerings to the issuer's private offering.303

If registration rights or exchange offer covenants are invoked after the private offering, or if the issuer reports under the Exchange Act, the disclosure made in response to the registration or reporting requirements will be compared by investors (and their lawyers) with the disclosure made in the private offering memorandum.

It is important to keep in mind that Rule 10b-5 allows investors to sue for damages where they have been provided with incorrect or misleading information. The rule applies not only to a registered public offering and to Exchange Act reports, but also to a private placement.[304]

---

302 Securities Act Rule 159 makes the disclosure provided during the course of a private placement subject to evaluation as of the time the investor entered into the contract to purchase. Generally, issuers or underwriters will provide a final term sheet at the time of pricing to include any additional information that was not in the original offering memorandum.

303 See *Yung v Lee*, 432 F 3d 142 (2d Circuit December 13 2005).

304 For more see the discussion of civil liability in "Securities litigation risks".

(a) *Private placement due diligence*

Even though Section 11 of the Securities Act does not apply in an unregistered private placement, an investment banking firm handling a private offering, as well as executives and employees of the issuer and others, will want to consider investigatory procedures prior to the distribution of an offering memorandum that are comparable in most ways to the due diligence procedures that are followed in a registered offering.

Claims of violation of the civil liability provisions of Rule 10b-5 under the Exchange Act can be countered by showing that an adequate investigation found no reason to believe that the offering memorandum contained material misstatements or omissions.

Generally, due diligence involves sessions with senior management, purchasers and counsel, often based on a management presentation, as well as the review of relevant information. Some of the procedures that are standard for a registered public offering and may also be followed in a private placement include:

- comfort letters from the issuer's auditors, and disclosure letters and opinions from outside counsel to both the issuer and the initial purchaser;
- examination of all significant contracts and corporate records, and interviews with senior management of the issuer;
- discussions with the issuer's auditors and outside advisers;
- purchase agreements between the issuer and initial purchaser, which will govern the transaction and include any applicable representations, warranties or covenants; and
- registration rights agreements between the issuer and initial purchaser setting out the procedures and timing of any required registration process.[305]

(b) *Major disclosure areas*

The following are examples of disclosure that may be necessary in a private placement in order to avoid a materially misleading offering memorandum. They reflect some of the significant disclosure requirements in a registered offering under the Securities Act and in periodic reports under the Exchange Act:

- Financial statements – a registered public offering prospectus must include detailed audited financial statements. A foreign private issuer must present its financial statements prepared:
  - in accordance with the English language version of International Financial Reporting Standards (IFRS);[306]
  - in accordance with US generally accepted accounting principles (GAAP); or
  - in accordance with its home-country accounting standards, but with a reconciliation to US GAAP.

---

305 See Appendix C for a sample checklist for due diligence review in international securities offerings, and the section on SEC review in "Public offerings" above.

306 In order to avoid having to provide a reconciliation to US GAAP, the notes to the financial statements must state "unreservedly and explicitly" that the financial statements are in compliance with IFRS (as adopted by the International Accounting Standards Board), and the independent auditor's report on the financial statements must attest to such compliance. The same applies to audited financial statements of significant companies that a foreign private issuer has recently acquired or is about to acquire, and companies in which the issuer has a significant equity investment.

It would be prudent to consider including financial statements meeting the same requirements in the offering memorandum.

- Segment disclosure – if two or more major segments of an issuer's overall business contribute disproportionately to its revenues and income (eg, a segment that operates at a great profit and a second that operates at a substantial loss), it is likely to be misleading in either a prospectus or offering memorandum to present overall issuer financial information without any indication that such circumstances exist.
- Management's discussion and analysis – in registered public offerings the management's discussion and analysis of the financial condition and the results of operations (MD&A)[307] provides both an explanation of past performance and a prospective disclosure of business trends and uncertainties. A foreign private issuer should consider an MD&A-type presentation in a private offering memorandum.
- Risk factor disclosure – foreign private issuers that register public offerings under the Securities Act or file reports under the Exchange Act must make so-called 'risk factor disclosure'. It has increasingly been the practice in drafting a private offering memorandum to include risk factor disclosure comparable to that which would appear in a public offering prospectus.

(c) Comparison with registered public offerings

When a foreign private issuer evaluates the relative advantages and disadvantages of a registered public offering as compared with an unregistered private offering (structured to permit exempt resales under Rule 144A), it will consider timing, cost and the extent of corporate disclosure. If it has not yet entered the Exchange Act reporting system, its main concern may be the immediate or long-term prospect of becoming a reporting company.

Appendix B presents a quick comparison of these advantages and disadvantages. This chart assumes that the issuer does not report under the Exchange Act and that shelf registration is therefore unavailable.

(d) Internet issues

Whether relying upon Securities Act Section 4(2), Regulation D or Rule 144A, conducting a private offering that makes use of the Internet in any way – including the posting of press releases – in a manner that complies with the requirements for a valid private offering poses special challenges. Particularly challenging are avoiding of general solicitation and general advertising, and limiting the number and type of offerees.[308]

Procedures: The SEC has indicated that the posting of a notice of a private offering on a password-protected web page operated by an affiliate of a registered broker-

307 See the section on other disclosure issues in "Periodic reporting requirements".

308 For a discussion of the distribution of disclosure documents over the Internet, see the section on other disclosure issues in "Periodic reporting requirements".

dealer and accessible only to accredited and sophisticated investors previously identified by that broker-dealer does not constitute general solicitation or general advertising.[309] There must be a pre-existing substantive relationship between the potential investors and the broker-dealer such that the private offering activities of the broker-dealer and any issuer on whose behalf it acts is not a general solicitation. However, SEC staff has indicated that similar activities by non-broker-dealers with pre-existing substantive relationships may be found to facilitate general solicitation.[310]

Special access concerns arise in the context of a private placement in the United States, concurrent with an offshore offering under Regulation S, as set forth below:

- Access should be restricted from the United States, or by US persons to web-posted offering materials for the offshore offering. Technology such as website blockers should prevent access from the United States or by US persons.
- Persons responding to the foreign internet offering should be prohibited from participating in the concurrent private placement in the United States even if they would be otherwise qualified to do so.
- Access to the offering materials posted online for the Regulation S offering should be limited to viewers that provide residence information.
- Where the offering materials posted online are in the English language, access should be limited to persons established to be foreign persons that are granted passwords in advance using both self-certification and independent residence verification. This is also true where the offering materials are not posted in the English language, but there is reason to believe that a large expatriate community resident in the United States may seek to invest in securities issued in their home country.
- If password protections are not put in place, the posted offering information should be limited to the offshore offering, except for information about the US offering required by applicable foreign law to be provided to participating investors.

Publicity activities: Issuers should refrain from including information on their unrestricted websites that can be reasonably expected to encourage direct or indirect interest in the offering or be deemed to have been released for that purpose. This includes:

- all information about any aspect of the offering;
- information about the operations, financial position or prospects of the issuer;
- the level of dividend payout;
- any forecasts, predictions, projections or opinions with respect to the issuer; and
- any advertising not in the ordinary course of the issuer's business or inconsistent with past practice.

---

309 IPONET, SEC No Action Letter (July 26 1996).
310 *Id.*

Information relating solely to the issuer's products or services that the issuer typically puts on the website may be kept. Issuers should not establish or expand their unrestricted websites until after the offering is completed.[311]

Electronic road shows: The SEC has approved the use of the Internet to conduct road shows for private offerings in the United States.[312] In order to comply with Section 4(2) of the Securities Act, the electronic road show must be transmitted on behalf of an issuer solely to persons reasonably believed to be qualified institutional buyers, or accredited investors in Regulation D private placements. Other protective measures include:

- presenting the entire unedited live road show on the website;
- making the offering memorandum available on the website, accessible through a button on the site;
- restricting downloading, videotaping or other copying and distribution of the road show's content; and
- consistency between the road show and the offering memorandum.

311 For sample publicity guidelines for private placements by foreign private issuers, see Appendix D.

312 Net Roadshow, Inc, SEC No Action Letter (January 30 1998); Net Roadshow, Inc, SEC No Action Letter September 8 1997).

4. Periodic reporting requirements

4.1 Background

A foreign private issuer will enter the Exchange Act reporting system following either:

- a registered Securities Act public offering; or
- the filing of an Exchange Act registration statement, which it will be required to do if:
  - it lists a class of securities on a US national securities exchange; or
  - its equity securities become owned by a sufficient number of US investors, unless it falls under the automatic exemption of Rule 12g3-2(b).

4.2 Rule 12g3-2(b) exemption

Unless it falls under the automatic exemption of Rule 12g3-2(b), a foreign private issuer is required to register under the Exchange Act if:

- it has an equity security with 500 or more shareholders worldwide (300 of which are US resident shareholders); and
- its assets exceed $10 million.

This is true even if the foreign private issuer has not conducted a registered public offering of securities in the United States or otherwise filed a registration statement with the SEC.

(a) Old rule

Prior to October 2008, Exchange Act Rule 12g3-2(b) allowed a foreign private issuer facing Exchange Act registration because of its US shareholding to avail itself of a registration exemption by electing to do so before registration was required. The foreign private issuer would have to:

- furnish to the SEC information that was material to an investment decision and that the issuer made or was required to make public during the last fiscal year:
  - under the law of its country of organisation or domicile;
  - by an exchange on which its securities were traded, after it was filed with that exchange; or
  - had otherwise distributed to its security holders, including press releases and articles;

- provide additional information concerning the number of US holders of each class of equity securities, the circumstances under which they were acquired and the date and circumstances of the most recent public distribution of securities by the issuer or an affiliate;[313] and
- furnish the SEC, after this initial submission, with any additional information made public as required under local law, the exchange on which it was listed or to its security holders promptly after it was made public.

(b) 2008 amendment

In September 2008 the SEC adopted an amendment, which became effective on October 10 2008, that drastically altered the methods of compliance with Rule 12g3-2(b).[314] The SEC adopted the 2008 amendment to encourage cross-border capital flows and to make it easier for US investors to gain access to the material foreign disclosure documents of foreign private issuers – and thus make better-informed investment decisions.[315]

Generally, the new version of the exemption eliminates the requirement that the foreign private issuer proactively apply for the exemption through a written application, substituting instead a conditional, automatic exemption. Under this amendment, a foreign private issuer qualifies for exemption if it:

- is not otherwise required to register under the Exchange Act;
- maintains a listing on one or more international exchanges that constitute the primary trading market for its equity securities. This means that at least 55% of worldwide trading in such securities occurs in one or more markets in no more than two foreign jurisdictions during the issuer's most recently completed fiscal year; and
- electronically publishes in the English language, usually on its website, whatever 'material'[316] information it:
    - has made or is required to make public pursuant to its home country laws;
    - has filed or is required to file under the requirements of a foreign stock exchange; or
    - has otherwise distributed or is required to distribute to its security holders.[317] The following include examples of information considered material to an investment decision, and which therefore must be included on the website of a foreign private issuer claiming an exemption under Rule 12g3-2(b) to the extent that such information is otherwise made publicly available under home country requirements:

313 Exchange Act Rule 12g3-2(b)(1)(v) (2005).

314 SEC Release No 34-58465, "Exemption from Registration under Section 12(g) of the Securities Exchange Act of 1934 for Foreign Private Issuers" (September 5 2008).

315 SEC Press Release, "SEC Votes to Modernize Disclosure Requirements to Help U.S. Investors in Foreign Companies" (August 27 2008).

316 The term 'material' usually refers to those matters that a reasonable investor would consider important is determining whether to make an investment, which can depend on the particular facts or circumstances.

317 Exchange Act Rule 12g3-2(b)(1)(iii).

- financial condition and results of operations;
- changes in business;
- acquisitions or dispositions of assets;
- issuance, redemption or acquisitions of securities;
- changes in management or control;
- granting of options or other payments of other compensation to directors or officers; and
- transactions with directors, officers or principal security holders.[318]

The Rule 12g3-2(b) exemption is applied separately to each class of a company's equity securities. In other words, each class must satisfy all of the requirements of the exemption (including the stock exchange listing and primary trading market requirements) in order for it to be exempt from Exchange Act registration. By contrast, before the 2008 amendment, if a company satisfied the conditions for exemption, all of its securities were exempt from Exchange Act registration and reporting.

As a result of this change, if a company has any class of equity securities that does not satisfy the conditions of the exemption (eg, because it is not traded on a stock exchange), in order to avoid Exchange Act registration triggered by the second class, it will need to monitor the number of holders of that class to make sure they stay below either 500 worldwide or 300 US holders. An important exception to this part of the rule is that if a class of securities satisfies all of the conditions for the exemption, then compensatory stock options to purchase that class of securities are also exempt.

The foreign private issuer must disclose the documents in English either:

- on its website; or
- through an electronic information delivery system that is available to the public in its primary trading market.[319]

All relevant information since the start of the issuer's last completed fiscal year is required to be posted.

The 2008 amendment also requires foreign private issuers to maintain the exemption by publishing the required foreign disclosure documents on an ongoing basis. The information required is essentially the same as what was previously required to be submitted to the SEC.

The required documents must be published in English. Generally, summaries of foreign disclosure documents are not permitted. However, the SEC has indicated that if, as a registrant, an issuer may submit an English language summary under cover of Form 6-K or pursuant to Exchange Act Rule 12b-12(d)(3), then the issuer may also do so to maintain the exemption. However, at least the following must be translated into English:

---

318 SEC Release No 34-58465, "Exemption from Registration Under Section 12(g) of the Securities Exchange Act of 1934 For Foreign Private Issuers", II-C (September 5 2008); Exchange Act Rule 12g3-2(b)(3)(i).

319 SEC Release No 34-58465, "Exemption from Registration Under Section 12(g) of the Securities Exchange Act of 1934 For Foreign Private Issuers", II-C (September 5 2008).

- an annual report, including or accompanied by annual financial statements;
- interim reports that include financial statements;
- press releases; and
- all other communications and documents distributed directly to security holders of each class of securities to which the exemption relates.[320]

Under Rule 12b-12(d)(3), a party may submit an English language summary instead of an English translation of a foreign language document as an exhibit or attachment to a filing or submission, as long as the applicable form permits the use of an English language summary and the foreign language document does not consist of:

- articles of incorporation, memoranda of association, bylaws and other comparable documents, whether original or restated;
- instruments defining the rights of security holders, including indentures qualified or to be qualified under the US Trust Indenture Act of 1939;
- voting agreements, including voting trust agreements;
- contracts to which directors, officers, promoters, voting trustees or security holders named in a registration statement, report or other document are parties;
- contracts upon which a registrant's business is substantially dependent; or
- audited annual and interim consolidated financial information.

There is no requirement in Rule 12g3-2(b) that the information published meet technical Exchange Act reporting standards, although liability under Rule 10b-5 can be invoked if disclosure is materially misleading or contains material omissions.

The Rule 12g3-2(b) exemption remains in effect until the issuer:

- no longer maintains a listing of the subject class of securities on one or more exchanges in a primary trading market (ie, it is no longer listed on a foreign exchange or the one or two principal foreign jurisdictions in which its securities trade no longer meet the primary trading market definition);[321]
- no longer satisfies the electronic publication requirement; or
- registers a class of securities under Section 12 of the Exchange Act or incurs reporting obligations under Section 15(d) of that act.[322]

While there is no grandfather clause in the 2008 amendment, the amended rule does provide a three-year transition period by which issuers which will no longer qualify for the exemption under this amendment must either comply with the conditions of the amended Rule 12g3-2(b) or file a registration statement under the Exchange Act.[323]

---

320 Exchange Act Rule 12g3-2(b)(3)(ii).

321 Note that the definition of a 'primary trading market' uses a trading volume standard for an issuer's most recently completed fiscal year, so that the issuer will have to redetermine its relative US and foreign trading volumes on an annual basis.

322 Rule 12g3-2(c) under the Exchange Act.

323 SEC Release No 34-58465, "Exemption from Registration Under Section 12(g) of the Securities Exchange Act of 1934 For Foreign Private Issuers" (September 5 2008).

Relationship to American depositary receipt programmes: In order to establish an American depositary receipt (ADR) programme, a foreign private issuer needs to be either exempt under Rule 12g3-2(b) or a reporting company under the Exchange Act. Prior to October 2008, issuers could limit the establishment of unsponsored ADR programmes by failing to submit, obtain and maintain a Rule 12g3-2(b) exemption. However, now that the 2008 amendment has created automatic exemption criteria, international companies are finding that new unsponsored ADR programmes are being established on the over-the-counter capital markets in the United States without their consent or participation. It is now possible for a depositary bank to set up an ADR without the issuer's involvement if the bank believes in good faith, after exercising reasonable due diligence, that the issuer has properly published the required disclosure information in English and satisfies the other requirements of Rule 12g3-2(b).

The 2008 amendment and the increasing demand for ADRs from US investors have led to a significant increase in unsponsored ADR programmes since the 2008 amendment was adopted. Many foreign private issuers negatively view these programmes, over which the issuers have very little or no control.[324]

(c) *Effects of using Rule 12g3-2(b)*

A foreign private issuer that has not entered the Exchange Act reporting system – such as an issuer falling under the Rule 12g3-2(b) exemption – is not within the Sarbanes-Oxley Act's coverage or within the coverage of the rules that the SEC has adopted in response to that act. The various disclosure, certification and corporate governance provisions of Sarbanes-Oxley are applicable to 'issuers', a term defined narrowly in that act as an issuer that is subject to the reporting requirements of the Exchange Act.[325]

Even though Rule 12g3-2(b) information is not filed with the SEC, since it is published on the issuer's website or otherwise publicly available, it will be absorbed into the overall body of data that the US markets possess concerning the foreign private issuer. If the information is materially misleading or contains material omissions, Exchange Act Rule 10b-5 gives investors the right to bring the same kind of civil damage claims that they could bring under that rule against companies filing under the Exchange Act reporting system.

This exposure to liability for Rule 12g3-2(b) information has so far proved more theoretical than real, mostly because securities transactions relying on Rule 12g3-2(b) do not result in raising capital for the issuer, so the consequences for investors are limited. Nevertheless, documents drafted primarily for a foreign audience are less likely to meet the disclosure standards of US federal securities laws than those specially prepared for US filing purposes.

4.3 Exchange Act reports

The Exchange Act reporting requirements are designed to provide a continuous

324 For more see the chapter on "American depositary receipts".
325 Sarbanes-Oxley Act §2(a)(7).

stream of business and financial information from issuers once they become subject to these requirements. This is done primarily through the annual report that is required to be filed each year with the SEC. As with a Securities Act prospectus, an Exchange Act report must not only respond to instructions for providing financial statements and making specific textual disclosures, but also provide "such further material information" as may be necessary to make the required statements "not misleading".[326] In 2009 there were more than 950 foreign private issuers reporting under the Exchange Act.[327]

(a) *Annual report*

The annual report (Form 10-K for most US issuers and Form 20-F for foreign private issuers) contains the latest fiscal year's audited financial statements and updates of the issuer's MD&A and business description. Both Form 10-K and Form 20-F have been amended to reflect the changes introduced by the Sarbanes-Oxley Act and the SEC's responsive rules.[328]

Form 10-K filing deadlines for US companies vary depending upon their size. For so-called 'large accelerated filers' – essentially the same companies that are treated as 'well-known seasoned issuers' for Securities Act purposes[329] – the deadline to file with the SEC is 60 days after the end of their fiscal years. Other US issuers have from 75 to 90 days after fiscal year-end.[330] The Form 20-F filing deadline for all foreign private issuers is four months after fiscal year-end for fiscal years ending on or after December 15 2011.[331] Previously, the deadline for Form 20-F was six months after fiscal year-end.

In September 2008 the SEC adopted new rules for Form 20-F's timing and reporting obligations.[332] Various amendments became applicable immediately in 2009, while others are being implemented over a five-year period. The SEC adopted these amendments to "effect changes in the disclosure and other requirements applicable to foreign private issuers in light of market developments, new technologies and other matters in a manner that promotes investor protection and cross-border capital flows".[333] The following is a summary of these new rules:

- Annual determination of status – rather that doing so on a continuous basis, companies are permitted to assess their foreign private issuer eligibility annually, on the last business day of their second fiscal quarter.
- Annual disclosures – the amended Form 20-F requires new information to be disclosed, as follows:
  - any changes in the registrant's certifying accountant;
  - information about the fees and other charges paid by holders of any

326 Exchange Act Rule 12b-20.
327 SEC Division of Corporate Finance, International Registered and Reporting Companies Market Summary (December 31 2009).
328 Form 40-F, which is available only to certain Canadian foreign private issuers and is not discussed in this book, has been similarly amended.
329 See "Public offerings".
330 Form 10-K, General Instruction A(2); see also SEC Release No 33-8644, "Revisions to Accelerated Filer Definition and Accelerated Deadlines For Filing Periodic Reports" (December 21 2005).
331 SEC Release No 33-8959, "Foreign Issuer Reporting Enhancements" (September 23 2008).
332 *Id.*
333 *Id.*

ADRs to depositaries; and
- information about the significant differences in the corporate governance practices of listed foreign private issuers compared to the corporate governance practices applicable to US companies under the relevant exchange's listing standards.

- Segment data – the amended Form 20-F eliminates the instruction from Item 17 that allowed foreign private issuers that present financial statements otherwise fully in compliance with US generally accepted accounting principles (GAAP) to omit segment data from their financial statements. Accordingly, such segment data must now be disclosed.
- Accelerated timing deadline – beginning in 2011, all foreign private issuers filing annual reports on Form 20-F will be required to do so within four months of their fiscal year-end.
- US GAAP reconciliation – in 2011, all foreign private issuers that are required to provide a US GAAP reconciliation with their financial statements will have to comply with Item 18 of Form 20-F, which lists more extensive requirements.[334] Third-party financial statements may continue to be prepared using the less stringent requirements of Item 17 of the same form. In summary, foreign private issuers may present their financial statements:
  - in accordance with US GAAP;
  - in accordance with International Financial Reporting Standards (IFRS) as adopted by the International Accounting Standards Board (IASB); or
  - in accordance with home country GAAP but with certain reconciliations to US GAAP.[335]

The term 'annual report' is used to describe not only such formal SEC-filed documents, but also the annual report to security holders that a US company reporting under the Exchange Act is required by the SEC's proxy rules to distribute prior to each annual meeting of its stockholders.[336]

While the annual report to security holders must contain financial statements and an MD&A meeting Form 10-K standards (and these will often be incorporated by reference into the Form 10-K to avoid repetition), it otherwise tends to be a glossy public relations document. Alternatively, some companies distribute their Form 10-K as their annual report to shareholders, sometimes with a glossy wrap-around cover.

Foreign private issuers may publish a comparable document, but they are not subject to the SEC's proxy rules and its regulations do not require them to do so.

(b) Interim reports

Both US companies and foreign private issuers that report under the Exchange Act are also subject to interim reporting requirements. There is, however, a substantial difference as far as the frequency and content of interim reports are concerned:

---

334 Form 20-F Item 18 requires various footnote disclosures relating to pension assets, financial instruments and derivatives, among other things, that Item 17 does not require.

335 See the section on international disclosure standards in this chapter.

336 Exchange Act Rule 14a-3.

US issuers that report under the Exchange Act are required to provide interim reports on Form 10-Q that contain unaudited financial and other prescribed information and updated MD&A information following the end of each of the first three quarters of the fiscal year. They are also required to file special reports on Form 8-K upon the occurrence of specified significant events.[337]

Foreign private issuers, by contrast, are required to provide as interim reports (on Form 6-K) only whatever information they have made, or are required to make, public pursuant to their home country corporate laws or an international stock exchange's requirements, or distribute to their security holders, and that "is material with respect to the issuer and its subsidiaries" concerning such matters as:

- changes in business;
- changes in management or control;
- acquisitions or dispositions of assets;
- bankruptcy or receivership;
- financial condition and results of operations;
- material legal proceedings;
- changes in securities or in the collateral for registered securities;
- defaults upon senior securities;
- material increases or decreases in the amount outstanding of securities or indebtedness; and
- transactions with directors, officers or principal security holders.

Form 6-K is required to be filed promptly after the information has been made public.[338]

Form 6-K does not list specific information or major matters that must be reported. A foreign private issuer might nonetheless consult the list of Form 8-K disclosure items in determining what other events could be considered material for US disclosure purposes and possibly reported under the Form 6-K catch-all phrase "other information that the issuer deems of material importance to security holders".

- In March 2004 the SEC amended its Form 8-K reporting rules to:
  - identify a large number of additional events to be reported on Form 8-K by a US issuer; and
  - shorten the time required to file mandatory Form 8-K reports to four business days.[339]
- Section 409 of the Sarbanes-Oxley Act amended the reporting provisions of the Exchange Act to authorise the SEC to institute a 'real-time issuer disclosure' system, "which may include trend and qualitative information and graphic presentations", as the SEC determines is necessary or useful. The Form 8-K amendments of 2004 were a movement in this direction, as is the SEC's experiment with interactive data discussed further in this chapter below.

---

337 Exchange Act Rules 13a-11 (Current Reports on Form 8-K) and 13a-13 (Quarterly Reports on Form 10-Q and Form 10-QSB).

338 Exchange Act Rule 13a-16; Form 6-K, General Instruction B.

339 SEC Release No 33-8400, "Additional Form 8-K Disclosure Requirements and Acceleration of Filing Date" (March 16 2004); amended in SEC Release No 33-8400A (August 4 2004).

(c) *SEC review*

The SEC staff does not review Exchange Act forms prior to their filing. This is different from the Securities Act public offering scheme, where registration statements may be reviewed before effectiveness.[340] If the staff of the SEC reviews a Form 10-K or Form 20-F annual report, or another Exchange Act report, it will do so after the issuer files the report.

If an issuer is selected for review, the staff of the Division of Corporation Finance may look not only at the 10-K or 20-F report, but also at its other filed documents and at such other materials as press releases and the issuer's website. However, a review is likely to focus principally – perhaps solely – on the financial statements and the MD&A.

When the staff finds what it believes are deficiencies in a reviewed report, it may ask that a formal amendment of the document be filed. If the deficiencies are not considered material, the issuer will be requested to adopt a different disclosure pattern in future filings instead of amending the report. Such so-called 'futures comments' are far more common than requests for amendments and are much less likely to provoke lawsuits from private parties.

The clamour for stricter enforcement following the revelation of deficiencies in the Exchange Act reports of Enron, WorldCom and other failed companies led to action by both the US Congress and the SEC.

Section 408 of the Sarbanes-Oxley Act specifies that every issuer reporting under the Exchange Act that is listed on a US national securities exchange shall be reviewed by the SEC "on a regular and systematic basis", and every issuer filing Exchange Act reports shall be reviewed by the SEC no less frequently than once every three years.

Independently, the SEC conducted a review of the annual reports of all of the Fortune 500 companies for the year 2002. The Division of Corporation Finance, in its summary of matters addressed in the review, reported that it issued comments on issuers' MD&A discussions more than on any other topic.

(d) *Interactive data for financial reporting*

In December 2008 the SEC adopted a final rule that requires foreign private issuers that prepare their financial statements in accordance with US GAAP or IFRS to provide the statements in an interactive format using eXtensible Business Reporting Language (XBRL). Foreign private issuers that file pursuant to their home country GAAP, although with US GAAP reconciliation, will not, as of yet, be required to use XBRL to disclose financial information. Effective from April 13 2009, the XBRL rule is being phased in over a three-year period for foreign private issuers that use US GAAP or IFRS. The interactive data requirement applies to annual report Form 10-K and Form 20-F, as well as interim report Form 10-Q, Form 8-K and Form 6-K that contain updated or revised versions of financial statements.[341]

The adoption of the new rules is consistent with the SEC's stated goal of continuing to update filing standards as technology improves. XBRL allows financial

340 For discussion of SEC review procedures, see "Public offerings".
341 SEC Release No 33-9002, "Interactive Data to Improve Financial Reporting" (January 30 2009).

information to be downloaded directly into spreadsheets and used in various off-the-shelf software programs. According to the SEC, interactive data will increase the speed, accuracy and utility of financial disclosure, reducing costs and making financial information easier for investors to analyse.

4.4 Sarbanes-Oxley Act

The Sarbanes-Oxley Act impacts on foreign private issuers in a number of respects. Most notably, it changes various auditor independence standards, internal control reports, officer certifications, disclosure controls and attorney obligations, and adds requirements involving other disclosure obligations.

(a) Auditor independence

The SEC has consistently emphasised the need for an auditor to remain independent – that is, to have neither mutual nor conflicting interests with its audit client and to exercise objective and impartial judgement. It has generally required foreign private issuers and the auditors of their financial statements to comply with US independence requirements when such issuers' audited financial statements are filed with the SEC. It is a requirement of Form 20-F that "the auditor must comply with the US standards for auditor independence".[342]

If an auditor cannot meet the SEC's independence standards, then the audited company's financial statements are not certified for purposes of inclusion in Securities Act or Exchange Act filings. A foreign private issuer should examine consulting and other non-audit business relationships with its audit firm, and discuss their possible effect on independence, to see whether they will present an impediment to entering the US capital markets.

Sarbanes-Oxley changes: Title II of the Sarbanes-Oxley Act required the SEC to change its rules on auditor independence in a number of respects. The SEC responded in January 2003 by amending its Regulation S-X rules on the qualifications of accountants.[343]

The SEC observed that its rules "will affect foreign accounting firms that conduct audits of both foreign private issuers and foreign subsidiaries and affiliates of US issuers":[344]

- Non-audit services – an auditor's rendition of non-audit services to an audit client – often more lucrative to the auditor than its performance of audit services – have always raised questions as to the auditor's independence. Rules of the accounting profession and the SEC have identified types of non-audit services that are considered to impair independence in most circumstances (eg, bookkeeping and management services), or that have been

342 Form 20-F, General Instruction E and Instruction 2 to Item 8.A.2.

343 Regulation S-X Rule 2-01; SEC Release No 33-8183, "Strengthening the Commission's Requirements Regarding Auditor Independence" (January 28 2003).

344 SEC Release No 33-8183, "Strengthening the Commission's Requirements Regarding Auditor Independence" (January 28 2003).

permitted only to a limited extent (eg, financial information systems design and implementation). Section 201 of the Sarbanes-Oxley Act prohibits an auditor from providing these and several other listed categories of non-audit services (including appraisal, broker-dealer and investment advisory services) to an audit client contemporaneously with the audit.[345]

- Tax and legal services – tax services are generally not on the prohibited list. Legal services and expert services provided in connection with litigation or regulatory proceedings are, on the other hand, proscribed. It appears that auditor independence would not be impaired by providing 'traditional' assistance in connection with governmental tax audits – although it could be adversely affected by representation before a tax court, a federal district court or court of claims. Characterisation of tax services as 'legal services' by foreign law would be irrelevant.[346] In 2006, however, the Public Company Accounting Oversight Board ruled that certain tax services impair auditor independence if provided to audit clients. The prohibited services include the marketing or planning of aggressive tax position transactions – a significant purpose of which is tax avoidance – and the provision of any tax service to a person in a financial reporting oversight role at the audit client.[347]
- Audit committee involvement – under Section 202 of the Sarbanes-Oxley Act and the SEC's January 2003 rules, all services provided by an auditor – both audit services and permitted non-audit services (with a *de minimis* exception) – must be approved in advance by the issuer's audit committee. In addition, the Public Company Accounting Oversight Board's 2006 rules on tax services require the auditor to provide the audit committee with written documentation of the scope of proposed tax services and discuss with the committee their potential impact on independence. Approval may be pursuant to pre-established committee procedures.[348] In Item 16C of Form 20-F, a foreign private issuer reporting company must give a breakdown by categories of the fees paid to its auditor over the preceding two years and disclose its audit committee's pre-approval policies.[349]
- Audit report – before an audit report is filed with the SEC, the auditor must advise the audit committee of the issuer's critical accounting policies and practices and alternative GAAP accounting treatments.[350]

---

345 Sarbanes-Oxley Act §201(a); Exchange Act §10A(g).

346 SEC Release No 33-8183, "Strengthening the Commission's Requirements Regarding Auditor Independence", I-B-9 (January 28 2003).

347 SEC Release No 34-53677, "Order Approving Public Company Accounting Oversight Board Ethics and Independence Rules" (April 19 2006); Public Company Accounting Oversight Board Rules 3522, 3523. The constitutionality of the oversight board was upheld by the US Supreme Court in June 2010, although the provision of the Sarbanes-Oxley Act required that its members be removed only for cause was struck down and in future the SEC may remove members without cause. *Free Enterprise v Public Accounting Oversight Board,* 130 S Ct 3139 (June 28 2010).

348 Sarbanes-Oxley Act §201; Exchange Act §10A(h); Sarbanes-Oxley Act §202; Exchange Act §10A(i); Regulation S-X Rule 2-01.

349 SEC Release No 33-8183, "Strengthening the Commission's Requirements Regarding Auditor Independence", II-H (January 28 2003).

350 Sarbanes-Oxley Act §204; Exchange Act §10A(k); Regulation S-X Rule 2-07(a). For more see the section on management's commentary on financial statements in this chapter.

- Present and former auditor personnel – auditing firms must rotate the partners who work on a particular issuer's audit.[351] An issuer that hires former auditor personnel who recently worked on its audit may impair the auditor's independence.[352] The SEC's January 2003 rules contain specifics regarding partner rotation and 'cooling-off' periods.[353] The lead and concurring partner must rotate after five years and cannot serve in those positions for five years thereafter. Other audit partners are subject to a rotation after seven years and cannot serve as audit partners for two years thereafter. Additionally, there is a one-year cooling-off period before a member of the audit engagement team may accept employment in certain designated positions with an issuer.

(b) Internal control over financial reporting

Financial statements – audited as well as unaudited – are basically the responsibility of the issuer's management.

Asking management to focus on internal controls is not new. Since 1977, the Exchange Act has required reporting issuers to keep "books, records and accounts, which, in reasonable detail, accurately and fairly reflect the transactions and dispositions of the assets" of the issuer.[354] Professional standards have long required auditors to consider the adequacy of issuers' internal controls in auditing their financial statements.[355]

Section 404 of the Sarbanes-Oxley Act added a requirement for an annual management report on internal controls over financial reporting that:

- states the responsibility of management for "establishing and maintaining an adequate internal control structure and procedures for financial reporting";
- contains a fiscal year-end assessment of the effectiveness of the internal control structure; and
- is accompanied by the auditor's attestation to management's assessment.

In June 2003 the SEC adopted rules that implement Section 404:[356]

- All issuers reporting under the Exchange Act must include such a management internal control report in their Form 10-K annual reports (US issuers) or Form 20-F annual reports (foreign private issuers).
- Management must make an affirmative statement that its internal control over financial reporting is effective (or that it is not, in which case it must disclose any material weaknesses).

---

351 Sarbanes-Oxley Act §203; Exchange Act §10A(j); Regulation S-X Rule 2-01(c)(6).

352 Sarbanes-Oxley Act §206; Exchange Act §10A(l); Regulation S-X Rule 2-01(c)(2).

353 SEC Release No 33-8183, "Strengthening the Commission's Requirements Regarding Auditor Independence" (January 28 2003).

354 Exchange Act §13(b)(2). See, for example, SEC Litigation Release No 19578, "*SEC v NetEase.com, Inc*" (February 27 2006); SEC Litigation Release No 8664, "In the Matter of Helen Haiwen He" (February 27 2006).

355 See SEC Release No 33-8618, "Management's Report on Internal Control Over Financial Reporting and Certification of Disclosure in Exchange Act Periodic Reports of Companies That Are Not Accelerated Filers", fn 13 (September 22 2005).

356 SEC Release No 33-8238, "Management's Report on Internal Control Over Financial Reporting and Certification of Disclosure in Exchange Act Periodic Reports" (June 5 2003).

- The Form 10-K or Form 20-F annual report must include the auditor's attestation to management's assessment of effectiveness, in accordance with standards promulgated by the Public Company Accounting Oversight Board and approved by the SEC in June 2004.[357] A perception of ineffective audit committee oversight of external reporting and internal control could present the auditor with strong indication of a material weakness.
- The Dodd-Frank Act exempted small issuers – foreign private issuers as well as US issuers – from the auditor attestation requirement if they have a market capitalisation of less than $75 million.[358]

SEC implementation of Section 404: Of the many changes introduced by the Sarbanes-Oxley Act, the requirement of Section 404 for a management assessment of internal control and auditor attestation of management's assessment has provoked the most complaints from reporting issuers. Foreign private issuers and smaller US companies in particular have objected to the costs and demands upon accounting and managerial personnel involved in compliance. By 2007, various companies had even published information detailing the cost of Section 404 compliance, with figures ranging from $860,000 to $5.4 million.[359] Responding to these concerns, in 2007 the SEC published management guidance[360] and adopted a new auditing standard.[361]

This management guidance provides a top-down, risk-based approach to evaluating internal control over financial reporting. In response to the concerns voiced about Section 404, the guide:

- explains how to vary evaluation approaches for gathering evidence based on risk assessments;
- explains the use of 'daily interaction', self-assessment and other ongoing monitoring activities as evidence in the evaluation;
- explains the purpose of documentation and how management may be flexible in its approaches to documenting support for its assessment;
- provides management with significant flexibility in making judgements regarding what constitutes adequate evidence in low-risk areas; and
- allows for management and the auditor to have different testing approaches.

The new auditing standard – Auditing Standard No 5, for the independent audit of internal controls over financial reporting required under Section 404(b) – provides

357 SEC Release No 34-49884, "Public Company Accounting Oversight Board; Order Approving Proposed Auditing Standard No 2, *An Audit of Internal Control Over Financial Reporting Performed in Conjunction with an Audit of Financial Statements* ('Auditing Standard No 2')" (June 17 2004).

358 Dodd-Frank Act § 989G.

359 See SEC Office of Economic Analysis, *Study of the Sarbanes-Oxley Act of 2002 Section 404 Internal Control over Financial Reporting Requirements* (September 2009).

360 See SEC Release No 33-8810, "Commission Guidance Regarding Management's Report on Internal Control Over Financial Reporting Under Section 13(a) or 15(d) of the Securities Exchange Act of 1934" (June 27 2007).

361 See SEC Release No 34-56152, "Order Approving Proposed Auditing Standard No. 5, *An Audit of Internal Control Over Financial Reporting that is Integrated with an Audit of Financial Statements, a Related Independence Rule, and Conforming Amendments*" (July 27 2007).

professional standards and related performance guidance for independent auditors to attest to, and report on, management's assessment of the effectiveness of internal controls over financial reporting under Sections 103 and 404 of Sarbanes-Oxley. Pursuant to this standard, the auditor's report will express one opinion – whether the company has maintained effective internal control over financial reporting as of its fiscal year-end.

In a contemporaneous press release, then SEC Chairman Cox stated: "this standard and the Commission's interpretive guidance for management represent the culmination of two years' work by the Commission and the [Public Company Accounting Oversight Board] and our respective staffs to make the implementation of Section 404 more effective and efficient."[362]

The following are some benefits of Auditing Standard No 5:

- It allows auditors to exercise their judgement.
- It scales the level of internal control testing to match the size of the corporation.
- It eliminates unnecessary procedures for audit and allows auditors to focus on matters that they consider to be most important for internal control.
- It allows auditors to use a principles-based approach to decide the extent to which they can rely on work already done by others, including the effort exerted by management in complying with Section 404(a).

Compliance dates for newly public companies: Newly public companies, whether they are US companies or foreign private issuers, must comply with these internal control over financial reporting requirements as of their second annual report.[363]

As discussed further below, certain officer certifications must accompany Form 20-F annual reports of foreign private issuers, as well as Form 10-K annual reports of US issuers. Such certifications must disclose certain recent changes in the issuer's internal control over financial reporting. The certifications must also state that the certifying officers have designed (or supervised the design of) internal control over financial reporting "to provide reasonable assurance regarding the reliability" of the issuer's financial reporting and published financial statements, and that they have concluded that internal control was effective (or not effective) as of year-end.[364]

(c) Cost-benefit analysis

Section 404 of the Sarbanes-Oxley Act has been the most controversial and costly aspect of compliance for domestic and foreign issuers alike.[365] The rules enacted by the SEC under this section have the stated purposes of "enhancing the quality of reporting and increasing investor confidence in the financial statements,"[366] but

---

362 See Press Release, SEC, "SEC Approves PCAOB Auditing Standard No. 5 Regarding Audits of Internal Control Over Financial Reporting; Adopts Definition of 'Significant Deficiency'" (July 25 2007).

363 SEC Release No 33-8934, "Internal Control Over Financial Reporting in Exchange Act Periodic Reports of Non-Accelerated Filers" (June 26 2008).

364 Exchange Act Rule 13a-14; see Form 20-F, Instructions to Exhibits, Item 12 for the text of the required certification with respect to foreign private issuers.

365 Cindy R Alexander *et al*, *The Economic Effects of SOX Section 404 Compliance: A Corporate Insider Perspective* (March 2010).

legislation often has unintended consequences. Section 404 contains two noteworthy requirements:

- Issuers must put in place, take responsibility for, disclose and evaluate the efficacy of their internal controls relating to financial reporting; and
- Independent auditors must affirm the accuracy of the issuer's assessment of the effectiveness of their financial reporting mechanisms.

There are both direct and indirect costs and benefits to foreign private issuers from compliance with the Sarbanes-Oxley Act, and specifically Section 404. These will be evaluated, in particular, by those foreign private issuers considering whether to take a course of action that will bring them into the Exchange Act reporting system.

Benefits of Section 404 compliance: Direct benefits from compliance with Section 404 of the Sarbanes-Oxley Act are those that are proximately caused by improvements in the company's financial reporting, such as the improved quality of the corporate governance structure. Indirect benefits are those that materialise due to improvements in financial reporting, such as increased shareholder confidence. Furthermore, it is important to acknowledge that some costs and benefits are tangible (ie, increased liquidity for the issuer's securities), while others are more intangible (ie, increased investor confidence).

A 2010 survey based on the opinions of corporate executives revealed some of the direct and indirect benefits of Section 404 compliance.[367] Notable direct benefits include:

- an increase in the quality of an issuer's internal control structure;
- increased audit committee confidence in an issuer's internal controls for financial reporting;
- an improvement in the quality of the issuer's financial reporting; and
- an enhancement of the issuer's ability to detect and prevent fraud.

Similarly, indirect benefits cited by the study were:

- the issuer's ability to raise capital;
- increased investor confidence in the issuer;
- increased liquidity of the issuer's securities; and
- confidence in financial reports.

Contrary to executives' opinions, a 2006 empirical study comparing share price movements during the implementation period of Section 404 found that companies that complied with Section 404 experienced significantly greater increases in share price than non-complying companies.[368] These increases in share price were of such

366 SEC Office of Economic Analysis, *Study of the Sarbanes-Oxley Act of 2002 Section 404 Internal Control over Financial Reporting Requirements* (September 16 2009).

367 Cindy R Alexander *et al*, *The Economic Effects of SOX Section 404 Compliance: A Corporate Insider Perspective* (March 2010).

368 *Do The Benefits Of 404 Exceed The Cost?*, The Lord & Benoit Report (2006).

a magnitude that they more than covered the costs of compliance.

Overall, however, the 2010 study discussed above found that while many issuers that comply with Section 404 recognise benefits relating to corporate governance, they do not perceive increased efficiency as a result of such compliance.

Foreign private issuers may experience further intangible benefits as a result of choosing to list on a US national securities exchange and comply with Section 404. For example, compliance may increase an issuer's publicity and credibility.[369] By voluntarily submitting to US securities regulation, foreign private issuers are signalling to their shareholders and the public that they are able to comply with this strict disclosure regime. Thus, they are in effect posting a surety bond – albeit an expensive one – for the benefit of their international investors.

Costs of Section 404 compliance: The costs of Section 404 compliance may be broken down into four main categories:

- audit fees paid to independent auditors, which averaged approximately $650,000 per company in 2009;
- annual fees paid to outside vendors, excluding audit fees, which averaged approximately $280,000 per company in 2009;
- in-house staff hours spent on compliance, which averaged approximately $1.3 million per company in 2009; and
- non-labour expenses, such as the cost of hardware, software and travel related to compliance, which averaged approximately $130,000 per company in 2009.

Overall, issuers complying with Section 404(b) spent an average of approximately $2.3 million per company on compliance in the 2009 fiscal year. There are additional costs of compliance relating to increased director and officer insurance, increased board compensation, lost productivity and legal fees. Compliance costs also vary with company size, as large companies (ie, those with a market value above $700 million) reported compliance costs of $3.9 million, while small companies (ie, those with a market value under $75 million) averaged $690,000, with the remaining companies reporting average compliance costs of $1 million.[370]

Another important cost may be the fear of increased liability imposed on issuers that are required to comply with Section 404. However, if compliance is accomplished effectively, fear of liability for financial and accounting fraud may in fact be reduced. Furthermore, researchers have noted that companies that are able to centralise their financial reporting systems can reduce the costs associated with Section 404 compliance.[371]

However, evidence suggests that these compliance costs are decreasing with time, as companies become more comfortable with reporting procedures and

369 Christopher Woo, *The Effects of the Sarbanes-Oxley Act on Foreign Private Issuers* (2006).
370 Cindy R Alexander *et al*, *The Economic Effects of SOX Section 404 Compliance: A Corporate Insider Perspective* (March 2010).
371 "Survey of SOX 404 Costs," *Financial Executives International* (2007).

knowledgeable about the risks posed by Sarbanes-Oxley. For example, a 2005 study found that the average cost of Section 404 compliance was under $3 million per company and predicted costs to decline in the future.[372] As discussed above, a 2009 study placed the average cost at a reduced $2.3 million per company.

There are additional costs unique to foreign private issuers complying with the Sarbanes-Oxley Act. For example, those issuers must consider how they will comply with Sarbanes-Oxley accounting standards. As of March 4 2008, foreign private issuers are no longer required to provide a reconciliation to US GAAP, and can instead conform to IFRS as issued by the IASB.[373] Alternatively, they may choose to use their own home-country standards (including local versions of IFRS), in which case they must provide financial statements that reconcile their accounting standards with US GAAP. In such cases foreign private issuers may also have to deal with the possibility of conflicting or inconsistent law in their home countries.

Issuers whose home countries enforce relatively weak regulatory standards have been found to experience benefits that outweighed the costs of complying with Sarbanes-Oxley.[374] One such benefit to these companies has been in the form of higher credit ratings. By contrast, issuers from countries that already have in place a strict securities regulatory regime incur the costs of compliance without many benefits, since they are already meeting the transparency requirements of their home country. Similarly, the extent of compliance benefits appears to be correlated with the extent of pre-existing regulation in the industry. Empirical analysis suggests that Sarbanes-Oxley Section 404 compliance imparts few – if any – benefits to companies already subjected to extensive disclosure requirements, such as in the financial industry, while companies in less regulated industries benefit more noticeably.[375]

(c) Conclusion

A major criticism of the Sarbanes-Oxley Act has been that it places a disproportionate financial burden on smaller issuers as compared to larger ones. Many costs of compliance with Section 404 are both fixed and non-scalable, making them the same whether the issuer paying them is large or small. This raises the cost of compliance for smaller companies, as a percentage of revenue. While audit costs were already disproportionately larger for smaller companies before the applicability of the Section 404 requirements, Sarbanes-Oxley has exacerbated this problem.

In practice, this means that larger issuers will be more likely to perceive net benefits from compliance than their smaller counterparts.[376] The Dodd-Frank Act has recognised the proportionately larger burden on smaller issuers by exempting both US and foreign private issuers from the auditor attestation component of Section 404

---

372 Larry Rittenberg & Patricia Miller, *Sarbanes-Oxley Section 404 Work: Looking at the Benefits*, The IIA Research Foundation (2005).

373 SEC Release No 33-8879, "Acceptance from Foreign Private Issuers of Financial Statements Prepared in Accordance with International Financial Reporting Standards without Reconciliation to US GAAP" (December 21 2007).

374 Kate Litvak, *The Effect of The Sarbanes-Oxley Act on Non-U.S. Companies Cross-Listed in the US*, 13 Journal of Corporate Finance 195 (2007).

375 Litvak, *supra*, note 299.

376 Jaimin Wang, *Sarbanes-Oxley Section 404 Places Disproportionate Burden on Smaller Public Companies*, The Heritage Foundation (August 2008).

if their market capitalisations are under $75 million.[377]

It is difficult to compare costs and benefits of Section 404 compliance because the benefits have a significant intangible component on which it is hard to place a monetary value, while the costs are very tangible. Notably, studies have shown that the costs of compliance with Section 404 are decreasing over time as issuers become more experienced in this area of securities regulation. Also, many of the compliance costs are related to start-up, and therefore may also decrease over time.

(d) Officer certifications

Section 302 of the Sarbanes-Oxley Act added a requirement for the SEC to adopt rules requiring the principal or chief executive officer (CEO) and the principal or chief financial officer (CFO) of reporting issuers to certify, in each annual report and quarterly report filed pursuant to Section 13(a) or 15(d) of the Exchange Act, that:

- the signing officer has reviewed the report;
- based on the officer's knowledge, the report does not contain any untrue statement of a material fact or omit to state a material fact necessary in order to make the statements made, in light of the circumstances in which such statements were made, not misleading;
- based on the officer's knowledge, the financial statements and other financial information fairly present in all material respects the financial condition and results of operations of the issuer;
- the signing officers:
  - are responsible for establishing and maintaining internal controls;
  - have designed such internal controls to ensure that material information relating to the issuer is made known to such officers by others;
  - have evaluated the effectiveness of the issuer's internal controls; and
  - have presented in the report their conclusions about the effectiveness of their controls based on the evaluation as of that date;
- the signing officers have disclosed to the issuer's auditors and audit committee of the board of directors (or persons fulfilling the equivalent function):
  - all significant deficiencies in the design or operation of internal controls that could adversely affect the issuer's ability to record, process, summarise and report financial data, and have identified for the auditors any material weaknesses in internal controls; and
  - any fraud, whether or not material, that involved management or other employees who have a significant role in the issuer's internal controls; and
- the signing officers have indicated in the report whether there were significant changes in internal controls or in other factors that could significantly affect internal controls subsequent to the date of their evaluation, including any corrective actions made with regard to significant deficiencies and material weaknesses.[378]

377 Dodd-Frank Act §989G.

As is discussed in "Securities litigation risks", knowing violations of the certification requirement can result in civil and criminal liability for CEOs and CFOs.

(e) *Disclosure controls and procedures*

According to the SEC's release of August 28 2002, which adopted the officer certification requirements mandated by Section 302, the 'disclosure controls and procedures' that the certifying officers are required to design and evaluate "are intended to cover a broader range of information than is covered by an issuer's internal controls related to financial reporting".[379] The SEC's release of June 5 2003, which imposes the requirement for a management internal control report, discusses both the differences between and overlaps of internal control and disclosure controls.[380]

The procedures should ensure timely collection and evaluation of information that is potentially subject to disclosure in required SEC reports. They will provide a framework for the exercise of due diligence in investigating the issuer's business and finances. The process of preparing certifications will involve both the use and review of disclosure controls and procedures. Some companies' disclosure controls and procedures may contemplate having other high-level officers and employees execute back-up certifications – not for filing with the SEC, but for internal support purposes. The SEC recommended that issuers "create a committee with responsibility for considering the materiality of information and determining disclosure obligations on a timely basis" – that is, a 'disclosure committee' – and suggested that officers and employees serving on such a committee could include the controller, general counsel and principal risk management and investor relations officers, and perhaps heads of key business units.[381] Many US issuers that report under the Exchange Act have followed the recommendation to create such a committee, including adopting a charter that is modelled after the audit committee charter required by the NYSE and NASDAQ. In addition to including officer certifications in its Form 20-F annual report, a foreign private issuer must report the conclusions of its CEO and CFO as to the effectiveness of its disclosure controls and procedures in Item 15 of Form 20-F.

(f) *Attorney obligations*

The SEC has adopted rules that establish minimum standards of professional conduct for attorneys appearing and practising before the SEC in the representation of issuers.[382] These rules, which implement Section 307 of the Sarbanes-Oxley Act, apply to both in-house and outside attorneys, including, in some cases, attorneys licensed

378 Sarbanes-Oxley Act §302. The text of the required certification, which must be used in the exact language, is set forth in Item 601(31) of Regulations S-K (for Form 10-K and 10-Q certifications) and Item 12 of the Instructions to Exhibits in Form 20-F (for Form 20-F certifications).

379 SEC Release No 33-8124, "Certification of Disclosure in Companies' Quarterly and Annual Reports", III-B (August 28 2002).

380 SEC Release No 33-8238, "Management's Report on Internal Control Over Financial Reporting and Certification of Disclosure in Exchange Act Periodic Reports", II-D (June 5 2003).

381 SEC Release No 33-8124, "Certification of Disclosure in Companies' Quarterly and Annual Reports", II-B-3, fn 60 (August 28 2002).

382 17 CFR §205; SEC Release No 33-8185, "Implementation of Standards of Professional Conduct for Attorneys" (January 29 2003).

outside the United States. Effective since August 5 2003, these rules:

- require an attorney to report evidence of a material violation of securities laws, a material breach of fiduciary duty or a similar material violation of any US federal or state law to the issuer's chief legal officer (CLO) or to both the CLO and the CEO; and
- require the attorney, in the absence of an appropriate and timely response from the CLO or CEO, to report the evidence 'up the ladder' to the issuer's audit committee, another independent committee of the board of directors or the full board. The rules permit an issuer to establish a 'qualified legal compliance committee' as an alternative procedure for addressing evidence of a material violation.

In a departure from the preliminary rules proposed by the SEC in November 2002, the final rules do not obligate an outside attorney to withdraw from representing the issuer and to notify the SEC if the attorney does not receive an appropriate response to a report of a material violation all the way 'up the ladder' to the issuer's CLO or qualified legal compliance committee. However, since 2003 the SEC has considered this so-called 'noisy withdrawal' proposal as well as an alternative proposal that would obligate the issuer, rather than the attorney, to notify the SEC.

Scope: The rules apply broadly to "attorneys appearing and practicing before the [SEC] in the representation of an issuer".[383] An attorney 'appears and practises' before the SEC when he:

- transacts any business with the SEC, including communications in any form;
- represents an issuer in an SEC administrative proceeding, investigation, inquiry, information request or subpoena;
- provides advice in respect of US securities laws or SEC rules regarding any document to be filed with or submitted to, or incorporated into any document that will be filed with or submitted to, the SEC; or
- advises an issuer as to whether information or a statement, opinion or other writing is required under the US securities laws or SEC rules to be filed with or submitted to, or incorporated into any document that will be filed with or submitted to, the SEC.[384]

Although the rules raise a number of interpretative issues, it is important to recognise that their scope clearly extends beyond traditional securities law practitioners. Attorneys in other practice specialties who review or prepare discrete portions of an issuer's disclosure documents may be covered, depending on the circumstances. While privately held companies are outside the scope of the rules, an attorney retained by a subsidiary of a publicly held issuer may be covered if, for example, he or she reviews or contributes to parts of the parent's SEC filings. An

383 17 CFR §205.1.
384 17 CFR §205.2(a).

attorney may be covered by virtue of exhibits to SEC filings and materials incorporated by reference into SEC filings, provided that the attorney has notice that the document will be filed or incorporated.

An attorney will be deemed to be appearing and practising before the SEC to the extent that he or she supervises an attorney who is appearing and practising before the SEC.[385] An attorney investigating a report of a material violation is also considered to be appearing and practising before the SEC, although that attorney does not have a reporting obligation if certain conditions are met.[386]

In the case of foreign private issuers, a threshold question is whether the issuer is a reporting company under the Exchange Act. If the issuer has not entered the Exchange Act reporting system (eg, an issuer that qualifies for the Rule 12g3-2(b) exemption), it is not considered to be an issuer for purposes of the rules.

The rules also contain special provisions applicable to foreign attorneys. 'Non-appearing foreign attorneys' are not covered by the rules, but other foreign attorneys are. A 'non-appearing foreign attorney' is an attorney who:

- is admitted to practise law in a jurisdiction outside the United States;
- does not hold himself out as practising, or give legal advice regarding, US law; and
- conducts activities that would constitute appearing and practising before the SEC:
  - only incidentally and in the ordinary course of their practice of law outside the United States; or
  - only in consultation with counsel admitted or licensed to practise law in the United States.[387]

Foreign attorneys who do not qualify as non-appearing foreign attorneys will be required to comply with the rules on the same basis as US attorneys, except to the extent that compliance is prohibited by applicable foreign law.

Triggering of reporting obligation: If an attorney is covered by the rules, the attorney's reporting obligations will be triggered when he or she "becomes aware of evidence of a material violation by the issuer or by any officer, director, employee, or agent of the issuer".[388] The rules do not contain a specific timing requirement for action by the attorney, but instead provide that the attorney must make his report "forthwith" after becoming aware of the evidence.

The SEC is concerned with more than material violations of US federal securities laws. 'Material violation', for purposes of the rules, also includes material violations of state securities law, a material breach of fiduciary duty arising under US federal or state law, or a similar material violation of any US federal or state law.[389] The term does not, however, include violations of foreign laws. The SEC chose not to define

385 17 CFR §205.4(a).
386 17 CFR §205.3(b)(5).
387 17 CFR §205.2(j).
388 17 CFR §205.3(b)(1).
389 17 CFR §205.2(i).

the word 'material' in the final rules, opting instead for the common law meaning of that term under US federal securities laws. Under current law, information is generally deemed to be material if there is a substantial likelihood that its disclosure would be considered significant by a reasonable investor.

'Evidence of a material violation' means "credible evidence, based upon which it would be unreasonable, under the circumstances, for a prudent and competent attorney not to conclude that it is reasonably likely that a material violation has occurred, is ongoing, or is about to occur".[390] In its release adopting the rules, the SEC characterises this evidentiary standard as an objective standard, but recognises that there is a "range of conduct" in which an attorney may engage without being unreasonable.[391] The circumstances relevant in assessing the reasonableness of an attorney's actions are those at the time the attorney decides whether he or she is obligated to report the information and may include, among others:

- the attorney's professional skills, background and experience;
- the time constraints under which the attorney is acting;
- the attorney's previous experience and familiarity with the client; and
- the availability of other attorneys with whom the attorney may consult.

The duty to report evidence of a material violation is not limited to instances when the attorney knows that a material violation has occurred or concludes that there has been a violation and no reasonable fact finder could conclude otherwise. Rather, the test is whether it is 'reasonably likely' that a material violation has occurred, is ongoing or is about to occur. According to the SEC, this means that "a material violation must be more than a mere possibility, but it need not be 'more likely than not'".

It is also important to note that the rules do not link the behaviour that causes the attorney to be covered by the rules with the event triggering the attorney's reporting obligation. An attorney who appears and practises before the SEC because he or she renders securities law advice to a client could, for example, be required to report a material tax law violation of which he or she becomes aware.

Procedures for reporting 'up the ladder': If an attorney covered by the rules becomes aware of evidence of a material violation, the attorney must report the evidence to the issuer and, possibly, take the report 'up the ladder' within the issuer. Alternatively, the issuer may establish a qualified legal compliance committee as a mechanism for addressing evidence of a material violation.

The first rung of the reporting ladder is the issuer's CLO or the equivalent thereof. Except for 'subordinate attorneys' (who are subject to special reporting procedures, as described below), an attorney who has evidence of a material violation must report the evidence 'forthwith' to the CLO, or to both the CLO and the CEO.[392]

The CLO must then conduct a reasonable inquiry. If the CLO determines that no

390. 17 CFR §205.2(e).

391 SEC Release No 33-8185, "Implementation of Standards of Professional Conduct for Attorneys" (January 29 2003).

392 17 CFR §205.3(b)(1).

material violation has occurred, is occurring or is about to occur, he or she must notify the reporting attorney of this conclusion and the basis for such determination. Unless the CLO reasonably believes that no material violation has occurred, is occurring or is about to occur, he or she must take all reasonable steps to cause the issuer to adopt an appropriate response, and must advise the reporting attorney of the steps taken.[393]

If the reporting attorney reasonably believes that the CLO or CEO has provided an appropriate and timely response to a report of evidence of a material violation, the attorney has no further reporting obligation under the rules.[394] A response is 'appropriate' if, as a result of the response, the reporting attorney reasonably believes that:

- no material violation has occurred, is ongoing or is about to occur;
- the issuer has adopted appropriate remedial measures, including steps or sanctions to stop, prevent and remedy any material violation; or
- the issuer, with the consent of its board of directors or a qualified committee of the board, has retained or directed an attorney to review the reported evidence of a material violation, and has either:
  - substantially implemented any remedial recommendations made by such attorney after a reasonable investigation and evaluation of the evidence; or
  - been advised that such attorney may assert a colourable defence on behalf of the issuer (or its officers) in any investigation or proceeding relating to the reported evidence.[395]

If the reporting attorney does not reasonably believe that the CLO or CEO has provided an appropriate and timely response to a report of evidence of a material violation, then the attorney must notify the CLO and report the evidence of a material violation further 'up the ladder' within the issuer:

- to the audit committee;
- if the issuer has no audit committee, to another board committee consisting solely of directors who are not directly or indirectly employed by the issuer (and who are not, in the case of a registered investment company, interested persons); or
- in the absence of such a committee, to the full board of directors.[396]

The rules permit an attorney who reasonably believes that it would be futile to report evidence of a material violation to the CLO and CEO instead to go directly 'up the ladder' as provided above.[397]

The SEC expressly rejects the notion that the reporting attorney should be able to rely completely on the assurance of the CLO that there was no material violation

393 17 CFR §205.3(b)(2).
394 17 CFR §205.3(b)(8).
395 17 CFR §205.2(b).
396 17 CFR §205.3(b)(3).
397 17 CFR §205.3(b)(4).

or that the issuer was adopting appropriate remedial measures. According to the SEC's release adopting these rules: "this information, while certainly relevant to the determination whether an attorney could reasonably believe that a response was appropriate, cannot be dispositive of the issue. Otherwise, an issuer could simply have its CLO reply to the reporting attorney that 'there is no material violation,' without taking any steps to investigate and/or remedy material violations." Thus, the CLO's response will not in and of itself relieve the reporting attorney of his obligation to consider whether to pursue the matter further 'up the ladder'.[398]

More limited reporting obligations apply to subordinate attorneys who appear and practise before the SEC under the supervision or direction of another attorney ('supervisory attorney').[399] A subordinate attorney need only report evidence of a material violation to his or her supervisory attorney. The supervisory attorney is then responsible for complying with the full range of reporting requirements prescribed under the rules, including going 'up the ladder' if appropriate.[400] A supervisory attorney must also use reasonable efforts to ensure that his subordinate attorneys comply with the rules. An attorney under the direct supervision or direction of the issuer's CLO is expressly not a subordinate attorney.[401]

Alternative reporting mechanism: As an alternative to 'up the ladder' reporting, issuers may utilise a qualified legal compliance committee.[402] An attorney covered by the rules who is aware of evidence of a material violation may report the evidence to a previously established legal compliance committee in lieu of going to the CLO (or CLO and CEO). In contrast to reporting 'up the ladder', disclosure in this way relieves the reporting attorney of any further reporting obligation.

Similarly, the issuer's CLO may refer a report of evidence of a material violation to a previously established legal compliance committee in lieu of causing an inquiry to be conducted. The CLO must notify the reporting attorney that he or she has taken such action. The committee, acting by a vote of the majority of its members, is then responsible for responding to the evidence.

A qualified legal compliance committee must satisfy several criteria.[403] It cannot be created after the fact – that is, it must already be in existence when evidence of a material violation is first reported. It must be composed of:

- at least one member of the issuer's audit committee or, in the absence of an audit committee, one member of an equivalent committee of independent directors; and
- two or more members of the board of directors who are not, directly or indirectly, employed by the issuer (and who are not, in the case of a registered investment company, interested persons).

---

398 SEC Release No 33-8185, "Implementation of Standards of Professional Conduct for Attorneys" (January 29 2003).
399 17 CFR §205.5.
400 17 CFR §205.4.
401 17 CFR §205.5(a).
402 17 CFR §205.3(c).
403 17 CFR §205.2(k).

The audit committee or another existing board committee may also serve as the qualified legal compliance committee if its membership satisfies the above requirements.

The committee must adopt written procedures and have the authority and responsibility:

- to inform the CLO and CEO of any report of evidence of a material violation;
- to determine whether an investigation is necessary and, if so, to notify the audit committee or the full board, initiate an investigation (which may be conducted by the CLO or outside attorneys) and retain any necessary experts; and
- at the conclusion of any such investigation, to recommend that the issuer implement an appropriate response, and to inform the CLO, the CEO and the board of directors of the results of the investigation.

Although the committee is not required to report outside the issuer to the SEC, the rules provide that it must have the authority and responsibility to take all appropriate action, "including the authority to notify the Commission in the event that the issuer fails in any material respect to implement an appropriate response that the [committee] has recommended the issuer to take".[404]

Attorney disclosure of confidential information: The rules contain a 'self-defence' exception to issuer confidentiality and permit an attorney to use any report or response prepared under the rules to defend against charges of non-compliance.[405] In addition, the rules allow an attorney to reveal to the SEC, without issuer consent, confidential information related to the attorney's representation of the issuer, to the extent that he or she reasonably believes is necessary to prevent (or in some cases rectify the consequences of):

- a material violation by the issuer that is likely to cause substantial injury to the issuer or investors; or
- the commission by the issuer of perjury or an act that the attorney reasonably believes is likely to perpetrate a fraud upon the SEC.

There is currently a question as to whether these permissive disclosures, though encouraged by the SEC rules, would still violate the ethics rules of many states, which are more restrictive in defining the circumstances under which permissive disclosures of client confidences are allowed.

Sanctions and discipline: An attorney who violates the SEC professional conduct rules will be subject to civil penalties and remedies violations of US federal securities laws, including injunctions, civil money penalties and cease and desist orders.[406] In addition, the SEC has administrative disciplinary authority over attorneys and may

404 17 CFR §205.2(k)(4).
405 17 CFR §205.3(d).
406 17 CFR §205.6(a).

censure an attorney or temporarily or permanently deny an attorney the privilege of appearing or practising before the SEC.[407] The rules include an express safe harbour provision stating that the new rules do not create a private right of action against an attorney, a law firm or an issuer based on compliance or non-compliance with such rules.[408]

4.5 Other disclosure issues

A number of other rules, regulations, requirements and provisions can directly affect foreign private issuers. Several of these are discussed below.

(a) Individual information

Executives and major shareholders of foreign private issuers often express concern that the requirements for issuer disclosure may entail disclosure of personal financial or business information.

In one important area – executive compensation – the SEC has accommodated international companies by making its Exchange Act proxy rules inapplicable to foreign private issuers and by allowing such issuers to avoid individual remuneration disclosure in their registration statements and reports. Under the proxy rules and in their registration statements and reports, US issuers must provide individual information as to remuneration received by each of the issuer's five most highly compensated executives. Under Form 20-F, foreign private issuer registration and reporting requires only aggregate compensation and pension accrual figures for all directors and officers as a group, unless individual information is disclosed in the home country.[409] The SEC has expanded the information that US issuers must provide as to executive compensation and personal benefits, also known as 'perquisites'. For foreign private issuers, this additional information would be reflected in Form 20-F only "if otherwise made publicly available".[410]

Shares in a foreign private issuer held by its directors and officers must be reported on an individual basis, under Form 20-F. Issuers are allowed simply to indicate that an individual's beneficial holdings are less than 1% of the class of shares where that is the case (paralleling the proxy rule requirements for US issuers).[411] As to other individual shareholding information, holdings of share options by directors and officers must be provided on an individual rather than simply on a group basis.[412]

Form 20-F calls for information as to persons known to own more than 5% of a foreign private issuer's voting securities.[413] A separate Exchange Act provision, applicable to shareholders of both US and foreign private issuers that have registered an equity security under that act, calls for public disclosure by the shareholder of beneficial ownership of more than 5% of the class of equity security.[414]

---

407 17 CFR §205.6(b).
408 17 CFR §205.7.
409 Form 20-F, Item 6.B.1.
410 SEC Release No 33-8732A, "Executive Compensation and Related Person Disclosure" (August 29 2006).
411 Form 20-F, Item 6.E and Instruction to Item 6.E.
412 Form 20-F, Item 6.E.
413 Form 20-F, Item 7.A.1. If the issuer is required to disclose shareholders owning a lesser percentage of its securities under home country rules, the more extensive disclosure must also be provided in Form 20-F.

Additionally, US issuers are subject to heightened disclosure requirements regarding risk management, compensation, director qualifications and corporate governance. These requirements were amended most recently in December 2009 and additional amendments are called for by the Dodd-Frank Act.[415] However, these heightened disclosure requirements are to be included only in proxy statements and thus are not applicable to foreign private issuers.

Form 20-F requires disclosure of the nature of any transactions between the issuer and certain related parties if the transaction is material to either the issuer or the related party, or is unusual in its nature or conditions.[416] By contrast, the corresponding disclosure requirement for US issuers relates to transactions in which the amount involved exceeds $120,000.[417] The SEC's January 2005 action against Mexican foreign private issuer TV Azteca claimed that undisclosed personal self-dealing by principal officers violated both Rule 10b-5 and the books-and-records requirements of Section 13 of the Exchange Act.[418] Under the 2006 settlement of the case, the principal officers agreed to pay penalties in excess of $8.5 million and not to serve as officers or directors of a US public company for five years.[419] In a proceeding brought in November 2004, the SEC contended that the Canadian foreign private issuer Hollinger, Inc was responsible for the failure of its publicly held US subsidiary to disclose self-dealing by its principal officers.[420] The SEC settled the case in 2007, with Hollinger's former deputy chairman and chief operating officer, David Radler, ordered to disgorge $23 million and pay $5 million in penalties.[421] In 2007 Hollinger, Inc chairman and CEO Conrad Black was convicted of fraud and obstruction of justice in connection with diverting funds for personal benefit from money due to the company, thereby defrauding shareholders out of millions of dollars. Black was sentenced to six and a half years in prison, fined $125,000 and ordered to pay $6.1 million in restitution. However, in July 2010 the US Supreme Court remanded Black's case to the lower court with respect to three counts of fraud after determining that the 'honest services fraud' clause of the federal law used to prosecute Black[422] could be used only to prosecute bribery or kickbacks.[423]

(b) *Selective disclosure and insider trading*

The anti-fraud provisions of the US federal securities laws not only prohibit the dissemination of false or misleading information by an issuer, but also make it illegal for any insider who is privy to undisclosed material information about the issuer to profit from the purchase or sale of its securities.[424] Both the SEC, in administrative

---

414 Exchange Act §13(d) and related rules and schedules in Regulation 13D.
415 See Dodd-Frank Act, §§951-956 and 972.
416 Form 20-F, Item 7.B.
417 Item 404 of Regulation S-K.
418 SEC Litigation Release No 19022, "*SEC v TV Azteca S.A. de C.V.*" (January 4 2005).
419 SEC News Digest, Issue 2006-179, Enforcement Proceedings (September 15 2006).
420 SEC Litigation Release No 18969, "*SEC v Conrad M. Black*" (November 15 2004).
421 SEC Litigation Release No 20043, "*U.S. Securities and Exchange Commission v Conrad M. Black, F. David Radler and Hollinger Inc*" (March 16 2007).
422 18 USC §1346.
423 *Black v United States*, 2010 WL 2518593 (June 24 2010).
424 Exchange Act Rule 10b-5; Exchange Act Rule 14e-3 (tender offers).

enforcement actions, and the federal courts, in private litigation – in suits brought by the SEC and in criminal prosecutions – have established principles for determining when there is unfair trading based on material undisclosed information:[425] a corporate officer, director or highly placed employee may have material confidential information concerning the issuer that the issuer has not announced to the public, such as its impending discontinuance of a business segment or its unexpectedly poor earnings performance for the last fiscal period. Trading in the issuer's securities by such insiders prior to public disclosure can violate Rule 10b-5 and expose the individuals to private damage actions as well as to SEC sanction. Such officers, directors or employees of a foreign private issuer are subject to both private and SEC lawsuits for insider trading – regardless of whether the issuer is a reporting company, uses Rule 12g3-2(b) or simply has its securities traded in the United States – if jurisdictional criteria are satisfied.[426] An example is the $1 million disgorgement and civil penalty payment imposed in January 2005 on a former executive of a NASDAQ-traded Chinese internet company.[427] If material undisclosed information is communicated selectively to one or a handful of securities analysts or other persons that trade on the basis of the information, there may be Rule 10b-5 liability for both the recipients and transmitters of the information.

Rule 10b5-2 contains a non-exclusive definition of circumstances in which a person has a 'duty of trust or confidence' for purposes of the 'misappropriation' theory of insider trading under Section 10(b) of the Exchange Act. Under this theory, anyone that steals information from his employer and uses that information to trade stock, even if it is not the employer's stock, is guilty of insider trading. Rule 10b5-2 specifically cites instances when a duty of trust or confidence exists. Under insider trading law, the insider holding the information is called the 'tipper', while the individual receiving the information is called the 'tippee'. Both can be held equally liable under the law as long as the tippee had knowledge of the breach of duty of trust; if either is found liable for insider trading, the consequences are severe.[428]

In recent years, insider trading enforcement has increased:

- In 2010, in the case of *SEC v Galleon Management*, LP, the SEC brought insider trading charges against a multi-billion dollar hedge fund company, where the alleged tippers and tippees were a number of senior executives and consultants at well-known companies such as IBM.[429]
- In 2009, in *SEC v Rorech*, the SEC brought an insider trading case involving a credit default swap, a type of investment contract previously thought to be excluded from the reach of insider trading laws. Responding to the claims brought, the defendants moved for judgment on the pleadings, basing their

425 See, for example, *US v O'Hagan*, 521 US 642 (1997) (misappropriation); *Dirks v SEC*, 463 US 646 (1983) (tipping); *Chiarella v US*, 445 US 222 (1980) (classical).

426 See Daniel J Kramer & Megan Elizabeth Murray, "The Extraterritorial Application of United States Securities Laws to Punish Insider Trading", *The Review of Securities & Commodities Regulation*, Vol 35 No. 7 (April 10 2002).

427 SEC Litigation Release No 19049, "*SEC v Jun Singo Liang*" (January 25 2005).

428 Exchange Act Rule 10b5-2(b).

429 *SEC v Galleon Management*, LP, 683 F Supp 2d 316 (SDNY February 9 2010).

argument on the notion that credit default swaps were not security-based. This proved unsuccessful.[430]

Fair disclosure: On August 15 2000 the SEC adopted Regulation FD,[431] aimed at reducing selective disclosure by issuers to favoured securities analysts. The SEC's concern is that selective disclosure of material non-public information threatens the fairness and integrity of the securities markets by enabling the recipients to profit from quick trading at the expense of members of the public.[432]

Under Regulation FD (the FD stands for 'fair disclosure'), whenever an issuer discloses material non-public information to any securities market professional or any holder of the issuer's securities that is reasonably likely to trade on it, the issuer has to disclose the same information publicly. The disclosures must be simultaneous (or prompt if the selective disclosure is made inadvertently). An issuer could make such public disclosure through the traditional means of an Exchange Act report or through a press release. Posting on the issuer's website, although encouraged, does not by itself constitute adequate public disclosure. An issuer's failure to comply with Regulation FD does not give private parties an additional right to sue the issuer, but the SEC has its usual enforcement power and has brought actions for violation of Regulation FD against US issuers.[433] Over the past two years, its enforcement has become more aggressive. In September 2009 the SEC brought an action against the CFO of American Commercial Airlines, while in March 2010 the SEC filed an injunction against Presstek, Inc for violations of Regulation FD.

Regulation FD applies to US issuers that have entered the Exchange Act reporting system. As originally proposed in December 1999, it also would have covered foreign private issuers that are Exchange Act reporting companies.[434] They were excluded in the final version,[435] but foreign private issuers still should be aware of the Regulation FD rules.

Regulation FD establishes patterns of communication for US companies. Foreign private issuers should consider whether their selective disclosure to analysts – even though not prohibited by FD – is any longer consistent with best practices. When dealing with the US investment community, such issuers are likely to find that securities analysts will accept such issuers' adherence to the principle of contemporaneous public release of material inside information that must be followed by US companies.

Many public companies have a longstanding practice of issuing an immediate

---

430 *SEC v Rorech*, 673 F Supp 2d 217 (SDNY December 10 2009).

431 17 CFR Part 243.

432 SEC Release No 33-7881, "Selective Disclosure and Insider Trading" (August 15 2000).

433 SEC Litigation Release No 19154, *"SEC v Flowserve Corp and C. Scott Greer"* (March 24 2005); SEC Litigation Release No 18330, *"SEC v Schering-Plough Corporation"* (September 9 2003); SEC Release No 34-46895, "In the Matter of Secure Computing Corp and John McNulty" (November 25 2002); SEC Release No. 34-4689, *"In the Matter of Siebel Systems, Inc"* (November 25 2002); SEC Release No 34-46897, *"In the Matter of Raytheon Company and Franklyn A Caine"* (November 25 2002). But see *SEC v Siebel Systems*, Inc 384 F Supp 2d 694 (SDNY, September 1 2005).

434 SEC Release No 33-7787, *"Proposed Rule: Selective Disclosure and Insider Trading"*, II-B-6 (December 20 1999).

435 17 CFR §243.101(b)

press release regarding the substance of discussions with analysts, in order to avoid Rule 10b-5 liability. Apart from Regulation FD, this private litigation risk remains a concern.

The SEC continues to issue guidance on how it interprets Regulation FD. In June 2010 the SEC updated its Compliance and Disclosure Interpretations relating to the regulation[436] to provide guidance to companies and clarify that:

- an issuer may selectively confirm a forecast that it has previously made to the public without triggering Regulation FD's reporting requirements;
- Regulation FD does not create a duty to update;
- an issuer may provide material non-public information to an analyst that expressly agrees to maintain confidentiality until the information is public; and
- Regulation FD does not prohibit directors from speaking privately with a shareholder or groups of shareholders, as long as the director takes steps to ensure that the company does not violate Regulation FD, such as pre-clearing discussion topics with the shareholders or having company counsel present at the meeting. Additionally, a private communication between a director and shareholder does not violate Regulation FD if the shareholder provides an express agreement to maintain the disclosed information in confidence.

Effects of Enron: Enron Corp executives sold stock of the company before its financial problems became generally known to the investing public. Some of their sales occurred while employee participants in Enron retirement plans were prohibited by the terms of the plans from instructing the plan administrators to sell Enron stock held for their accounts.

The resulting public outcry – asserting both classic insider trading abuse and unfairness to rank-and-file employees – prompted the US Congress to include three special provisions in the Sarbanes-Oxley Act that apply to foreign private issuers as well as US issuers, with the exception noted below:

- Section 304 of the Sarbanes-Oxley Act provides that if an issuer is required to restate its financial statements due to material non-compliance "as a result of misconduct" with any securities law financial reporting requirement, the CEO and the CFO of the issuer shall reimburse it for:
  - any bonus or 'other incentive-based or equity-based compensation' they received during the 12-month period following the first publication of the financial document embodying such financial reporting requirement; and
  - any profits realised from the sale of the issuer's securities during that 12-month period.
- Section 306(a) of the Sarbanes-Oxley Act, as implemented by SEC Regulation BTR (standing for 'blackout trading restrictions'),[437] makes it unlawful for any

436 SEC Compliance and Disclosure Interpretations, "Regulation FD" (June 4 2010).

437 17 CFR Part 245, adopted in SEC Release No 34-47225, "Insider Trades During Pension Fund Blackout Periods" (January 22 2003).

director or executive officer to buy, sell or otherwise acquire or transfer any equity security of the issuer during any pension plan 'blackout period' – when plan participants are subject to restrictions on trading such securities – if the equity security was acquired in connection with service or employment as a director or executive officer. Any profit realised from such a prohibited transaction is recoverable by the issuer or by any shareholder of the issuer on its behalf.

The rule is limited to blackout periods that affect trading by 50% or more of plan participants or beneficiaries located in the United States (determined on an aggregate basis under all individual account plans of the company and its subsidiaries). To accommodate foreign private issuers, the SEC's rules further limit the application of Section 306(a) to situations where the number of employees located in the United States that are affected by the suspension exceeds either 15% of total worldwide employees or 50,000.

- Section 306(b) of the Sarbanes-Oxley Act contains an amendment to the Employee Retirement Income Security Act[438] – the US statute governing retirement plans – requiring 30 days' advance notice of a blackout period to all affected plan participants and beneficiaries. Unlike the two provisions described above, which apply only to 'issuers' under the Sarbanes-Oxley Act (defined as Exchange Act reporting companies and companies that have filed a registration statement under the Securites Act), the amendment to the Employee Retirement Income Security Act applies to all companies that sponsor US-based individual account plans (eg, 401(k) plans), whether or not their securities are publicly traded.

(c) Exhibits and confidential information

Registration statement and report requirements under the Securities Act and Exchange Act, respectively, call for the filing of specified 'exhibits'. These are made available to the public along with the rest of the statement or report. Form 20-F contains such exhibit requirements.[439] Contracts of material importance to the issuer's business are among the documents covered by the exhibit requirements.[440]

Issuers may have no problem with a general textual discussion of the contract, yet have a concern over disclosure of particular contract terms.

The SEC revised the Form 20-F exhibit instructions to require foreign private issuers to file an individual employment contract or compensatory plan only if the contract or plan is required to be filed in the foreign private issuer's home country or the issuer otherwise publicly discloses it.[441]

Rules under the Securities Act and the Exchange Act contain provisions for withholding confidential information,[442] but they require an application to the SEC and are of limited practical use. If disclosure of price or other terms would create a

---

438 29 USC §1001 *et seq*. The provision added by Section 306(b) is at 29 USC §1021(i).
439 Form 20-F, Item 19 and Instructions to Exhibits.
440 Form 20-F, Instructions to Exhibits, Item 4.
441 Form 20-F, Instructions to Exhibits, Item 4(c)(v).
442 Securities Act Rule 406; Exchange Act Rule 24b-2.

competitive problem for the issuer, the SEC may allow the omission of the particular portion – but not the entirety – of the document.

The legal staff of the SEC's Division of Corporation Finance has published a useful summary of practices to be followed by issuers wishing to obtain confidential treatment for particular portions of documents.[443]

(d) *Management's commentary on financial statements*

SEC rules require both Securities Act and Exchange Act documents to accompany their financial statements with a management's discussion and analysis of financial condition and results of operations (MD&A). The MD&A is designed not only to explain significant variations in historical financial performance and provide a qualitative analysis of balance-sheet items, but also to disclose "presently known trends, events or uncertainties" that the issuer's management reasonably perceives as likely to affect its future performance and financial health. Management is asked to pay particular attention to the effects of trends and uncertainties on the issuer's liquidity, capital resources and results of operations. According to the SEC, the MD&A is "intended to give the investor an opportunity to look at the company through the eyes of management by providing both a short- and long-term analysis of the business of the company"[444]

US issuers must supply an MD&A under the instructions contained in Item 303 of Regulation S-K.

Foreign private issuers must provide an MD&A in a registration statement or report under the requirements of Form 20-F, which contains essentially the same substantive MD&A requirements that apply to US issuers under Item 303 of Regulation S-K.[445]

The MD&A requirements have always been worded broadly, as principles rather than detailed disclosure rules, in order to stimulate issuers to draft material that is tailored to the situation of the particular company and its industry. This generality has caused issuers to look for guidance in their drafting.

The SEC published a comprehensive interpretive release in 1989 that has been treated as a complement to the formal MD&A instructions. On December 19 2003 it issued new interpretive guidance that applies – as did the 1989 release – both to US issuers and to foreign private issuers.[446]

The December 2003 release offers suggestions as to the substantive content of the MD&A and as to the manner and style of presenting information. It urges issuers to avoid complex language and eliminate immaterial disclosures. One recommendation is for an introductory summary or overview to help readers to sift out the really significant financial and business data.

Issuers are urged to have senior management focus on the areas of major

443 SEC Division of Corporation Finance, Staff Legal Bulletin No 1 "Confidential Treatment Requests" (February 28 1997, addendum added on July 11 2001).

444 SEC Release No 33-8177, "Disclosure Required by Sections 406 and 407 of the Sarbanes-Oxley Act of 2002" (January 23 2003).

445 See Appendix A for more on the disclosure requirements of Form 20-F.

446 SEC Release No 33-8350, "Interpretation: Commission Guidance Regarding Management's Discussion and Analysis of Financial Condition and Results of Operations" (December 19 2003).

importance at the outset of the drafting process. Those foreign private issuers that are concerned with the MD&A – either as reporting companies under the Exchange Act or in connection with securities offerings – would do well to see that their directors and officers are familiar with these interpretive releases.

Supplementing these general interpretive guides, the SEC from time to time publishes advice on specific MD&A topics (eg, in September 2010, regarding disclosure with respect to liquidity and capital resources).[447]

The SEC and the US Congress have focused on two areas discussed below in adopting the Sarbanes-Oxley Act and the regulations thereunder. Although the areas are arguably covered by the general language of Regulation S-K, Item 303 and Form 20-F, Item 5, amendments and proposed amendments call for specific MD&A disclosure regarding off-balance sheet arrangements and critical accounting policies.

Off-balance sheet arrangements: A major complaint about the opacity of financial statements has been the failure to explain the significance of off-balance sheet structures. Section 401(a) of the Sarbanes-Oxley Act instructed the SEC to issue rules requiring Exchange Act reports to disclose all material off-balance sheet arrangements.

On January 28 2003 the SEC amended the MD&A rules to call for a separately captioned subsection requiring:

- an explanation of the issuer's off-balance sheet arrangements (defined as guaranty obligations, contingent interests in assets transferred to the off-balance sheet entity and specified derivative and variable interest obligations); and
- an overview in a tabular format of specified categories of contractual obligations.[448]

Both Item 303 of Regulation S-K and Item 5 of Form 20-F were revised to add these requirements. In Form 20-F:

- foreign private issuers must discuss off-balance sheet arrangements that have or are reasonably likely to have a material current or future effect on financial presentation. Specifically required disclosures include:
  - the nature and business purpose of the arrangements and their importance to liquidity, capital resources, market risk support or credit risk support;
  - various specific financial information as to the effect of the arrangements on the issuer; and
  - any known event, demand, commitment, trend or uncertainty reasonably likely to result in termination or material reduction in availability to the issuer of the arrangements;[449] and
- a foreign private issuer must further provide, as of its latest fiscal year end,

447 SEC Release No 33-9144, "Commission Guidance on Presentation of Liquidity and Capital Resources Disclosures in Management's Discussion and Analysis" (September 17 2010).

448 SEC Release No 33-8182, "Disclosure in Management's Discussion and Analysis about Off-Balance Sheet Arrangements and Aggregate Contractual Obligations" (January 28 2003).

449 Form 20-F, Item 5E.

information in a tabular format as to the aggregate amounts of payments due under obligations for long term debt, capital leases, operating leases, purchase obligations and other long-term obligations reflected on the balance sheet under US GAAP or IFRS.[450]

During December 2007, the SEC made public an illustrative letter sent to various registrants to give guidance regarding off-balance sheet obligations. The letter focused on three topics in relation to Item 303 of Regulation S-K:

- items that companies might want to consider disclosing, to the extent they are applicable and material, for any non-consolidated conduit or collateralised debt obligation for which the company has material exposure;
- disclosure in relation to a company's critical accounting policies; and
- the requirement to discuss any known trends or uncertainties that the company expects to have a material favourable or unfavourable impact on income from operations, liquidity and capital resources.[451]

Critical accounting policies and estimates: On December 12 2001 the SEC issued cautionary advice that public companies should include in their MD&As full explanations – in plain English – of their 'critical accounting policies', the judgements and uncertainties affecting the application of those policies, and the likelihood that materially different amounts would be reported under different conditions or using different assumptions.[452]

On May 10 2002 the SEC proposed to amend the MD&A rules to make this cautionary advice into a formal – and more specific – disclosure requirement to be addressed by US issuers in an amended Item 303 of Regulation S-K, and by foreign private issuers in a new paragraph of Item 5 of Form 20-F:[453]

- There would be special disclosure regarding accounting policies adopted by the issuer within the prior year that would have a material impact on the issuer;
- There would be a requirement for issuer disclosure of its 'critical accounting estimates' and the significance of such estimates to the issuer's reported financial condition and results of operations; and
- An accounting estimate would be considered 'critical' if:
  - it required management to make assumptions about matters that are highly uncertain; and
  - different reasonable estimates or foreseeable changes in management's estimate would have a material impact on the issuer's financial presentation.

450 Form 20-F, Item 5F.

451 SEC Corporation Finance, Sample Letter Sent to Public Companies That Have Identified Investments in Structured Investment Vehicles, Conduits or Collateralized Debt Obligations (Off-balance Sheet Entities) (December 11 2007).

452 SEC Release No 33-8040, "Action: Cautionary Advice Regarding Disclosure about Critical Accounting Policies" (December 12 2001).

453 SEC Release No 33-8098, "Proposed Rule: Disclosure in Management's Discussion and Analysis about the Application of Critical Accounting Policies" (May 10 2002).

These proposals have not been adopted. The SEC's December 2003 comprehensive interpretive release stated that the May 2002 amendatory proposals remain under consideration, although no further action has been taken on the matter.[454] Through the release, the SEC has made clear that it already expects the MD&A to discuss critical accounting estimates and policies along the lines of the proposals and advises companies on what disclosure materials to provide.

(e) Press releases and issuer websites

Once a US public trading market has arisen in the securities of a foreign private issuer, the issuer must be concerned with the accuracy and completeness of the issuer information that the market possesses. Such initiatives as press releases, conference calls with securities analysts and postings on websites can be valuable tools in amplifying the body of publicly available information. Press release disclosure of material business or financial developments can inform investors on a more immediate basis than issuer SEC filings. Form 6-K reports and Rule 12g3-2(b) disclosure by foreign private issuers may reflect the text of prior press releases, as may Form 8-K filings of US issuers.

Press release requirements: There is no general requirement under the Exchange Act for the issuance of a press release whenever there is a material corporate development,[455] except for the Regulation FD requirement (applicable only to US issuers) of contemporaneous public release of material non-public information that is aimed at avoiding problems of insider trading and selective disclosure discussed above.

For issuers listed on a US national securities exchange, the rules of the particular exchange may call for continuous disclosure of material events through the medium of the press release. The listing agreement that a US or foreign private issuer must enter into with the NYSE when it lists securities on that exchange requires the issuer to "release quickly to the public any news or information that might reasonably be expected to materially affect the market for its securities".[456] The NYSE notes that the normal method of publication of important corporate data is by means of a press release marked 'For Immediate Release'.

The SEC recently approved changes relating to press-release requirements for NASDAQ-listed companies. Its March 2010 release amends the NASDAQ rules to eliminate requirements that duplicate Form 8-K requirements by permitting companies to fulfil their NASDAQ disclosure obligations through a press release or by filing Form 8-K, when required by the SEC.[457]

Furthermore, foreign private issuers were required under the prior rules to disclose interim financial results in a press release and Form 6-K, but the March 2010 changes eliminate the requirement to publish interim results in a press release.

---

454 SEC Release Nos 33-8350, "Interpretation: Commission Guidance Regarding Management's Discussion and Analysis of Financial Condition Results of Operations" (December 19 2003).

455 See *Basic, Inc v Levinson*, 485 US 224 (1988).

456 NYSE Listed Company Manual §202.05.

457 SEC Release No 34-61713, "Self-Regulatory Organizations; The NASDAQ Stock Market LLC; Order Granting Approval of Proposed Rule Change to Modify the Press Release Requirements for Listed Companies" (March 15 2010).

However, foreign private issuers are still required to publish their interim results in a Form 6-K filed with the SEC.[458]

Website information: As already discussed in "Periodic reporting requirements", an issuer must publish certain material information, typically on its website, in order to qualify for the reporting exemption provided by Exchange Act Rule 12g3-2(b).

In its September 5 2002 release accelerating the filing deadlines for US issuers' Exchange Act reports, the SEC observed that the development of the Internet "has revolutionized information production, availability and dissemination" and enabled companies to make information available "quickly and in a cost-effective manner".[459] The release encourages companies to provide website access to their Exchange Act reports and requires larger seasoned US issuers – essentially, those entitled to use short-form registration – to disclose in their Form 10-K reports whether they make Exchange Act reports available free of charge on the website on the same day that the material is electronically transmitted to the SEC.

Most larger companies – foreign private issuers as well as US issuers – post business and financial press releases on their websites. Many post their annual reports there as well. Practices vary as to how long they remain available. As discussed below, there is a duty to update information posted online whenever that information is restated, reissued or republished.

While generally urging issuers to broaden investor access to information through website postings, the SEC has not generally accepted that the effect of internet communication is the same as the effect of a press release.[460] Not all investors have Internet access. Nevertheless, the SEC has acknowledged that more and more companies continue to use websites as a means of publicly disseminating information, and has therefore issued an interpretive release to provide companies with guidance on a number of issues relating to the disclosure of information on websites.[461] The release does not contain any adoption or amendment of rules.

(f) Prospective information and duty to update

A Securities Act registration statement and an Exchange Act registration statement or annual report are required to present current and historical business and financial trends, events or uncertainties in 'risk factor' disclosure and in the MD&A.

It is often unclear whether prospective information falls within the category of "presently known trends, events or uncertainties" that is mandatorily disclosable in an issuer's MD&A or is only 'forward-looking information' whose disclosure is "encouraged but not required" by the SEC.[462]

---

458 See NASDAQ Marketplace Rule 520(c)(2).

459 SEC Release No 33-8128, "Acceleration of Periodic Report Filing Dates and Disclosure Concerning Website Access to Reports" (September 5 2002).

460 SEC Release No 33-7881, "Selective Disclosure and Insider Trading", II-B-4b (August 15 2000); SEC Release No 33-7856, "Use of Electronic Media" (April 28 2000).

461 SEC Release No 34-58288, "Commission Guidance on the Use of Company Websites" (August 1 2008).

462 See SEC Release No 33-6835, "Management's Discussion and Analysis of Financial Condition and Results of Operations; Certain Investment Company Disclosures", III-B (May 18 1989). Compare Form 20-F, Item 5 Instruction 3 with Regulation S-K, Item 303(a) Instruction 7. See also Commission Regulation (EC) No. 809/2004, Recital (8) (April 29 2004).

Cautionary statements: It can be difficult for a foreign private issuer to appreciate the need for discussions of future uncertainties or trends. There is a natural inclination to avoid negative predictions, particularly if the company's investor relations literature has been generally optimistic. As they familiarise themselves with the US federal disclosure system, however, most foreign private issuers come to perceive that negative disclosure of future uncertainties and trends is expected not just by the SEC, but also by the investment community.

On the positive side, prospective disclosure of investment risks, uncertainties and trends can establish credibility with securities analysts and protect against civil liability for material misstatements and omissions in offering literature and reports.

A foreign private issuer evaluating the business and financial disclosures it may have to make in a Securities Act registration statement or an Exchange Act registration statement or annual report will want to study materials published by its competitors and other companies in the same business. Not only the SEC, but also federal courts entertaining securities law litigation, will take note of significant differences in the quality of disclosure by companies that are similarly situated.

Projections and 'forward-looking information': Foreign private issuers entering the US securities market will face the same requests for estimates of future revenues and earnings that are faced by managements of US issuers. Making such projections of future economic performance is optional; probably, most US companies do not formally predict their future earnings per share in documents (eg, prospectuses and reports) that are responsive to SEC disclosure requirements. Increasingly, however, companies address earnings expectations in press releases and analyst conference calls. Regulation FD has stimulated public projections by companies seeking to avoid differential disclosure to securities analysts.

Analysts who follow the affairs of publicly traded companies regularly come up with their own estimates of future performance. If requested by analysts, most corporate managements will review pre-publication drafts of analyst reports for egregious errors. Issuers should be aware that the accompanying verbal exchange may result in management being perceived as having adopted or sanctioned the analysts' estimates.[463]

Issuers that are normally disinclined to issue forecasts may have to do so in particular circumstances. For example, issuers negotiating private placements with institutional investors are often asked for projections of future revenues and income, especially where the funds received in the offering will be applied to the construction of a specific new project. Investors will want to examine management's projections and the stated assumptions underlying them to reach a conclusion as to the project's viability.

Federal courts have held that management projections of future economic performance – often called 'soft' information and characterised by the SEC as

463 See, for example, *Elkind v Liggett & Myers, Inc*, 635 F 2d 156 (2d Circuit 1980); *SEC v Bausch & Lomb, Inc*, 565 F 2d 8 (2d Circuit 1977); SEC Release No 33-7881, "Selective Disclosure and Insider Trading", II-B-7 (August 14 2000).

'forward-looking information' – can create civil liability on the part of the issuer if the projections are found to have been made without a reasonable basis or in bad faith.[464] In the Private Securities Litigation Reform Act of 1995, amending the Securities Act and the Exchange Act, the US Congress introduced a statutory safe harbour designed to encourage issuers to make projections and provide other forward-looking information by giving protection to forward-looking statements that satisfy specified conditions. The principal condition is that an issuer's forward-looking statements be accompanied by 'meaningful cautionary statements'. Both mandatory forward-looking statements (eg, MD&A trend information) and optional forward-looking statements (eg, earnings projections) are covered. These cautionary statements cannot be merely boilerplate warnings, but rather must convey substantive information about the realistic factors that could cause results to differ materially from those projected in the forward-looking statement.[465] The statutory safe harbour is available only where the issuer is subject to the ongoing reporting requirements of the Exchange Act; but it will cover forward-looking statements in materials not required to be filed with the SEC (eg, private offering memoranda and press releases) as well as SEC-filed documents (eg, registration statements and reports).

The Second Circuit recently analysed the safe harbour provision in *Slayton v American Express Co*, providing some guidance on forward-looking statements. In this case, the plaintiffs alleged that American Express failed to disclose the true nature of its expected losses. The question considered was whether the safe harbour provided by the Private Securities Litigation Reform Act protected American Express from liability for forward-looking statements made in its Form 10-Q report filed with the SEC in May 2001. Ultimately, the Second Circuit held that American Express's language was too vague to be meaningful, because it essentially warned merely that "if [American Express's] portfolio deteriorates, then there will be losses in [their] portfolio".[466] Furthermore, according to the court, meaningful cautionary statements require substantive company-specific warnings based on a realistic description of the risks applicable to the particular circumstances. American Express, however, had used exactly the same language in an earlier SEC filing, even though they had received new information by the time they filed their Form 10-Q in May. This undercut any argument that the cautionary language was tailored to the specific future projection.[467]

Duty to update: Whenever an issuer discloses information to investors or the markets, the disclosure must be accurate and complete. This standard applies not only to disclosures in response to specific regulatory requirements, but also to voluntary statements. If an issuer's disclosure later proves to have been wrong when made, it has a duty to correct it.

---

464 See, for example, *Isquith v Middle South Utilities, Inc*, 847 F 2d 186 (5th Circuit), cert denied, 488 US 926 (1988); Securities Act Rule 175; Exchange Act Rule 3b-6.

465 Securities Litigation Reform, US House of Representatives Report No 104 -369, 104th Congress, 1st Session, at 31-49 (November 28 1995).

466 *Slayton v American Express Co*, 604 F 3d 758, 773 (2d Circuit May 18 2010).

467 *Id.*

It is less clear that an issuer has a duty to update and correct a statement that, although truthful when made, subsequently becomes misleading. Courts have had difficulty with this question in the area of prospective or forward-looking information.[468] For example, a projection of future earnings may be reasonable under the circumstances existing at the time it is made, but may become unrealistic if the prospects of the business change materially. If the markets could reasonably expect that the maker of the projection would revise it to reflect material changes, the courts could find such a duty to update.

A particular area of concern to reporting companies, including foreign private issuers, is whether, once they post information on their websites, the information will be considered to be republished each time it is accessed, subjecting such companies to a duty to correct and update continually the previously posted information. In August 2008 the SEC issued an interpretive release that, among other things, provided guidance on this very question.[469] This release clarified that information originally published on a company's website that simply remains available on such website as historic information, but is not later affirmatively restated, reissued or republished, is not subject to a duty to correct or update.

A foreign private issuer should consider the following as part of an ongoing US disclosure programme:

- Review the forward-looking information in SEC-filed documents, particularly information included in response to the MD&A requirements, to see whether updating is called for. MD&A information should be brought up to date in succeeding documents, whether it was provided mandatorily (in response to requirements for disclosing trends, uncertainties and the like) or voluntarily.
- Analyse other forward-looking statements – such as those made in press releases or on the issuer's website – to see whether investors are still likely to be relying on them and, if so, publish updated information if necessary.
- Consider the utility of disclaiming in press releases and on the issuer's website a duty to correct or update.
- For issuers reporting under the Exchange Act, seek to take advantage of the safe harbour for forward-looking statements referred to above and in "Securities litigation risks" below, and periodically update the 'cautionary statements' that are necessary for safe harbour protection, to make them meaningful.
- Consider clearly identifying information posted on an issuer's website as historical or previously posted (eg, by dating posted materials) or posting it in a separate section that contains historical or previously-posted materials.

(g) *Electronic communications and EDGAR system*

The greatly expanded use of electronic communication has led the SEC to:

---

468 Compare different circuit court approaches in *Backman v Polaroid Corp*, 910 F 2d 10 (1st Circuit 1990); *In re International Business Machines Corp Securities Litigation*, 163 F 3d 102 (2d Circuit 1998); *Oran v Stafford*, 226 F 3d 275 (3d Circuit 2000); *Gallagher v Abbott Laboratories*, 269 F 3d 806 (7th Circuit 2001).

469 SEC Release Nos 34-58288, "Commission Guidance on the Use of Company Websites" (August 1 2008).

- address the impact of the Internet on the mechanics of corporate disclosure; and
- adopt its own electronic filing system.

Use of the Internet generally: The SEC has permitted electronic communication as a substitute for traditional methods, under varying conditions and limitations. It has allowed both registered and private offerings to be made on the Internet and has accepted the use of internet communication in such aspects of the public offering process as underwriter road shows and prospectus delivery. In its releases leading to the Offering Reform Rules (discussed in "Public offerings" above), the SEC pointed to the investment community's increasing reliance on electronic communication as a major reason for its streamlining of the Securities Act registration process.[470]

The SEC's September 5 2002 rule amendment release relating to the timing of Exchange Act reports summarises the effects of internet communication.[471] Its earlier proposing release lists several SEC pronouncements commencing in 1995 "to encourage companies and market intermediaries to take advantage of electronic media to communicate with, and deliver information to, investors".[472]

Use of the Internet in offshore offerings: The Internet enables issuers to disseminate advertisements and information regarding securities across national borders. Foreign private issuers engaged in offshore offerings have been uncertain whether offshore offerings that involve the use of the Internet in some fashion – although not intended for US persons – could fall foul of the registration or other provisions of the US securities laws.

In a March 1998 interpretive statement[473] the SEC gave these views on the use of websites to disseminate offshore offering materials:

- Issuers should implement precautionary measures "that are reasonably designed to ensure" that offshore Internet offers do not target the US market. Suggested (although not exclusive) procedures are:
  - including on the website a prominent disclaimer of any intent to offer in the United States or to US persons; and
  - avoiding transmission of materials to persons at US addresses or phone numbers.

  Where a foreign private issuer is not planning a concurrent offering in the United States and complies with Regulation S, these procedures should be sufficient to avoid Securities Act registration problems.
- Where a foreign private issuer plans to make a US private offering concurrently with its offshore offering, it should implement the above

470 SEC Release No 33-8501, "Securities Offering Reform", I-B-1 (November 3 2004); SEC Release No 33-8591, "Securities Offering Reform", I-B-1, III-B-1 (July 19 2005).

471 SEC Release No 33-8128, "Acceleration of Periodic Report Filing Dates and Disclosure Concerning Website Access to Reports" (September 5 2002).

472 SEC Release No 33-8089, "Acceleration of Periodic Report Filing Dates and Disclosure Concerning Website Access to Reports", II-B-1 (April 12 2002).

473 SEC Release No 33-7516, "Statement of the Commission Regarding Use of Internet Web Sites to Offer Securities, Solicit Securities Transactions or Advertise Investment Services Offshore" (March 23 1998).

procedures and, in addition, either:

  - not permit persons responding to the offshore internet offer to participate in the US private offering (even if otherwise entitled to do so); or
  - limit access to the offshore offering materials on its website to viewers first providing residence information that does not suggest they are US persons.

  Access may be limited by the use of website blockers, as discussed in "Private placements" above. The offshore offering material should contain no more information concerning the private US offering than is required by foreign law to be provided in the offshore offering.
- Where a concurrent US offering is registered under the Securities Act, foreign private issuers should avoid 'gun jumping' that could arise from the premature internet posting of offshore offering material.

The SEC reaffirmed these views in October 1999 in its Cross-Border Release.[474] It noted that website posting of tender and exchange offer and rights offering materials "presents special problems not present in the context of public underwritten offerings" because US security holders are already familiar with the subject company and are more likely to have an incentive to find an indirect way to participate in the offer. For transactions that are not exempted under Rule 801 or Rule 802, or the Tier I or Tier II tender offer exemptions, foreign private issuers are given "additional guidance as to what constitutes adequate precautions" to prevent participation by US persons.[475]

SEC filing requirements and the EDGAR system: Since November 4 2002, the SEC has required foreign private issuers to file most of their Securities Act and Exchange Act materials electronically under its EDGAR system rather than in traditional paper form.[476] They thus joined US issuers, which have been required to file under EDGAR since the mid-1990s.

Generally, Securities Act registration statements and Exchange Act registration statements and reports, as well as various other specified securities materials, have to be filed electronically on EDGAR by a foreign private issuer. However, the SEC currently permits first-time foreign private issuers, upon request, to submit paper drafts of their initial Securities Act or Exchange Act registration statements for staff review on a confidential basis.

Interim reports of a foreign private issuer on Form 6-K may be filed in paper form:

- if the sole purpose of the Form 6-K report is to provide a copy of the issuer's annual report to security holders (the annual report to security holders will continue to be submitted in paper form, as is the case of annual reports to security holders of US issuers); or

---

474 See "International offerings with US participants".

475 SEC Release No 33-7759, "Cross-Border Tender and Exchange Offers, Business Combinations and Rights Offerings", II-G-1 (October 22 1999).

476 SEC Release No 33-8099, "Mandated EDGAR Filing for Foreign Issuers" (May 14 2002).

- if the foreign private issuer requests confidential treatment.

As discussed in "Periodic reporting requirements" above, the Rule 12g3-2(b) exemption from registration no longer requires that any information be submitted to the SEC, and instead relies on disclosure via the issuer's website or through an electronic information delivery system generally available to the public.

The SEC's Regulation S-T provides the mechanical rules for making EDGAR filings. It is regularly updated by the SEC.

Interactive data: The SEC has investigated ways to broaden the utility of information stored on EDGAR. In February 2005 it adopted a programme for issuers voluntarily to submit supplemental 'tagged' financial information using XBRL.[477]

In a May 2006 speech the chairman of the SEC characterised the subject matter of the programme as 'interactive data' and saw it as progress toward the real-time disclosure system envisaged by Section 409 of the Sarbanes-Oxley Act.[478] On August 19 2008 the SEC introduced plans to replace the EDGAR system with the IDEA (Interactive Data Electronic Applications) system. This can be seen as another modernisation step taken by the SEC. Based on a new architecture, IDEA will at first supplement and then eventually replace the EDGAR system. Similar to XBRL, IDEA will facilitate the use and analysis of information submitted to the SEC in interactive data format.[479]

4.6 Delisting and deregistration

Since the Sarbanes-Oxley Act was adopted in 2002, many foreign private issuers have tried to leave the US capital markets in order to avoid regulation under this act. These issuers would attempt to 'delist' – that is, terminate their listing on one of the US national securities exchanges – and also 'deregister' the securities they had registered under the Exchange Act. However, foreign private issuers often found the process for delisting and deregistering to be cumbersome. Recent rule changes have made this process much easier.

Delisting: A foreign private issuer of a class of securities may voluntarily terminate its listing on one of the US national securities exchanges by complying with the rules set forth in Exchange Act Rule 12d2-2(c), which require the following:

- The issuer must file an application, Form 25, with the SEC to notify the SEC of its withdrawal of the securities from the US national securities exchange and its intention to withdraw the securities from registration;
- The issuer must comply with any specific delisting rules set forth by the national securities exchange;

---

477 SEC Release No 33-8529, "XBRL Voluntary Financial Reporting Programme on the EDGAR System" (February 3 2005). XBRL is discussed in the section on interactive data in "Periodic reporting requirements".

478 Christopher Cox, SEC chairman, speech at the American Enterprise Institute, "The Interactive Data Revolution: Improved Disclosure for Investors, Less Expensive Reporting for Companies" (May 30 2006).

479 Press Release, SEC, "'IDEA' Will Make Company and Fund Information Interactive" (August 19 2008).

- The issuer has 10 days after it files Form 25 with the SEC to provide written notice to the national securities exchange that it is delisting the class of securities or deregistering on that exchange. The notice must describe the security involved along with all of the material facts relating to the reason for delisting;
- The issuer must issue a press release contemporaneously with its Form 25 filing, containing its intention to delist and reasons for delisting, and post the press release on its publicly accessible website (if it has one) until the time that the delisting on Form 25 has become effective. The press release must specify if the issuer has not arranged for listing on another national securities exchange; and
- The national securities exchange must provide notice on its website that the issuer intends to delist once it receives notice from the issuer.

The Form 25 application is effective 10 days after it is filed with the SEC for delisting. However, the SEC has the right to postpone the effectiveness of the delisting application in order to determine whether the Form 25 application was properly made and whether any terms should be imposed to protect investors.[480]

Deregistration: Once a foreign private issuer registers a class of securities under Section 12(g) of the Exchange Act and commences filing reports as required under Section 13(a) and Section 15(d) of that act, it must continue in the reporting system indefinitely – unless and until it becomes entitled to terminate its Exchange Act reporting obligations. Until recently, foreign private issuers could delist from a US national securities exchange, but they faced many obstacles in deregistering their securities from the SEC's reporting system.[481] Without deregistration, a foreign private issuer could only suspend, and not terminate, its duty to report under the Exchange Act even if there was little interest in the issuer's securities registered in the United States.

The primary determinant used by the SEC to allow an issuer to terminate its registration of a class of securities or suspend its reporting obligations was whether the securities were held of record by fewer than 300 US residents. If the issuer's number of US record holders remained below 300, its reporting obligations would merely be suspended. However, if the number of US holders rose above 300, it would have to resume its reporting obligations despite the fact that there were relatively low levels of interest in its securities by US residents. As a result, foreign private issuers were trapped in the US capital markets long after there was any meaningful interest in their securities in the United States.

The SEC acknowledged that the burdensome and costly nature of the deregistering process was discouraging foreign private issuers from entering the US public capital markets in the first place. Thus, in order to make the US markets more attractive to

480 Exchange Act Rule 12d-2.

481 Craig Doidge, *et al*, *Why Do Foreign Firms Leave U.S. Equity Markets? An Analysis of Deregistration under SEC Exchange Act Rule 12h-6*, The Ohio State University, Fisher College of Business, Charles A Dice Centre for Research in Financial Economics (August 2008).

foreign private issuers, it adopted Exchange Act Rule 12h-6 in 2007 to make it easier for foreign private issuers to deregister, thereby eliminating conditions considered a barrier to entry into the US markets while still ensuring investor protections.[482]

A major change adopted by the SEC in Rule 12h-6 was to move from the record holder standard to a quantitative benchmark based solely on a comparison of the average daily trading volume of a foreign private issuer's equity securities in the United States with the trading volume in the foreign private issuer's primary trading market. The SEC's rationale was that a comparison of US trading volume with the foreign private issuer's primary trading market would provide a more direct measure of the issuer's connection with the US market, and trading volume data would be easier to obtain than record holder data or a comparison of US public float with worldwide public float. As a result, Rule 12h-5 enables a foreign private issuer to qualify for termination of its Exchange Act reporting obligations by meeting a quantitative benchmark not tied to the number of its US record holders or the percentage of its securities held by those holders.

In order to deregister, the foreign private issuer must file Form 15F with the SEC, certifying that:

- its reporting obligations under Section 13(a) and Section 15(d) of the Exchange Act have been met for the last year and at least one annual report has been filed pursuant to Section 13(a);
- the foreign private issuer's securities have not been sold in the United States in a registered offering under the Securities Act for the last year, except for securities issued to employees, securities sold in non-underwritten offerings and a few other exceptions;
- the foreign private issuer has maintained a listing of that class of securities for the previous year on a foreign exchange that is the securities' primary trading market; and
- the average daily trading volume of the securities in the United States for the last year has been no greater than 5% of the volume of that class of securities on a worldwide basis for the same period, or that within 120 days of the Form 15F filing, the securities were held of record by fewer than 300 persons worldwide or who are US residents.

Rule 15h-6 includes directions on how to count the number of US residents holding a foreign private issuer's securities.

If the issuer's securities trade in the form of American depositary receipts (ADRs), it must calculate the average daily trading volume of these in terms of the number of securities that they represent.

The foreign private issuer must, before or contemporaneously with its Form 15F filing, publish a notice in the United States of its intent to deregister the securities and its reporting obligations. This notice must be published via a means reasonably

482 SEC Release No 34-55540, "Termination of a Foreign Private Issuer's Registration of a Class of Securities Under Section 12(g) and Duty to File Reports Under Section 13(a) or 15(d) of the Securities Exchange Act of 1934" (March 27 2007).

designed to provide broad dissemination of the information to the US public and must also be submitted to the SEC. However, a foreign private issuer must wait 12 months to file a Form 15F if:

- the issuer delisted securities from a national securities exchange and at the time of delisting the average daily trading volume in the United States exceeded 5% of the average daily trading volume on a worldwide basis for the last year; or
- the issuer terminated a sponsored ADR facility and at that time the average daily trading volume in the United States of these exceeded 5% of the volume of the underlying securities on a worldwide basis for the last year.

Immediately upon filing Form 15F, the foreign private issuer's duty to file reports under Section 13(a) or Section 15(d) of the Exchange Act is suspended. After 90 days, if the SEC has no objections, the registration of a class of securities under Section 12(g) is terminated and the foreign private issuer's duty to file reports is terminated as well.

The prior regulatory scheme was likened to the Hotel California, where you can check in any time you like, but you can never leave. Hopefully, the new scheme will facilitate timely exits.

4.7 International disclosure standards

US and foreign rules for textual disclosure and financial statement presentation have been moving towards convergence. But they have yet to reach the stage of agreement upon all significant standards and principles governing financial statements. However, the US Financial Accounting Standards Board (FASB) and the IASB have made the convergence of US GAAP and IFRS a high priority.[483] The SEC has been very active in this area, eliminating the requirement for foreign private issuers to reconcile their IFRS results to GAAP[484] and also proposing a roadmap for the voluntary adoption of IFRS by certain large domestic companies.[485]

(a) International securities regulation

In 1998 the International Organisation of Securities Commissioners (IOSCO) endorsed a core set of disclosure standards for the textual portions of securities disclosure documents.[486] The SEC revised its Form 20-F disclosure requirements for foreign private issuers, effective from September 30 2000, to conform to IOSCO's standards and promote the aim of creating a single disclosure document that would be accepted in multiple jurisdictions.[487] The incorporated international standards cover all types of registration statements, not just those where equity securities are offered for cash.

The incorporation of IOSCO standards in Form 20-F did not affect the financial

483 Ernst & Young, *U.S. GAAP v IFRS: The Basics* (January 2009).

484 See SEC Release No 33-8879, "Acceptance from Foreign Private Issuers of Financial Statements Prepared in Accordance with International Financial Reporting Standards without Reconciliation to U.S. GAAP" (December 21 2007).

485 See SEC Release No 33-9109, "Commission Statement in Support of Convergence and Global Accounting Standards" (February 24 2010).

486 See the IOSCO website at www.iosco.org.

487 SEC Release No 33-7745, "International Disclosure Standards" (September 28 1999).

statement reconciliation rules that apply when a foreign private issuer prepares financial statements on the basis of accounting principles other than US GAAP; nor did it alter a foreign private issuer's liabilities under federal securities laws or change existing SEC practices for reviewing filed documents.

(b) *International Financial Reporting Standards*

New and extended International Accounting Standards are known as IFRS. The SEC considers that this term encompasses previously published International Accounting Standards as well as such new and extended standards – in other words, the entire body of international standards:[488]

- In 2002 the European Union adopted a requirement that publicly traded issuers incorporated in an EU member state prepare financial statements under IFRS, commencing with their first fiscal year starting on or after January 1 2005.[489] Countries outside the European Union, such as Japan, Australia and Norway, have done the same.
- More broadly, the technical committee of IOSCO has recommended to all its member organisations that they "allow multinational issuers to use IFRS in cross-border offerings and listings, as supplemented by reconciliation, disclosure and interpretation where necessary to address outstanding substantive issues at a national or regional level".[490]
- In December 2007 the SEC issued a release adopting rules under which foreign private issuers may file their financial statements using IFRS without including a reconciliation to US GAAP, in order to satisfy Exchange Act reporting requirements. However, the SEC notes that a foreign private issuer must continue to include a reconciliation to US GAAP in its SEC filing if it uses any other basis of accounting, such as a jurisdictional variation of IFRS.[491]
- In September 2008 the IASB and FASB issued a memorandum of understanding to discuss a convergence of all major accounting standards by 2011 in light of a possible IFRS adoption.[492]
- In November 2008 the SEC released for public comment a roadmap for the potential use of financial statements prepared in accordance with IFRS.[493]
- In February 2010 the SEC voted to issue a statement reaffirming its position regarding the desirability of global accounting standards, making it clear that the SEC believes that a single set of high-quality, globally accepted accounting standards would be beneficial.[494]

---

488 SEC Release No 33-8397, "First-Time Application of IFRS", fn 12 (March 11 2004).
489 Regulation (EC) No 1606/2002 (July 19 2002).
490 IOSCO Technical Committee, Statement on the Development and Use of IFRS in 2005 (February 2005).
491 SEC Release No 33-8879, "Acceptance From Foreign Private Issuers of Financial Statements Prepared in Accordance With International Financial Reporting Standards Without Reconciliation to U.S. GAAP" (December 21 2007).
492 See Financial Accounting Standards Board, "Completing the February 2006 Memorandum of Understanding: A progress report and timetable for completion" (September 2008).
493 SEC Release No 33-8982, "Roadmap for the Potential Use of Financial Statements Prepared in Accordance with International Financial Reporting Standards By U.S. Issuers" (November 14 2008).
494 SEC Release No 33-9109, "Commission Statement in Support of Convergence and Global Accounting Standards" (February 24 2010).

However, convergence efforts alone will not totally eliminate all differences between US GAAP and IFRS. As international standards were developed, the IASB drew upon accounting standards from a variety of countries and took a different approach from US standards in order to avoid perceived problems in US GAAP. Additionally, the board reviews its existing standards annually to enhance their clarity and consistency. As a result, some of the differences between US GAAP and IFRS are intentional deviations from US requirements. Other differences have emerged through interpretation, as IFRS are broader than US GAAP and have limited interpretive guidance. Implementation of IFRS has been left to preparers and auditors. In contrast, the US market's strong regulatory and legal environment has resulted in more 'bright-line' rules and comprehensive implementation guidance and industry interpretations.[495]

The ability to use IFRS in satisfying Exchange Act reporting requirements is an important development in lowering the threshold for foreign private issuers to enter the US capital markets. Despite the high quality of IFRS, it should be taken into account that US investors, especially institutional investors, so far tend to prefer US GAAP.[496] Such a preference could be reflected in stock prices.

(c) Multi-jurisdictional disclosure system

In 1991 the SEC adopted rules, forms and schedules that implemented a 'multi-jurisdictional disclosure system' with Canada. This system basically permits use of Canadian disclosure documents and procedures to satisfy US as well as Canadian registration, reporting and tender offer obligations.[497]

Canadian foreign private issuers, if they meet specified conditions, may satisfy the registration requirements of the Securities Act by filing with the SEC a Canadian prospectus or comparable disclosure document meeting the requirements of Canadian regulatory authorities, with minimal additional information.

The SEC staff will not normally review such registrations. The Canadian disclosure requirements governing the preparation of Canadian offering materials are in essence adopted by the SEC as its own disclosure requirements. Offerings under the multi-jurisdictional disclosure system will still be subject, however, to those provisions of the Securities Act and the Exchange Act that create civil liability for misleading or omitted material information.

Canada is the only partner of the United States in a multi-jurisdictional disclosure initiative that allows foreign country disclosure standards to suffice automatically for US federal securities law disclosure purposes. The SEC staff has indicated that there are no plans to negotiate comparable arrangements with other countries. Indeed, the staff has stated that much of the system may eventually be integrated into the SEC's general foreign private issuer disclosure system.

---

495 Ernst & Young, *U.S. GAAP v IFRS: The Basics* (January 2009).

496 Hopkins, Patrick E, *et al*, *Response by the Financial Reporting Policy Committee of the Financial Accounting and Reporting Section of the American Accounting Association to the SEC Release: Acceptance from Foreign Private Issuers of Financial Statements Prepared in Accordance with International Financial Reporting Standards Without Reconciliation to U.S. GAAP* (January 1 2008) (working paper).

497 SEC Release No 33-6902, "Multijurisdictional Disclosure and Modifications to the Current Registration and Reporting System for Canadian Issuers" (June 21 1991).

5. International offerings with US participants

5.1 Overview

Foreign private issuers usually have at least some securities holders in the United States. When they are involved in transactions that are directed at an entire class of securities holders, even though the transactions are basically international in nature, US as well as foreign securities laws may apply. Regulation S, discussed in "Private placements" above, makes the Securities Act registration requirements inapplicable to 'offshore' offerings that are not accompanied by directed selling efforts in the United States, but it does not apply to a US component of an international offering. These offerings may be any of the following:

- rights offerings;
- tender offers;
- exchange offerings; or
- business combination transactions.

To avoid having to meet US securities law requirements, foreign private issuers often exclude their US securities holders from full participation in these transactions. However, the SEC wants to give US holders opportunities to participate in these offshore offerings.

In a release that became effective on January 24 2000 (the '2000 Cross-Border Release'),[498] the SEC established formulas for determining when transactions directed at foreign private issuers with US security holders need to comply with US federal securities laws. In rights offerings, exchange offers and business combinations, the key is having no more than 10% of the relevant class of the foreign private issuer's securities owned by US holders. Tender offers are exempted from registration based on a tiered system:

- Issuers with less than 10% US ownership ('Tier I') are exempt from almost all registration requirements; and
- Issuers with less than 40% US ownership ('Tier II') are exempt from some limited registration requirements.[499]

The SEC amended these formulas and sought to lessen cross-border conflicts of

498 SEC Release No 33-7759, "Cross-Border Tender and Exchange Offers, Business Combinations and Rights Offerings" (October 22 1999).

499 SEC Release No 33-7759, "Cross-Border Tender and Exchange Offers, Business Combinations and Rights Offerings" (October 22 1999). See also the discussion of US ownership below.

law through a second release (the '2008 Cross-Border Release').[500] The amendments in the 2008 Cross-Border Release change the formula for determining how to calculate these percentages. Under the old rules, securities held by a person or entity that individually holds more than 10% of the relevant class, whether US or foreign, were excluded from the formula. After the 2008 Cross-Border Release, these securities are included in both the numerator (US ownership) and denominator (worldwide ownership) when calculating the US ownership percentage.[501]

5.2 Determination of US ownership

The size of US ownership of a class of a foreign private issuer's securities is critical to determining whether the exemptive provisions adopted in the 2000 Cross-Border Release and the 2008 Cross-Border Release apply to rights offerings, exchange offers, business combinations or tender offers involving that class of securities. The exemptions provided by Rules 801 and 802 under the Securities Act[502] and the amended tender offer rules under the Exchange Act[503] refer to 'US holders'.

(a) Look-through analysis

In addressing who is a US holder, an offeror is required to 'look through' the record ownership of brokers, dealers, banks or nominees and, if such record owners hold securities for the accounts of customers, the offeror must determine the residency of those customers. As such, the determination of 'US holders' comes down to an examination of beneficial ownership.

The 2000 Cross-Border Release and the 2008 Cross-Border Release establish ground rules for such determinations:[504]

- US ownership is to be calculated at any date up to 30 days after, or 60 days before, the public announcement of the exchange offer, solicitation for a business combination or tender offer. If the buyer cannot perform the analysis within this period, it may perform the look-through analysis at a practical date no more than 120 days before the announcement.
- The inquiry as to the amount of securities represented by accounts of customers resident in the United States may be limited to brokers, dealers, banks and other nominees that are located in the United States, in the jurisdiction of incorporation of the subject company or of each participant in a business combination or in the jurisdiction that is the primary trading market for the subject securities. If, after reasonable inquiry, information cannot be obtained as to customer accounts, it may be assumed that the

---

500 SEC Release No 33-8957, "Commission Guidance and Revision to the Cross-Border Tender Offer, Exchange Offer, Rights Offering, and Business Combination Rules and Beneficial Ownership Reporting Rules for Certain Foreign Institutions" (September 19 2008).

501 See Securities Act Rule 800(h)(2); Exchange Act Rules 13e-4(h)(8) and (i), Instruction 2.ii; Exchange Act Rules 14d-1(c) and (d), Instruction 2.ii.

502 17 CFR §230.801-802.

503 See Exchange Act Rules 13d-1, 13e-3, 13e-4, 14d-1, 14d-11, 14e-15 and 16a-1.

504 SEC Release No 33-7759, "Cross-Border Tender and Exchange Offers, Business Combinations and Rights Offerings" (October 22 1999); SEC Release No 33-8957, "Commission Guidance and Revision to the Cross-Border Tender Offer, Exchange Offer, Rights Offering, and Business Combination Rules and Beneficial Ownership Reporting Rules for Certain Foreign Institutions" (September 19 2008).

customers are residents of the jurisdiction in which the broker, dealer, bank or nominee has its principal place of business.

- Reports of beneficial ownership provided to the person making the determination or that are publicly on file constitute information as to ownership by US holders that may be used in determining the number of beneficial owners.

(b) *Alternate test*

The 2008 Cross-Border Release provides an alternate test for determining whether a transaction was eligible to rely on the cross-border exemptions. Under certain circumstances, such as in most rights offerings and hostile takeovers, the purchaser may be entitled to rely on a presumption that the US ownership limits of the applicable exemption are not exceeded. This presumption applies if one of the following conditions is met:

- The transaction is non-negotiated (eg, a rights offering that is not made in response to an agreement with the issuer of the securities, or in the case of an unsolicited or 'hostile' tender offer); or
- The purchaser is unable to conduct the required look-through analysis because of specific circumstances. Examples of such situations, specifically provided by the SEC, include a target company that has not generated any list of security holders within the required timeframe, where the target securities are in bearer form and where nominees are prohibited by law from disclosing information regarding the beneficial owners of securities. The SEC has declined to provide a complete list of the circumstances where the look-through analysis is impossible and has stated that it will deal with situations on a case-to-case basis. The SEC has also stressed that concerns about the dedication of time or resources, or concerns about accuracy of information, are not sufficient to rely on the alternate test.[505]

However, the presumption that the US ownership limits of the applicable exemption are not exceeded will be lost if:[506]

- the average daily trading volume of the subject securities in the United States over a 12-month period that ended no more than 60 days before the announcement of the transaction is more than 10% (or 40% in the case of Tier II tender offers) of the average worldwide daily trading volume;
- reports filed by the subject company show US ownership levels that exceed the limits for the applicable exemption; or
- the offeror knows or has reason to know that US ownership levels exceed the limits for the applicable exemption.

505 SEC Release No 33-8957, "Commission Guidance and Revision to the Cross-Border Tender Offer, Exchange Offer, Rights Offering, and Business Combination Rules and Beneficial Ownership Reporting Rules for Certain Foreign Institutions" (September 19 2008).

506 SEC Release No 33-8957, "Commission Guidance and Revision to the Cross-Border Tender Offer, Exchange Offer, Rights Offering, and Business Combination Rules and Beneficial Ownership Reporting Rules for Certain Foreign Institutions", II-A-2 (September 19 2008).

In order for a purchaser to use the alternate test, the rules require that there be a foreign 'primary trading market', outside of the United States, for the subject securities. This means that at least 55% of the trading volume must take place in no more than two foreign jurisdictions during a recent 12-month period. In addition, if trading occurs in two foreign markets, the trading volume in at least one of the two must exceed the trading volume in the United States for that class.

(c) *Qualifying issuer*

The general definition of 'foreign private issuer[507] similarly requires a 'look through' the record ownership of brokers, dealers, banks or nominees.[508] If more than 50% of the outstanding voting securities of a foreign issuer are directly or indirectly owned of record by residents of the United States, then the issuer cannot qualify as a foreign private issuer. The method of calculation is essentially the same as that adopted in the 2000 Cross-Border Release.

5.3 Rights offerings

A rights offering is a public offer of equity securities for cash to the existing holders of a particular class of equity securities. This provides a way to raise capital without diluting the security holders' proportionate ownership of the foreign private issuer. A rights offering has to be registered under the Securities Act by a publicly held issuer, just as would a public offering to an unrelated group. While rights offering are very common in Europe, they are not common in the United States.

Rule 801 of the Securities Act exempts a foreign private issuer's rights offering from the registration requirements of that act if the following conditions are met:

- US holders own 10% or less of the foreign private issuer's securities that are the subject of the rights offering. As discussed above, as long as certain conditions are met, the buyer may rely on a rebuttable presumption that less than 10% of the holders of the class of securities are US holders;[509]
- The offer is made on a *pro rata* basis to existing security holders of the same class;
- The rights to purchase granted to US holders are not transferable by such holders except to purchasers outside the United States in accordance with Regulation S; and
- US holders participate in the offer on terms at least as favourable as those offered to any other holders.

5.4 Tender offers

A 'tender offer' is a public offer by a bidder to purchase shares directly from a target company's shareholders. Each shareholder then decides individually whether it will

---

507 See the "Introduction" for further discussion of the definition of 'foreign private issuer'.

508 SEC Release No 33-7745, "International Disclosure Standards" (September 28 1999) (amending Securities Act Rule 405 and Exchange Act Rule 3b-4).

509 Securities Act Rule 800(h); SEC Release No 33-8957, "Commission Guidance and Revision to the Cross-Border Tender Offer, Exchange Offer, Rights Offering, and Business Combination Rules and Beneficial Ownership Reporting Rules for Certain Foreign Institutions" (September 19 2008).

tender their shares. Tender offers provide a mechanism for acquiring control of a company by buying a large amount of its stock. However, even if a tender offer is successful, the buyer is unlikely to receive all of the shares. Tender offers may serve as an alternative to proxy contests for control. A tender offer may also be used in conjunction with a merger proposal, if the bidder is attempting to acquire the company. A tender offer in which shares are purchased for securities of the issuer or a combination of cash and securities is often referred to as an exchange offer.

If the target company has US holders, special Exchange Act rules and certain anti-fraud rules will apply, whether or not the target has entered the Exchange Act reporting system.[510] If the target is a reporting company under the Exchange Act, additional rules apply.[511]

Regardless of whether the target is a reporting company under the Exchange Act, US securities law requires that, among other general anti-fraud and related provisions:

- the tender offer remain open for at least 20 US business days;[512]
- after any changes in consideration offered, number of securities sought or solicitation fees, the tender offer again remain open for at least 10 US business days;[513] and
- the purchaser not buy shares outside the offer while it is in progress.[514]

These requirements apply if the tender offer is made by any means of US interstate commerce, whether intentionally or unintentionally.

If a purchaser extends a tender offer to the shareholders of a reporting company target, the purchaser must comply with the above rules, and must also comply with rules that, among other things:

- require disclosure to the target's shareholders of information about the terms and background of the tender offer;
- require that the purchaser afford certain protections to offerees (eg, treating them equally and giving them rights of withdrawal of shares they have tendered); and
- allow security holders to withdraw tendered securities that have not been purchased within a certain period of time after the offer has expired.[515]

In the 2000 Cross-Border Release, the SEC revised its tender offer rules to characterise some foreign private issuers as either Tier I or Tier II companies, based on the percentage of US ownership of the company, and afforded partial exemptions from the rules based on whether Tier I or Tier II applies. These tiers are intended to "address conflicts between US and foreign regulation, thereby facilitating the inclusion of US investors in cross-border transactions".[516]

---

510 Exchange Act §14(e).
511 Exchange Act Regulations 14D and 14E; Exchange Act §14(d).
512 Exchange Act Rule 14e-1(a).
513 Exchange Act Rule 14e-1(b).
514 Exchange Act Rule 14e-5.
515 Exchange Act §14d(5); Exchange Act Rules 14d-6 and 14d-7(a).
516 SEC Release No 33-7759, "Cross-Border Tender and Exchange Offers, Business Combinations and Rights Offerings" (October 22 1999).

The SEC also made substantial general revisions in its tender offer, proxy and other rules. Like the exemptions in the 2000 Cross-Border Release, the revisions took effect on January 24 2000. The revisions:

- eliminated certain timing and other differences between cash tender offers and exchange offers;
- simplified and integrated disclosure requirements for tender offers and certain other transactions;
- updated the financial statement requirements in certain types of takeover and business combination transactions; and
- relaxed restrictions on pre-filing or pre-commencement communications with security holders – under the Securities Act in transactions involving the issuance of securities, under the Exchange Act proxy rules and under the Exchange Act tender offer rules – in connection with acquisition and business combination transactions.[517]

In the 2008 Cross-Border Release, the SEC further revised the Tier I and Tier II exemptions. These changes are intended to expand and refine the exemptions created by the 2000 Cross-Border Release and to decrease conflicts of law.[518]

(a) *Tier I exemptions*

A tender offer for shares of a foreign private issuer will be exempt from most of the rules referred to above if US security holders own 10% or less of the class of securities being sought in the tender offer. If the initial bidder relies on this exemption, subsequent competing bidders may also rely on it without meeting the requirement of the 10% ceiling on US ownership. The Tier I exemptions apply to schemes of arrangement, cash mergers and compulsory acquisitions for cash, in addition to tender offers.[519] The Tier I exemption will apply if, among other requirements, the following conditions are met:

- US holders participate in the offer on terms at least as favourable as those offered to any other holders. Purchasers have the option to offer US holders cash, even if other holders are offered securities (provided that the bidder has a reasonable basis to conclude that the value of the different forms of consideration is substantially equivalent). This is referred to as the 'cash only' exemption.
- Offering documents are provided in English to US security holders on the same basis as that provided to foreign holders.
- Tier I offers are exempt from the rule that prohibits a bidder that has announced or commenced a tender offer from purchasing the target's securities outside the offer. The tender offer documents must disclose the possibility of such purchases.

---

517 SEC Release No 33-7760, "Regulation of Takeovers and Security Holder Communications" (October 22 1999).

518 SEC Release No 33-8957, "Commission Guidance and Revision to the Cross-Border Tender Offer, Exchange Offer, Rights Offering, and Business Combination Rules and Beneficial Ownership Reporting Rules for Certain Foreign Institutions" (September 19 2008).

519 Exchange Act Rule 14d-1(c).

Requirements for disclosure of 5% beneficial ownership (on Schedule 13D under the Exchange Act) are not affected by the exemption.[520]

It should be noted that there is no exemption from the anti-fraud rules of the Exchange Act.[521]

(b) *Tier II exemptions*

Limited exemptive relief from the tender offer rules will be available to a bidder when US security holders own 40% or less of the class of securities of a foreign private issuer being sought in a tender offer.[522] This exemption codifies certain SEC exemptive and interpretive positions. Among other provisions, the Tier II exemption provides as follows:

- The bidder may make separate offers to US and foreign holders, provided that the US offer is on terms at least as favourable as those offered to any other holder. The 'cash only' exception applicable to Tier I offers does not apply to Tier II offers, but the staff of the SEC will consider requests for relief on a case-by-case basis. ADR holders in the United States may be included in the US offer and, in certain situations, US holders may be included in the foreign offer.
- The bidder and its affiliates may purchase the target's securities outside of the tender offer, so long as:
  - those purchases are in compliance with the rules of the target's home jurisdiction;
  - there is a reasonable expectation that the tender offer qualifies for the Tier II exemption;
  - no purchases are made in the United States other than pursuant to the tender offer;
  - the US tender offer documents disclose the possibility of purchases outside of the tender offer;
  - disclosure of such purchases is made in the United States to the extent that such information is made public in the home jurisdiction; and
  - the tender offer price is raised to equal any higher price paid outside the tender offer.
- A financial adviser's affiliate may purchase the target's securities outside of the tender offer if, in addition to satisfying the first five conditions listed above for purchases by the bidder and its affiliates:
  - it enforces policies designed to prevent the flow of information between itself and the financial adviser that might in result in federal securities laws violations;
  - the affiliate has no officers or employees in common with the financial adviser that will also be involved in providing the bidder with financial

---

520 See SEC Release No 33-8957, "Commission Guidance and Revision to the Cross-Border Tender Offer, Exchange Offer, Rights Offering, and Business Combination Rules and Beneficial Ownership Reporting Rules for Certain Foreign Institutions" (September 19 2008).

521 See *id*, fn 24.

522 Exchange Act Rule 14d-1(d).

advisory services;
    - the financial adviser has a registered broker-dealer affiliate under Section 15(a) of the Exchange Act; and
    - the purchase is not made to facilitate the tender offer.
- Payment for shares tendered may be made, interest on securities tendered may be paid and notice of extensions of the offer may be given in accordance with the requirements of the home jurisdiction, rather than complying with the strict requirements of US securities law.
- The issuer may terminate the initial offering period prior to the scheduled expiration date if:
    - the conditions of the offer have been satisfied;
    - the bidder institutes a subsequent offering period;
    - the offer has been open for at least 20 US business days; and
    - the bidder has made the required disclosures.
- The bidder may reduce or waive the minimum acceptance condition without extending withdrawal rights during the remainder of the offer, if certain conditions are met.
- Bidders may suspend withdrawal rights while tendered securities are being counted if:
    - the withdrawal rights are suspended only during the period where the tendered securities are being counted;
    - the offer has been open a minimum of 20 US business days; and
    - all of the offer conditions have been satisfied.
- Bidders may suspend withdrawal rights between the closing of the initial offering period and the start of a subsequent offering period if:
    - the subsequent offering period commences immediately; and
    - payment and disclosure of the results of the offer are made in accordance with the laws of the target's home jurisdiction.
- Similarly, bidders may institute a subsequent offering period without first announcing the results of the initial offering period in accordance with US securities law if:
    - the subsequent offering period commences immediately; and
    - payment and disclosure of the results of the offer are made in accordance with the laws of the target's home jurisdiction.
- For certain types of tender offers, bidders may create separate pools of consideration for securities tendered during the initial and subsequent offer periods.

Tender offers that are eligible for the Tier II exemption are still required to meet the requirements of Rule 13e-3 under the Exchange Act, including filing information regarding the offer, disclosing information to certain security holders and complying with anti-fraud provisions. Certain procedural, disclosure and filing requirements of US tender offer laws still apply, as set forth below:

- Tier II exemptions do not provide relief from the requirement that an offer be open for at least 20 US business days and be extended for a minimum

amount of time in the event of certain changes in the offer.
- The specific disclosure requirements of Regulation 14D or requirements of Rule 13e-3 apply if the transaction would result in the company going private and disclosure requirements and anti-fraud provisions thereunder.[523]

(c) ***No-action letter exemptions***

A multi-jurisdictional tender offer must be structured to meet the requirements of the laws of the target's home country as well as US tender offer rules. If foreign and US regulatory requirements or offering procedures are in conflict, it may be necessary to obtain special SEC exemptive relief.

The staff of the SEC addresses requests for such relief on a case-by-case basis. If it agrees with the bidder, it may confirm that it will take no action adverse to the bidder if the US aspects of the offer are conducted without meeting all applicable Tier exemption conditions.[524] Many of the provisions that had been regularly instituted previously through no-action letters were formalised in the 2008 Cross-Border Release.[525]

5.5 Exchange offers

An exchange offer is a form of tender offer in which securities are given instead of, or in addition to, cash. For example, an issuer may seek to acquire a publicly held company and will offer its securities directly to the shareholders of the target as full or partial consideration for the exchange of their shares. This exchange offer is a public offer of the acquirer's securities that must be registered under the Securities Act, just as would a public offer to raise capital. The costs, delay and Exchange Act reporting obligations related to Securities Act registration disincentivise foreign bidders from extending exchange offers to US holders of securities of foreign private issuers that become targets of such offerings.

The SEC adopted Rule 802 under the Securities Act to encourage exchange offers to be extended to US security holders. Under this rule, the offer and sale of securities in exchange for a class of a foreign private issuer's securities will be exempt from the registration requirements of the Securities Act if the following conditions are met:

- US holders own 10% or less of the foreign private issuer's securities that are the subject of the exchange offer. As long as certain conditions are met, the buyer may rely on a rebuttable presumption that the issuer is a foreign private issuer and that less than 10% of the holders of the class of securities are US holders, as long as there is a primary trading market for the subject securities outside the United States. However, this presumption is unavailable if:
  - the average daily trading volume of the securities in the United States for

---

523 See SEC Release No 33-8957, "Commission Guidance and Revision to the Cross-Border Tender Offer, Exchange Offer, Rights Offering, and Business Combination Rules and Beneficial Ownership Reporting Rules for Certain Foreign Institutions", fn 24 (September 19 2008).

524 Publicis Groupe SA, SEC No-Action Letter (January 13 2006).

525 SEC Release No 33-8957, "Commission Guidance and Revision to the Cross-Border Tender Offer, Exchange Offer, Rights Offering, and Business Combination Rules and Beneficial Ownership Reporting Rules for Certain Foreign Institutions" (September 19 2008).

  - the past year has exceeded 10% of the average daily trading volume of that class of securities;
  - the most recent annual report submitted by the issuer with securities regulators in its home jurisdiction or the SEC indicates that US holders hold more than 10% of the outstanding class of securities; or
  - the acquirer or issuer knows, or has reason to know, that the level of US ownership exceeds 10% of such securities.[526]
- The terms and conditions of the offer are at least as favourable for US security holders as for foreign holders.
- Any information or documents distributed by the bidder concerning the exchange offer to the foreign holders are also distributed to the US security holders in English on at least a comparable basis as in its home jurisdiction. As such, the bidder must provide the information to US security holders at the same time as it provides it to the foreign holders.
- The information provided to the US security holders includes a legend stating that the exchange offer is being conducted according to foreign disclosure requirements, which may be different from US disclosure requirements.[527]

Generally, these requirements coincide with the requirements for the Tier I exemption for tender offers. If the initial bidder relies on this exemption, subsequent competing bidders may also rely on it without meeting the requirement of the 10% ceiling on US ownership.

5.6 Business combinations

Business combinations may involve the Securities Act if the target is a publicly held company (and the Exchange Act as well, if a publicly held target is a reporting company under that act). Business combinations may be statutory mergers, corporate mergers or acquisitions or other combinations where the security holders of the participating companies vote to approve the transaction. Business combinations are different from tender offers in that one party acquires the entire company from the other party, rather than only a substantial portion of its stock.

If the business combination takes the form of a transaction at the corporate level – a merger or an acquisition of the assets of the target – the shareholders of the target will be asked to authorise the target to enter into the transaction. In a business combination where securities of the acquiring company are to be issued and distributed to them, the solicitation of their votes in favour of the transaction will be regarded as an indirect public offer of the securities of the acquirer. This will require Securities Act registration.[528]

Such solicitation of the votes of the target's shareholders need not be made in

526 Rule 800(h)(7); SEC Release No 33-8957, "Commission Guidance and Revision to the Cross-Border Tender Offer, Exchange Offer, Rights Offering, and Business Combination Rules and Beneficial Ownership Reporting Rules for Certain Foreign Institutions" (September 19 2008).

527 Securities Act Rule 802(b). See Appendix H for a sample legend for exchange offers by foreign private issuers.

528 Securities Act Rule 145, Preliminary Note.

accordance with the Exchange Act proxy rules if the target meets the definition of 'foreign private issuer' and is hence exempt from the proxy rules.

Rule 802 under the Securities Act also applies to mergers and acquisitions where securities of the purchaser are issued and delivered to shareholders of a target that is a foreign private issuer. Such issuance and delivery will be exempt from the registration requirements of the Securities Act if the following conditions are met:

- US holders own 10% or less of the foreign private issuer's securities that are the subject of the business combination transaction. As discussed above, the purchaser may rely on a rebuttable presumption that the issuer is a foreign private issuer, and that less than 10% of the holders of the class of securities are US holders, as long as certain conditions are met. See the section on tender offers above.[529]
- The terms and conditions of the offer are at least as favourable for US security holders as for foreign holders.
- The offering materials are provided to US security holders on a comparable basis to how they are provided to other holders.
- Like exchange offers, the information provided to the US security holders must include a legend stating that the business combination is being conducted according to foreign disclosure requirements, which may be different from US disclosure requirements.[530]

Generally, these requirements coincide with the requirements for the Tier I exemption for tender offers. If the initial bidder relies on this exemption, subsequent competing bidders may also rely on this exemption without meeting the requirement of the 10% ceiling on US ownership.

5.7 Information requirements

(a) Generally

Rules 801 and 802 under the Securities Act do not require that any specific information be sent to US security holders in a rights offering, exchange offer or business combination solicitation in order to obtain the benefits of these rules. Nor do the tender offer rules call for any special information to be sent to US holders in order to claim Tier I or Tier II status. However, any offering documents or other information published overseas must be provided in English to US security holders. Internet dissemination alone of such offering materials would not constitute adequate dissemination.[531] For example, publishing the offering documents on the foreign private issuer's website would not constitute adequate publication in the

529 Securities Act Rule 800(h); SEC Release No 33-8957, "Commission Guidance and Revision to the Cross-Border Tender Offer, Exchange Offer, Rights Offering, and Business Combination Rules and Beneficial Ownership Reporting Rules for Certain Foreign Institutions" (September 19 2008).

530 Securities Act Rule 802(b). See Appendix H for a sample legend for exchange offers by foreign private issuers.

531 Exchange Act Rule 14e-5; SEC Release No 33-8957, "Commission Guidance and Revision to the Cross-Border Tender Offer, Exchange Offer, Rights Offering, and Business Combination Rules and Beneficial Ownership Reporting Rules for Certain Foreign Institutions", II-G (September 19 2008).

United States. In addition, all US informational documents must include certain specific material, including statements that the securities in question are those of a foreign company and that the transaction is being conducted under foreign disclosure requirements.[532] Such information must also be provided to the SEC, for notice purposes only. This information must be submitted electronically to the SEC on Form CB and a foreign purchaser must consent to service of process in the United States through Form F-X. These documents must be submitted to the SEC by the first business day after dissemination or publication.

(b) *Anti-fraud rules*

The SEC emphasised in its 2000 Cross-Border Release and 2008 Cross-Border Release that the anti-fraud and anti-manipulation rules and civil liability provisions of US federal securities laws will continue to apply to the exempted transactions discussed above, despite the permitted omission of information ordinarily required.[533] This is consistent with other SEC exemptive provisions, such as the private offering exemption and the Rule 144A safe harbour for offers to qualified institutional buyers, where practitioners often seek to reduce civil liability exposure by drafting offering documents that in most important respects resemble the offering materials that would be required if the particular transaction were not exempt.

The SEC's goal is to encourage foreign private issuers and bidders to extend offshore offerings, such as tender and exchange offers, rights offerings and business combinations to their US holders. US holders are often excluded from these transactions because the foreign private issuers would prefer to avoid application of the US securities laws, particularly in those cases where the US holders own only a small amount of the foreign private issuer's securities. However, excluding US holders denies them investment opportunities where they may receive a premium for their securities. These rules attempt to put US holders on an equal footing with foreign securities holders.

(c) *Internet issues*

Issues arise when the Internet is used to facilitate an international offering with US participants. As discussed above, when offering materials must be distributed directly to US security holders, the mere posting of information online is not adequate dissemination or publication under the exemptions for Tier I and Tier II offerings without something more. In addition, the bidder must obtain the US holder's consent to receive the materials electronically. Because a posting of materials on the Internet may be construed as an offer requiring registration under the Securities Act, a bidder must implement precautionary measures to ensure that the offer does not

---

532 SEC Release No 33-8957, "Commission Guidance and Revision to the Cross-Border Tender Offer, Exchange Offer, Rights Offering, and Business Combination Rules and Beneficial Ownership Reporting Rules for Certain Foreign Institutions" (September 19 2008). See Appendix H for a sample legend for exchange offers by foreign private issuers.

533 SEC Release No 33-7759, "Cross-Border Tender and Exchange Offers, Business Combinations and Rights Offerings", I-A (October 22 1999); SEC Release No 33-8957, "Commission Guidance and Revision to the Cross-Border Tender Offer, Exchange Offer, Rights Offering, and Business Combination Rules and Beneficial Ownership Reporting Rules for Certain Foreign Institutions" (September 19 2008).

target US persons and guard against sales to US persons in order not to subject itself to registration under that act.

Often, a private offering in the United States occurs simultaneously with an international offshore internet offering. In that case, foreign private issuers must take particular care to ensure that the Internet offering is not construed as a 'general solicitation', which is prohibited in private placements by Section 4(2) of the Securities Act and Regulation D. A foreign private issuer may take the following steps to ensure that the internet offering is not used to solicit US investors for the private US offering:

- US investors that respond to the offshore Internet offering should not be placed in the US offering;
- The US private offer should be extended only to US investors that were solicited before or independently from the posting of the offshore internet offering;
- Different contact persons should be used for both offerings;
- The US private offering should not be referred to in the offshore internet offering, unless and only to the extent required by foreign law; and
- The issuer should obtain representations by the investor that it is not a US person in addition to avoiding the mailing of cash or securities into the United States.

6. American depositary receipts

6.1 Overview

American depositary receipts (ADRs) have significantly enhanced the marketability of equity securities of foreign private issuers in the United States. ADRs facilitate the trading of foreign securities by US investors because they enable the holder to transfer title to the underlying foreign security simply by transferring the ADR. Investors in the United States often prefer ADRs over directly purchasing foreign shares because price information is more readily available, transaction costs are often lower and the trading is conducted in US dollars during US trading hours and using US settlement procedures.

6.2 Definition and characteristics

An ADR is a transferable certificate issued in the US by a bank or trust company (referred to as the 'depositary') evidencing the ownership of a specified amount of securities of a foreign private issuer deposited with the depositary's office or agent in a foreign country (referred to as the 'custodian'). The deposited securities are held by the custodian for as long as ADRs representing them are outstanding in the United States.

A holder of ADRs may at any time demand delivery of the underlying foreign securities indirectly owned by such holder. A holder may also return ADRs to the depositary for cancellation in the event the holder cannot find a US investor to purchase them at an acceptable price and wants to effect a sale of the underlying securities in the home market. The underlying securities will then be released to the holder's broker in the home country for sale (or retention in that form) under instructions from the holder.

The exchangeability of ADRs for the underlying securities makes possible an international arbitrage market based on the price differential between ADRs in the United States and the underlying securities in the home market, as well as on currency fluctuations and other international economic conditions.

The SEC observed in its December 30 2003 US federal court complaint against Parmalat Finanziaria SpA that "ADRs are tradable in the same manner as any other registered American security, may be listed on any of the major exchanges in the US or traded over the counter, and are subject to the US federal securities laws".[534] While the vast majority of ADRs represent ordinary shares or common stock of a foreign private issuer, they may also be used to represent debt securities or preferred stock of

534 SEC Litigation Release No 18527, "*SEC v Parmalat Finanziaria SpA* Complaint" (December 30 2003).

a foreign private issuer. ADRs have the following characteristics:

- Dividends, interest and principal are paid in US dollars;
- They are traded in US dollars;
- Trades are settled according to US rules;
- Holding ADRs may avoid inheritance tax or death duties imposed on the deposited securities by the home country of the foreign private issuer;
- The depositary will assist in obtaining refunds for or a tax credit with respect to foreign taxes withheld on dividends or interest;
- Holding shares in ADRs may result in better terms for a foreign shareholder in the event of expropriation by the home country; and
- Significant information relating to the issuer can be provided by or through the depositary.

In addition to the foregoing characteristics, ADRs have several cross-border aspects:

- An ADR is subject to market or trading conditions in at least two countries. For example, ADRs may be listed on the New York Stock Exchange (NYSE), and the underlying ordinary shares may be traded on the London Stock Exchange, with the result that two different trading environments in New York and London become relevant. On a US market, securities tend to trade at a different price-earnings ratio than in United Kingdom;[535]
- An ADR is subject to two currency fluctuations, both in US dollars and in a foreign currency; and
- It is common to find that the issuer of the underlying shares conducts operations in both countries, with the risks and benefits resulting from those different economies.

An imbalance produced in any of these three areas will tend to affect trading because, depending on where a favourable disparity appears, arbitrageurs will buy ADRs on the NYSE, return them to the depositary and sell the underlying ordinary shares in London – or, alternatively, buy ordinary shares in London, deposit them with the depositary and sell the resultant ADRs on the NYSE. Arbitrage trading in ADRs and their underlying shares theoretically prevents persistent deviation in trading prices.

An ADR structure is not a prerequisite to trading foreign private issuer securities in the US markets. Shares of a number of Canadian issuers have simultaneously traded on the NYSE and in Canada, and the NYSE has been testing the expansion of single-security trading of shares of foreign private issuers located in other countries. For example, in late 1998 it listed "global registered shares" of DaimlerChrysler AG that are capable of being traded in local currencies on different securities markets. Other companies that subsequently issued these global shares include Celanese AG in 1999, UBS AG in 2000[536] and Deutsche Bank in 2001.[537]

535 See, for example, "Country P/E/ Ratios: Nasdaq Highest, Netherlands Lowest", Bespoke Investment Group (July 9 2007).

536 Press Release, "NYSE Global Shares Growing as a New Class of Security," NYSE Euronext (March 2003).

537 Deutsche Bank Share – Global Share, Deutsche Bank Investor Relations.

6.3 Types of ADR programmes

(a) Unsponsored ADR programmes

An unsponsored ADR programme is established by a US bank as depositary, without the cooperation of the issuer, because of perceived significant US investor interest in the securities of a foreign private issuer. The depositary then acts as agent for ADR holders: the foreign private issuer is not a party to the deposit agreement. ADR holders pay all fees to the depositary for servicing and maintaining the unsponsored ADR programme. Unsponsored ADRs trade on the over-the-counter market. They may not be listed on a US national stock exchange.

After the amendments to Rule 12g3-2(b) adopted in October 2008, any depositary bank may now unilaterally establish unsponsored ADR programmes in anticipation of or in response to demand in the United States for an issuer's securities.[538] Depositary banks have an incentive to create these programmes because they generate substantial revenues as fees for issuing and cancelling ADRs for investors.

The following are several disadvantages of unsponsored ADR programmes for foreign private issuers:

- Because foreign private issuers may not even be notified of the creation of such unsponsored ADR programmes, issuers will be unable to negotiate their terms. These include any fees and charges payable by participating investors, the extent of any pre-release lending transactions and of any collateral securing such transactions, as well as the responsibilities of the depositary bank in managing the programme.
- The creation of unsponsored ADR programmes eliminates the ability of foreign private issuers to control how and when their shares will trade in the US capital markets. Accordingly, if a foreign private issuer did not previously have any of its shares traded in the United States, its debut would be determined by a depositary bank that may not have the issuer's long-term business strategy in mind.
- It is possible that multiple depositary banks set up ADR programmes for the same security. Due to each bank's own fee structure or inconsistent exchange rates, differences in dividend payments could result, leading to investor confusion.
- Communication between the issuer and shareholders is not fostered by unsponsored ADRs. The depositary of an unsponsored ADR programme is under no obligation to distribute shareholder communications received from the issuer. The depositary is also under no obligation to exercise voting rights on behalf of ADR holders or notify ADR holders about shareholder meetings. Therefore, this can complicate the issuer's ability to communicate with its shareholder base.
- The SEC will not permit an unsponsored ADR programme to coexist with a sponsored programme for the same deposited securities. A foreign private

538 See the section on the Rule 12g3-2(b) exemption in "Periodic reporting requirements".

issuer seeking to establish a sponsored ADR programme after the establishment of an unsponsored programme is required to ensure that the depositary of the unsponsored programme effect a transfer of the deposited securities and of the related ADR holders to the new sponsored programme, and terminate the unsponsored programme. Typically, the depositary of the sponsored programme will negotiate and buy out the unsponsored programme in order to carry out this transfer.

- Foreign private issuers could be forced to register with the SEC under the Exchange Act if, at some point in the future, they do not comply with the Rule 12g3-2(b) exemption requirements and at that time their securities are held by 300 or more US residents.

International companies dealing with undesirable, unsponsored ADR programmes may consider working with a depositary bank to establish a sponsored ADR programme as a way both to establish control and to combat the negative effects of the 2008 amendments to Rule 12g3-2(b) and Form F-6.[539]

(b) *Sponsored ADR programmes*

Under a sponsored ADR programme, the foreign private issuer appoints a single US bank to act as depositary, thereby enabling the foreign private issuer to monitor the US market for its ADRs. The depositary provides basic shareholder services, such as mailing annual reports and notices, responding to inquiries, record maintenance, transferring certificates, proxy solicitation and dividend and stock disbursements. These services are rendered at the expense of the foreign private issuer. Only sponsored ADRs may be listed on a US national securities exchange.

Because of the disadvantages of unsponsored ADR programmes listed above, foreign private issuers may consider working with a depositary bank to establish a sponsored ADR programme to control the trading of their equity securities, including:

- negotiating the terms of the deposit agreement;
- improving communications with their equity security-holders;
- consolidating all US trading in a sponsored ADR programme; and
- ensuring continued compliance with the Rule 12g3-2(b) exemption from registration with the SEC.

6.4 Levels of ADR programmes

There are three levels of ADR programmes commonly considered:

- Level 3 ADR programmes involve an offering of new securities to raise capital. The securities are listed on a US national securities exchange, such as the NYSE or NASDAQ. This type of ADR programme is established pursuant to a public offering registered under the Securities Act. The issuer must file a Form F-1 with the SEC, in addition to Form F-6 filed by the depositary covering the ADRs, and its financial statements must be reconciled with US generally

539 See the section on legal requirements in this chapter.

accepted accounting principles (GAAP) or International Financial Reporting Standards (IFRS). The issuer must also thereafter comply with the Sarbanes-Oxley Act and is subject to the reporting requirements applicable to foreign private issuers under the Exchange Act.

- Level 2 ADR programmes permit ADRs to be traded on a US national securities exchange, such as the NYSE or NASDAQ, and the disclosure requirements are essentially the same as for a Level 3 programme. However, a Level 2 programme does not enable the issuer to raise capital and instead constitutes only a listing of existing securities.
- Level 1 ADR programmes permit ADRs to be traded in the over-the-counter capital markets in the United States. This type of programme is the simplest and least expensive method for foreign private issuers to access the US capital markets and establish an initial investor base.

(a) OTCQX International

In 2007 an electronic over-the-counter listing service, OTCQX International, was created that offers a respected, fully electronic trading market for Level 1 ADR programmes similar to the NYSE and NASDAQ Stock Market, but without requiring registration with the SEC, thereby avoiding the often costly disclosure requirements related to SEC registration. About 140 foreign private issuers were listed on OTCQX International as of late 2010, including large-cap international companies such as Adidas, Air France-KLM, BASF, Deutsche Telekom, Wal-Mart de Mexico and Roche.[540] The advantages of OTCQX International include the following:

- OTCQX International provides a way for foreign private issuers that raise money in their home country to access US investors for additional liquidity and diversify their shareholder base without much cost. As a result, foreign companies can cross-list and access US investors without the regulatory costs that are required as part of listing on a US national securities exchange;
- A listing on OTCQX International does not require SEC registration; and
- US investors have access to information that foreign private issuers make available under Rule 12g3-2(b).

OTCQX International is reserved for foreign private issuers listed on one of 54 qualified stock exchanges around the world that meet the Rule 12g3-2(b) exemption requirements. In addition, OTCQX International companies are required to have either:

- a sponsored Level 1 ADR programme in the United States; or
- a foreign ordinary share that is Depositary Trust Company eligible.

All OTCQX International companies appoint a qualified, third-party principal US liaison (usually an investment bank) to help with the listing process, post disclosure in English and serve as a resource for US market protocols.

540 List of OTCQX Companies, OTCQX.com (as of December 27 2010).

(b) *Advantages of sponsored level 1 ADR programmes*

Like all other ADR programmes, sponsored Level 1 ADR programmes are subject to the rules of the SEC. However, the SEC imposes few requirements on the foreign private issuer:

- The depositary bank must file a Form F-6 with the SEC covering the ADRs, which the SEC must approve, in order for the Level 1 ADR programme to be established. Form F-6 summarises the terms of the deposit agreement.
- The foreign private issuer need not comply with US GAAP nor file any specially prepared disclosure documents with the SEC, provided that it falls under the Rule 12g3-2(b) exemption.
- Level 1 ADR programmes do not have to comply with the provisions of the Sarbanes-Oxley Act.

Compared to Level 2 and Level 3 ADR programmes, Level 1 ADR programmes have a relatively low cost. Level 2 and Level 3 ADR programmes require more time and resources from the issuer. The legal and accounting expenses associated with preparing disclosure documents required by SEC registration are high. In the case of a Level 2 ADR programme, the issuer raises no capital to pay the costs of registration. In the case of a Level 3 ADR programme, the cost of placing the securities in the market is also high; however, it permits the raising of capital in the US capital markets.

Level 1 ADR programmes are easier to establish than Level 2 and Level 3 ADR programmes. Depending on the foreign private issuer and its financial information, the programmes require only two to three months to set up. Level 1 ADR programmes are also easy to terminate. The only requirement is that, in accordance with the depositary agreement, a notice of termination be sent to all ADR holders no later than 90 days from the termination. There is no need to count or reduce the number of ADR holders. Level 1 ADR programmes, however, may not be used by the foreign private issuer's controlling shareholders and other affiliates to offer and sell their shares in ADR form to the investing public in the United States.

6.5 Legal requirements for ADR programmes

For purposes of the Securities Act, the underlying securities represented by ADRs are separate securities distinct from the ADRs themselves and each must either be registered or qualify for an exemption before being sold in the United States.

Unsponsored ADR programmes, and most sponsored ones, are open to the public. To implement any public ADR programme, the ADRs must be registered under the Securities Act. A special Securities Act registration form – Form F-6 – is used for this purpose. Form F-6 is relatively simple and requires only limited information about the ADR programme and no additional disclosures about the underlying security or about the foreign private issuer.

In order to qualify to file a Form F-6, three conditions must be met:

- The foreign private issuer of the underlying securities must be either a reporting company under the Exchange Act or exempt from registration by reason of Rule 12g3-2(b);

- The deposited securities must be either registered with the SEC or acquired through an exempt transaction; and
- The holders of the ADRs must generally be entitled to withdraw the underlying deposited securities freely.

Unlike a regular Securities Act registration, a Form F-6 does not automatically subject the foreign private issuer to the Exchange Act reporting system. The issuer will be exempt from Exchange Act registration by virtue of Rule 12g3-2(b), if it is not otherwise a reporting company.

(a) Sponsored ADR programmes

If a foreign private issuer wishes to raise capital in the United States by a public offering of ADRs, it must file two registration statements under the Securities Act:

- one with respect to the underlying securities (Form F-1, Form F-2 or Form F-3); and
- one with respect to the ADRs (Form F-6).

If there is to be no public offering of ADRs and the underlying securities, the foreign private issuer need only register the trading of ADRs on Form F-6.

In addition, as of the first fiscal year ending on or after December 15 2009, new disclosure rules require foreign private issuers that are reporting companies under the Exchange Act and have a sponsored ADR programme to disclose:

- all fees and charges payable by ADR holders to that sponsored depositary; and
- all incentive payments made by the sponsored depositary to the issuer, on Form F-20.

The SEC has stated that this disclosure is intended to benefit ADR holders because sponsored ADR programmes have increased fees as compared to unsponsored ADR programmes, and many investors purchase ADRs without having the opportunity first to review the associated fees. This disclosure must be made on a per-payment basis.[541]

(b) Unsponsored ADR programmes

The depositary of an unsponsored ADR programme must:

- determine, in good faith, either that the issuer of the underlying securities is a reporting company under the Exchange Act, or that the issuer publishes (usually on its website) information sufficient to qualify for a Rule 12g3-2(b) exemption to Exchange Act registration; and
- register trading in ADRs under the Securities Act by filing with the SEC a registration statement on Form F-6.

The SEC has explicitly declined to require that ADR programmes obtain the

541 SEC Release No 33-8959, "Foreign Issuer Reporting Enhancements" (September 19 2009).

consent of the underlying issuer as a precondition to filing Form F-6.[542]

As already described in "Periodic reporting requirements" above, the SEC has made significant changes to both Rule 12g3-2(b) and Form F-6. Previously, US depositary banks could not establish unsponsored ADR programmes unless the foreign issuer had formally applied for the Rule 12g3-2(b) exemption by filing with the SEC (or was a reporting company). Thus, foreign private issuers that did not wish to establish sponsored ADR programmes, but that also did not want the establishment of unsponsored ADR programmes, could deliberately fail to apply for the Rule 12g3-2(b) exemption. As a result of the 2008 amendments to Rule 12g3-2(b), this exemption is now automatic once an issuer complies with its requirements.[543]

The foreign issuer may determine whether an unsponsored ADR programme has been established with respect to its shares by checking the SEC's website to see whether a Form F-6 has been filed. If an unsponsored ADR programme has been established, the issuer has a few options:

- It may establish a sponsored ADR programme and compensate the depositary of the unsponsored ADR programme for the termination of the unsponsored programme, thus allowing the issuer to control the ADR programme.
- It may be able to eliminate current unsponsored ADR programmes and prevent the establishment of such programmes in the future by being obviously non-compliant with the Rule 12g3-2(b) website disclosure requirements (and even posting, for example, a notice on its website that the disclosure on that site does not meet the requirements of Rule 12g3-2(b)). This would negate the depositary from having a good-faith belief, after reasonable due diligence, that the issuer has properly published the required disclosure information in English. The advantage of preventing unsponsored ADR programmes should be weighed against the danger that shareholders and others will disapprove of this lack of transparency.

6.6 Uses of ADR programmes

An increasing number of foreign private issuers with an equity security traded in their home country are using ADRs in connection with their US operations. The principal uses of ADRs are to raise capital, to acquire a US business and to compensate US employees.

(a) Raising capital

As a security readily acceptable to US investors, an ADR may be privately placed with sophisticated investors or may be sold to the public in an underwritten offering registered under the Securities Act. ADRs may be listed on a US national securities exchange. Additionally, a foreign private issuer may use Rule 144A and/or Regulation S ADR offerings to raise capital. Rule 144A ADR offerings are those in which the depositary receipts are privately placed with qualified institutional investors in the

---

542 SEC Release No 34-58465, "Exemption from Registration under Section 12(g) of the Securities Exchange Act of 1934 for Foreign Private Issuers", Section II-I (September 5 2008).

543 See the section on the Rule 12g3-2(b) exemption in "Periodic reporting requirements".

United States. A Regulation S offering allows the offshore placement of depositary receipts to non-US investors in reliance on Regulation S. The mechanics of an ADR offering are basically no different from those in any other US security offering, so far as the form and content of the offering material and any underwriting and SEC review procedures (if it is a public offering) are concerned. Similar investigatory and analytical work is required and the liability of the issuer, underwriters, officers and directors does not change.

(b) Acquisitions

If a foreign private issuer uses its equity securities to acquire a US business, it will probably find that ADRs will be more desirable to US sellers than a security traded only abroad. ADRs can be used both in acquisitions of closely held companies and in acquisitions of publicly traded corporations.

(c) Compensation

For the reasons stated above, a US security, such as an ADR, is more readily acceptable as compensation in the United States than is a security denominated in a foreign currency, traded only abroad and paying dividends that require a costly currency conversion when deposited in US banks.

Generally, all US compensation techniques using equity securities are as available with ADRs as they are when paid in common stock of a US company. A foreign private issuer that has an ADR programme could offer its US employees a stock benefit plan in which awards are denominated in ADRs. Alternatively, such a company could offer employees a benefit plan with awards denominated in parent company securities and assist the employees in depositing such securities with the ADR programme, so that the employees end up with ADRs.

6.7 Compensation of US employees

There has been a growing interest on the part of foreign private issuers in providing compensation arrangements for US employees using stock of the foreign private issuer or related ADRs.

When a foreign private issuer establishes an employee benefit plan that uses its stock or ADRs, it is making an offer of its securities to the plan participants and therefore must consider whether the Securities Act requires registration of the offering or affords an exemption from registration. There is no automatic exemption for an offering to employees of an issuer. If registration is to be avoided, an exemption must be found for the issuer's offer and sale to the employees and, before the securities can be resold by the employees, an exemption must be found for their resale. Of course, the ability to resell securities freely enhances the value of the plan as a compensation device.

A foreign private issuer's employee benefit stock plan can be confined to a select group of key US employees or can be extended generally to all or a large number of US employees. Examples of the first type include grants of stock options, restricted stock units or performance shares, as well as executive bonuses paid in stock, while examples of the second type include a wide variety of 'tax qualified' plans such as employee stock ownership plans (ESOPs), profit sharing plans and 401(k) plans, as well as broad-based stock option plans, stock bonus ('free share') plans and stock purchase plans.

If the plan is being extended to a limited number of high-level executives in the United States, the foreign private issuer may be able to structure the offering of benefit plan shares or ADRs as a private offering that is exempt from Securities Act registration. This would be the case if all the eligible US employees met the Regulation D test of 'accredited investor' and could well be so even if certain members of the group did not meet the test (although the Regulation D requirement for providing information to non-accredited investors could prove onerous in stock option or other offerings that are outstanding for an extended period). The employee recipients of the stock or ADRs would need either to have their resales registered under the Securities Act or to find an exemption. The most likely exemption options would be Rule 144 and Regulation S.[544]

If the eligible US employee group is large or is not confined to sophisticated or key personnel, the offering may be regarded as a public rather than a private one, in which case a private offering exemption would not be available.[545] Because the standard Securities Act registration will likely be an excessive burden, the SEC has adopted provisions dealing with securities offerings to employees that permit such offerings to be made without going through the full registration process:

- Companies that are subject to the Exchange Act's reporting requirements will generally be able to register offerings to their US employees on simplified SEC registration Form S-8.
- For companies that are not subject to these requirements, Securities Act Rule 701 provides a limited exemption from registration.

Both registration on Form S-8 and the Rule 701 exemption from registration are available only for offerings to employees of the issuer or its parent or subsidiaries. Although the criteria for the availability of Rule 701 and Form S-8 are generally the same, there are some differences. For example, for purposes of Rule 701 (but not Form S-8), the issuer's 'subsidiaries' are limited to majority-owned subsidiaries. Rule 701 (but not Form S-8) is available not only for employees of the issuer's majority-owned subsidiaries, but also for employees of majority-owned subsidiaries of the issuer's parent. Both Form S-8 and Rule 701 define 'employee' to include the following:

- employees, directors, general partners, trustees (of a business trust) and officers;
- insurance agents who are exclusive agents of the issuer, its parent or its subsidiaries, or who derive more than 50% of their annual income from those entities;

---

544 For more on these exemptions see "Periodic reporting requirements".

545 See SEC Release No 33-8523, "In the Matter of Google, Inc. and David C. Drummond, Order Instituting Cease-and-Desist Proceedings, Making Findings, and Imposing a Cease-and-Desist Order Pursuant to Section 8a of the Securities Act of 1933" (January 13 2005) (imposing a cease-and-desist order against Google, Inc and its general counsel in connection with grants of stock options to employees and consultants without either registration or an exemption from registration).

- consultants, if:
  - they are natural persons;
  - they provide *bona fide* services to the issuer, its parent or its subsidiaries (as defined above); and
  - their services do not promote or maintain a market for the issuer's securities and are not in connection with the offer or sale of securities in a capital-raising transaction.[546]

Rule 701 and Form S-8 are also available for former employees (as defined above), but under somewhat different conditions. Rule 701 is available only if the former employees were employed by or providing services to the issuer at the time the securities were offered. For example, a person that was granted a stock option while an employee would be able to exercise the option under Rule 701 even after termination of employment. Form S-8 can be used to register sales to former employees only if the transaction involves:

- the exercise of stock options and subsequent sale of the securities acquired on exercise; or
- the acquisition of issuer securities pursuant to intra-plan transfers among plan investments (eg, as is permitted under a 401(k) plan), in each case if the transaction is permitted under the terms of the plan.

Form S-8 may also be used for sales by executors or beneficiaries of the estates of deceased employees for the transactions described in the preceding sentence.

Rule 701 and Form S-8 are also available for sales to specified family members of the employee who acquired the securities as a gift or under a domestic relations order. (In the case of Form S-8, family members can be covered only with respect to the exercise of stock options and sale of the acquired securities.)

Under both Rule 701 and Form S-8, an 'employee benefit plan' includes a written compensatory agreement. Thus, these provisions would also apply to sales of securities made pursuant to an individually negotiated employment agreement or to a grant of an equity award made outside a formal plan.

(a) Companies subject to the Exchange Act

A foreign private issuer that is subject to the reporting requirements of the Exchange Act may register the underlying securities to be issued under employee benefit plans on Form S-8. If it has a related ADR programme, it may register the ADRs on the same form. If it has already registered sufficient ADRs on Form F-6, the foreign private issuer could instead merely register the underlying securities on Form S-8.

Sale by issuer: Use of Form S-8 is limited to offerings of securities under employee

546 Securities Act Rule 701(c); Form S-8, General Instruction A.1.

547 Form S-8, General Instruction A.1.(a). Employee benefit plans are defined as: "[A]ny written purchase, savings, option, bonus, appreciation, profit sharing, thrift, incentive, pension or similar plan or written compensation contract solely for employees, directors, general partners, trustees (where the registrant is a business trust), officers, or consultants or advisers." Securities Act Regulation C, Rule 405.

benefit plans or written compensation agreements.[547] Both domestic and foreign private issuers are eligible to use it if they have entered the Exchange Act reporting system and have previously filed all required Exchange Act reports in the previous 12 months (or since the issuer registered, if less). Form S-8 registration is not available to a foreign private issuer that is exempt from Exchange Act registration under Rule 12g3-2(b).

Registration on Form S-8 is a relatively simple process. The focal point is the delivery to a plan's participants of a prospectus that contains a description of the plan, the tax consequences of participation and the ADRs (if utilised), as well as certain other information.[548] A description of the business of the issuer and its financial statements (and financial statements of the employee benefit plan, where applicable)[549] are incorporated by reference into the prospectus from the issuer's (or plan's) Exchange Act reports.[550] Financial statements of the plan are required where the registration statement registers so-called 'interests in the plan' – generally, where securities of the employer are held in a trust (as is the case in a 401(k) plan), the participant has an account in the trust rather than owning the employer securities directly and funds of the participant have been used to acquire employer securities.

The non-prospectus part of the registration statement, containing such items as undertakings and exhibits, is filed with the SEC, but – in a feature unique to Form S-8 registration – the prospectus is not filed with the SEC[551] (although it must be provided to employees). Moreover, except for incorporated Exchange Act reports, the prospectus does not give rise to Section 11 liability (although it is subject to anti-fraud provisions such as Rule 10b-5).[552] A Form S-8 registration is effective upon filing, without prior SEC review.[553]

The Form S-8 prospectus incorporates by reference not only Exchange Act reports that are on file at the time of preparation of the prospectus, but also Exchange Act reports that are filed thereafter.[554] There is thus no need to update and redistribute the prospectus continually to include current information about the issuer. In order to provide employees with current information about the issuer, the rules require the issuer to deliver a copy of its annual report to each participant at the time of delivery of the prospectus, and thereafter, for as long as the person remains a participant (eg, as a holder of stock options), to deliver a copy of all reports, proxy statements and other communications delivered to shareholders generally.[555] Changes to the description of plan provisions and tax consequences (and to the other information actually stated in the prospectus) can be made by distributing to participants a supplement to the prospectus, which need not repeat previously provided information. This 'evergreen' feature also distinguishes registration on Form S-8 from

548 Form S-8, Items 1 and 2.

549 See SEC Release No 33-6188, "Employee Benefit Plans" (February 1 1980). The financial statements of the plan are filed using Exchange Act on Form 11-K.

550 Form S-8, Items 2 and 3.

551 Form S-8, Note to Part I.

552 See SEC Release No 33-6867, "Registration and Reporting Requirements for Employee Benefit Plans", II.C (June 6 1990).

553 Form S-8, General Instruction D.

554 Form S-8, Item 3.

555 Securities Act Rule 428.

most of the other Securities Act registration forms. The issuer is required to retain (and deliver to the SEC upon request) each document constituting part of the prospectus for a period of five years after its last use as such.

Resales by employees: An offering that is registered under the Securities Act is an offering to the public. Ultimate purchasers of securities in a public offering are generally able to resell without further registration. Registration on Form S-8 makes it possible for all plan participants except affiliates to resell freely the securities received under the plan. Affiliates may not resell the securities received under the plan unless an exemption applies or the affiliate's sale is itself registered.

Generally, only executive officers, directors or significant stockholders of a foreign private issuer would be its 'affiliates'. US employees of the foreign private issuer or its US subsidiaries seldom would be. In cases where US employees are affiliates, resales would normally be made pursuant to the exemption from registration provided by Rule 144:[556]

- Since the securities would have been acquired in a registered public offering, they would not be 'restricted securities' and no Rule 144 holding period would be necessary.
- The volume limitation of Rule 144 is not likely to be a problem. In any three-month period, an affiliate (and related persons and entities) may sell up to the greater of:
  - 1% of the outstanding securities of that class; or
  - the average weekly trading volume over the last four weeks of the securities on all US national securities exchanges.[557]

  The SEC staff has taken the position that the class of securities for purposes of the 1% test is that of the company's underlying securities, not the number of shares represented by ADRs.

As alternatives to Rule 144:

- the securities received by the affiliate can be registered for resale by means of a separate registration statement or, more realistically, by means of a resale prospectus filed with the plan registration statement on Form S-8;[558]
- the affiliate may be able to resell the securities on a foreign stock exchange pursuant to Regulation S; or
- at least in theory, the affiliate may resell in a privately negotiated transaction (pursuant to Rule 144A or Section 4(1½)).[559]

Bonus stock plans: A company may choose to offer securities to its employees under a plan in which they do not pay for them except through continued service. In such a situation, where the amount of the securities received is not individually negotiated with the employee and does not represent a significant portion of the

---

556 For more on Rule 144 see the overview to "Private placements".
557 Securities Act Rule 144(e).
558 Form S-8, General Instruction C.
559 See "Private placements" for more information on Rule 144A and Regulation S.

employee's total compensation, the SEC has taken the position that there has been no sale of a security and thus that no registration is required.[560] In such a situation, the securities in the hands of the employees would technically be 'restricted securities' – because they were received from the issuer without Securities Act registration – and thus could not be resold by the employees without registration or an exemption.

However, the staff of the SEC has articulated an administrative exception – limited to securities issued under broad-based bonus plans of companies subject to the reporting requirements of the Exchange Act – that permits shares issued under such a plan without registration to be resold in the United States by non-affiliates without restriction (and by affiliates under Rule 144, but without the otherwise-required holding period) if:

- the stock is actively traded in the open market; and
- the number of shares being distributed to plan participants during a fiscal year is "relatively small".[561]

The SEC has further stated that this second test will always be satisfied if the number of shares distributed during the year does not exceed 1% of the outstanding shares of the class. However, larger amounts may also satisfy the test if the distribution would have no measurable impact on the public market for the securities. This has been found to be the case in several individual situations where the shares distributed were approximately 2% or 3% of the outstanding shares.[562]

(b) *Companies not subject to the Exchange Act*

A foreign private issuer that is not subject to the registration and periodic reporting requirements of the Exchange Act, including an issuer that is exempt from registration by virtue of Rule 12g3-2(b), may utilise a special exemption from Securities Act registration provided by Rule 701 under that act to issue securities in limited amounts to employees pursuant to employee benefit plans (or written compensation agreements) – even if the employees would not qualify for a private placement.[563]

Sale by issuer: Rule 701 applies only to offers and sales of an issuer's securities under written compensatory benefit plans or agreements. The number of securities that may be offered under Rule 701 is not limited. However, the amount of securities that may be sold in any 12-month period without Securities Act registration in reliance on this rule (under all benefit plans and agreements in the aggregate) may not exceed the greatest of the amounts set forth below:

- securities having an aggregate purchase price of $1 million;

---

560 SEC Release No 33-6188, "Employee Benefit Plans" (February 1 1980). See Securities Act §2(a)(3).

561 SEC Release No 33-6188, "Employee Benefit Plans" (February 1 1980).

562 SEC Release No 33-6281, "Employee Benefit Plans" (January 15 1981); SEC Release No 33-6867, "Registration and Reporting Requirements for Employee Benefit Plans" (June 6 1990).

563 Securities Act Rule 701(b); SEC Compliance and Disclosure Interpretations, Q&A 271.03 (January 26 2009).

- securities having an aggregate purchase price of 15% of the issuer's total assets; or
- the number of securities equal to 15% of the outstanding class.[564]

In applying these limits with respect to stock options, the sale is treated as occurring at the time that the option is granted, not when it is exercised.[565] As a result, stock options are counted against the limits of this rule only at the time of grant. For purposes of the above limits, the issuer's assets and voting securities may be measured as reflected on its balance sheet as of either the end of its last fiscal year or a more recent date, whichever is more favourable to the issuer.[566] In addition, for a limited period after the end of a fiscal year, before the year-end balance sheet is available, the issuer may use a balance sheet as of a date in its last fiscal quarter.[567] The 12-month period used for applying the above limits may be either a fixed 12-month period (eg, the calendar year or a fiscal year) or a rolling period (consisting of the 12 months immediately preceding the sale or option grant in question), as long as the chosen method is used consistently.[568]

The numerical limitations described above apply only to sales made under Rule 701 and do not prevent contemporaneous offers and sales under other Securities Act exemptions.[569] Thus, sales to non-US employees made under Regulation S can be disregarded for purposes of these limits, even if made under the same global plan as sales to US employees. Similarly, sales to US employees under one of the exemptions in Regulation D can also be disregarded.[570]

Rule 701 requires that the issuer deliver to employees a copy of the benefit plan or contract under which the securities are being sold. In addition, if the aggregate sales price of the securities sold in any 12-month period (including the aggregate exercise price of the stock options granted in the period) exceeds $5 million, the following additional disclosure is required to be provided "a reasonable time" before the date of sale or, in the case of options, before the date of exercise:

- a summary of the terms of the plan;
- information about "the risks associated with investment in" the plan securities; and
- financial statements that are no more than 180 days old, which may be unaudited (unless the issuer otherwise prepares audited financial statements), but must either be prepared in accordance with IFRS (as issued by the International Accounting Standards Board) or must be presented in accordance with (or reconciled to) US GAAP.[571]

In addition to these specific disclosure requirements, all sales made pursuant to

564 Securities Act Rule 701(d)(2).
565 Securities Act Rule 701(d)(3).
566 SEC Compliance and Disclosure Interpretations, Q&A 271.09 (January 26 2009).
567 American Bar Association, SEC No-action letter (December 7 2000).
568 SEC Compliance and Disclosure Interpretations, Q&A 271.06 (January 26 2009).
569 Securities Act Rule 701(d)(3)(iv) and (f).
570 Securities Act Rule 701(d)(3)(iv).
571 Securities Act Rule 701(e).

this rule are subject to the general requirement (embodied in Exchange Act Rule 10b-5) that they not be based on false or misleading information.

The rule's requirement that the financial statements be as of a date no more than 180 days before the option exercise or other sale effectively results in a requirement that the financial statements (including reconciliation to US GAAP, if not presented using IFRS) be available on at least a quarterly basis, unless option exercises are limited to particular times of the year. Moreover, in order to permit uninterrupted option exercisability, the financial statements (and any required reconciliation) must be completed within three months of the end of each quarter. Foreign private issuers that are unable to satisfy the timing requirements for this enhanced disclosure need to structure their US equity compensation programmes so as to stay below the $5 million threshold that triggers this level of disclosure.

Resales by employees: Securities acquired by employees in a Rule 701 offering are 'restricted securities', as defined by Rule 144, just like securities acquired in a private offering.[572] Resales cannot be made by employees without Securities Act registration unless an exemption from registration is available. For securities issued by foreign private issuers, the most likely exemptions are those afforded by Regulation S and Rule 144.

Regulation S permits securities acquired in unregistered transactions to be resold in offshore transactions (which include sales on a foreign securities exchange or through the facilities of a designated foreign securities market), so long as the resale is accompanied by no directed selling efforts in the United States.[573] If the selling employee is an affiliate of the issuer, the employee may not pay any amounts other than customary broker's commissions in connection with the resale of the shares. If the securities acquired under the plan are ADRs, the employee may deposit them in the ADR programme and withdraw the underlying securities, which may then be sold abroad pursuant to Regulation S.

Shares acquired pursuant to Rule 701 may also be sold under Rule 144 if all conditions of that rule, including the applicable holding period (either six months or one year, depending on whether the issuer is a reporting company under the Exchange Act), are satisfied.[574] Under the 2008 revisions to Rule 144, these securities may be resold by non-affiliates after the applicable holding period has been satisfied, without further restrictions.[575] The securities may be resold by affiliates after the applicable holding period only if the public information, volume limitations, manner of sale and filing requirements of Rule 144 are met. In addition, securities acquired under Rule 701 may be resold under Rule 144 without a holding period 90 days after the issuer has become subject to the reporting requirements of the Exchange Act.

---

572 Securities Act Rule 701(g).

573 See the section on Regulation S offshore transactions in "Private placements".

574 Securities Act Rule 144(d).

575 SEC Release No 33-8869, "Revisions to Rules 144 and 145" (December 17 2007), effective on February 15 2008.

(c) *Exemption from Exchange Act registration*

A foreign private issuer that is issuing its securities to a large number of US employees needs to consider the effect of its benefit programmes on its status under the Exchange Act. If the issuer has more than $10 million in total assets and a class of equity securities held by 300 or more US holders – and 500 or more holders worldwide – it must either register under the Exchange Act or operate under either the Rule 12g3-2(b) or Rule 12h-1 exemptions from registration. The SEC has clarified that in addition to common stock or ordinary shares, stock options constitute a class of securities for this purpose.

Rule 12g3-2(b): As described in more detail in "Periodic reporting requirements" above, Exchange Act Rule 12g3-2(b) provides an exemption from Exchange Act registration for foreign private issuers. Among the conditions of the rule are that the issuer:

- have a class of equity securities listed on a non-US stock exchange in its 'primary trading market'; and
- post specified information, in English, on its website.

The Rule 12g3-2(b) exemption is applied separately to each class of a company's equity securities. Thus, with one exception, in order for a particular class of equity securities to be eligible for the exemption, that class of equity securities must be listed on a non-US stock exchange. The sole exception is that compensatory stock options do not need to be listed on a stock exchange if the securities to be acquired on exercise of the stock options are so listed.[576] However, to the extent that equity awards other than stock options are deemed to be a class of securities different from the underlying listed class of securities, such awards (which presumably are not themselves listed on a stock exchange) would not be eligible for the exemption.

Rule 12h-1(f): Rule 12h-1(f) provides an exemption from Exchange Act registration for compensatory stock options issued by companies that are not subject to that act. In order to use this exemption, all of the issuer's compensatory stock options – whether issued to US or foreign employees, and whether or not issued under the same plan – must satisfy all of the conditions for the exemption.[577] These conditions include the following:

- The stock options must be issued under one or more written compensatory plans established by the issuer, the issuer's parent, its majority-owned subsidiaries or majority-owned subsidiaries of the issuer's parent.
- The options may be granted only to those categories of individuals who are eligible to be granted stock options under Rule 701.
- Transferability of the options must be:
  - limited to transfers to 'family members' (as defined in Rule 701) by gift or domestic relations order; or to executors or guardians of the option

576 Exchange Act Rule 12g3-2(b)(1)(ii) and Note 3 to Paragraph (b)(1).
577 Exchange Act Rule 12h-1(f)(1).

  holder in the event of his or her death or disability; or
  - made in connection with an acquisition of the issuer in certain circumstances.

  (These transfer restrictions do not apply to the securities received on the exercise of the options.)
- The options (and, prior to exercise, the underlying shares) may not be pledged or subject to hedging transactions.
- The issuer must deliver to the option holders every six months the same information as is required to be provided under the enhanced disclosure provision of Rule 701 – that is, information about the terms of the plan, risks associated with the investment in plan securities and financial statements that are no more than 180 days old. This information must be provided as a condition to availability of the Rule 12h-1(f) exemption, whether or not the issuer triggers the enhanced disclosure requirement under Rule 701.

These restrictions generally must be embodied in the terms of the stock option plan or in another binding agreement. However, the issuer may provide that the restrictions will terminate in the event that the issuer becomes subject to the Exchange Act or qualifies for the Rule 12g3-2(b) exemption.

Rule 12h-1(f) applies only to stock options. Thus, if a foreign private issuer seeks to issue compensatory equity awards other than stock options, it needs to stay below the thresholds that would trigger Exchange Act registration (300 US holders and 500 worldwide holders of the class of securities), register the class under the Exchange Act (and become subject to the act's ongoing reporting requirements), qualify for an exemption to registration or seek individual relief from the SEC.

Rule 12h-1(g): The registration requirements of the Exchange Act generally apply to each class of equity securities held by the requisite number of holders. However, Rule 12h-1(g) provides an exemption from registration for compensatory stock options where the issuer of the shares underlying the stock options is already subject to the act's reporting requirements. This exemption is available only if substantially all of the compensatory stock options relating to the issuer's securities are held by persons that qualify as option holders under either Rule 701 or Form S-8.

7. Securities litigation risks

7.1 Background

US federal securities laws are enforced in three ways:

- through the regulatory activities of the SEC in reviewing disclosure documents, monitoring trading and market practices, and bringing civil and administrative enforcement proceedings;
- through civil liability provisions that allow private investors to bring suits for monetary damages; and
- through criminal law sanctions, in cases of egregious violations.

Issuers and persons associated with issuers, such as directors, officers and controlling shareholders, may be liable to investors for damages if the issuer's securities are sold or traded on the basis of incorrect or misleading disclosure. The US federal courts have procedural rules that permit the bringing of class actions for damages on behalf of large bodies of security holders, creating significant contingent liabilities. A plaintiffs' bar is active in the United States in prosecuting such civil class actions, and litigation costs can be high even where claims are ultimately determined to be baseless or settled for low amounts. Foreign private issuers are generally unaccustomed to the kind of exposure to private civil damage claims and the intensity of litigation that exist in the United States.

Because the thrust of most securities law claims is failure of proper disclosure, issuers can minimise litigation risks by publishing offering materials, periodic reports and other business and financial documents that are materially accurate and complete and that adequately describe the risks of investment.

Amendments to the Securities Act and the Exchange Act, discussed in this chapter below, were intended by Congress to reduce the cost and liability burdens of securities claims. Both foreign private issuers and US issuers should find these legislative changes helpful, given that the volume of US private securities class actions continues to be substantial – although recently the filings have dropped, in part due to the global financial crisis.[578]

(a) *The US legal system*

Many features of the US legal system are unique compared to other systems around the world. Understanding the framework in which potential lawsuits would take

578 PricewaterhouseCoopers, 2009 Securities Litigation Study 6 (2009).

place can help to inform a competent defence strategy on the front end. This chapter provides information on some of the critical areas within the US legal system that may differ from foreign legal systems, especially those with a civil code tradition.

The US legal system is the product of English common law, contrasted with the civil code tradition that prevails in the rest of Europe. Accordingly, in the United States, judge-made case law is prevalent, as is the principle of *stare decisis* or respect for precedent. However, all case law must comply with the US Constitution, which was adopted in 1789, and with the relevant federal statutes. US securities laws are almost exclusively governed by federal law, because securities transactions generally involve interstate commerce.

There were no federal statutes or regulatory agencies of note relating to securities transactions until the New Deal introduced the Securities Act in 1933, and the Exchange Act and the SEC in 1934. Thereafter, the rules for securities transactions emanate from the SEC, the federal courts and Congress.

Contingency fees: In the United States, attorneys working for plaintiffs in private securities litigation may work on a contingency fee basis.[579] Under this system, plaintiffs do not pay the attorney fees unless they receive an award or settlement, at which point they pay a negotiated percentage to their attorney, typically between 20% and 40%. Such a fee structure is either uncommon or even banned in many countries around the world and it remains controversial. Supporters of contingency fees argue that the system allows equal access to the courts and justice, while critics allege that they promote speculative litigation.

Loser does not pay: In the United States, a plaintiff that brings a lawsuit and loses generally does not have to bear any of the defendant's costs. Many European nations, on the contrary, require that the loser pay some or all litigation costs.

Juries: In the United States, juries decide issues of fact, which tend to be most of the issues in a lawsuit, and trial judges decide issues of law. Juries are composed of ordinary citizens[580] and can range in size from six to 12 members, depending on the jurisdiction. The process of selecting juries also varies, but generally there is a process called *voir dire* that permits the parties to eliminate jurors who may be biased.[581] In addition, in some courts the parties may have a limited right to eliminate a few jurors without having to show that the juror had any bias.[582]

Discovery: The discovery process is an important part of litigation in the United

579 See Mark A Behrens *et al*, "Global Litigation Trends", 17 *Michigan State Journal of International Law* 165, 183-187 (2009).

580 US Constitution, Amendment VII.

581 See *Mu'min v Virginia*, 500 US 415, 431 (1991) ("*Voir dire* examination serves the dual purposes of enabling the court to select an impartial jury and assisting counsel in exercising peremptory challenges").

582 See *State v Howell*, 868 S W 2d 238, 247 (Tenn 1993) ("The ultimate goal of *voir dire* is to see that jurors are competent, unbiased, and impartial, and the decision of how to conduct *voir dire* of prospective jurors rests within the sound discretion of the trial court").

States and one that foreign companies likely find most surprising. Once a lawsuit is initiated, each party may ask the other for any information (eg, witnesses, documents or emails) that may be relevant to the lawsuit; the other party is then required to produce such information.[583] There are some limits to what a party may request, but the inclination of the US judicial system is towards full disclosure. Discovery tends to account for a substantial portion of litigation costs, typically around 50% of the total sum.[584]

Class actions: In the United States, a person that purports to represent a whole class of persons that have been injured in the same way may bring a single lawsuit on their behalf. This procedure, called a class action lawsuit, allows one individual or a small group to represent thousands of individuals.[585] In order to file a class action, the plaintiff must prove the following elements:

- The class is so large that other legal remedies are impractical;
- There are questions of law and fact that are common to the class;
- The claims and defences of the representatives filing the actions are typical and representative of the other class members; and
- Representative parties will accurately and fairly represent the interests of all other class members.

Class actions are of particular concern to defendants because one verdict for a large class could result in damage awards of millions of dollars. Until recently, the United States was one of only a handful of countries that permitted class action lawsuits.

Derivative lawsuits: Derivative lawsuits allow shareholders of a corporation to bring a lawsuit on behalf of the corporation against directors or officers of the same corporation that may have breached their fiduciary duty.[586] Because it is ordinarily the responsibility of management to bring a lawsuit on behalf of the corporation, there are procedures that dictate when shareholders may proceed with a derivative lawsuit.[587] For example, shareholders may proceed only when management has failed to pursue the same lawsuit on behalf of the corporation.[588]

Consolidations and coordinations: Claims of multiple plaintiffs may be brought in a single lawsuit; or different lawsuits may be joined into a single lawsuit.[589] This is sometimes called consolidation. Like a class action, there will be a single trial for all

583 Federal Rules of Civil Procedure 26.

584 Thomas E Willging *et al*, "An Empirical Study of Discovery and Disclosure Practice Under the 1993 Federal Rule Amendments", 39 *Boston College Law Review* 525, 548 (1998).

585 Federal Rules of Civil Procedure 23.

586 *Schrag v Dinges*, 825 F Supp 954 (D Kansas 1993) ("As a matter of general corporation law, an action for damages to a corporation may be brought either by the corporation or, in some circumstances, as a derivative action by the shareholders").

587 See, for example, *White v Panic*, 783 A 2d 543, 546-547 (Delaware 2001).

588 In most cases the shareholders must make demand on the corporate management requesting that management initiate the lawsuit on behalf of the corporation. In certain cases this demand requirement may be excused if the court determines that demand would be futile. See, for example, *Brehm v Eisner*, 746 A 2d 244, 256-257 (Delaware 2000).

of the claims in a consolidated action. Defendants may oppose consolidations if there are fundamental differences between each plaintiff's claims. A US district court's decision as to whether to consolidate is discretionary and depends on the following factors:[590]

- risk of prejudice and the confusion of consolidating;
- risk of potential inconsistencies arising from separate litigation;
- length of time required to conduct multiple lawsuits; and
- relative expense of options.

In addition to consolidation, procedures in state and federal courts permit the coordination of claims.[591] Coordination procedures deal mainly with procedural aspects such as discovery, evidence and various other motions. In US federal courts, cases may be coordinated in a so-called 'multidistrict litigation court'. This court handles all discovery and motions filed before trial. The cases are then returned to the courts where they were originally filed. In coordinated actions, unlike class actions or consolidated actions, each lawsuit is treated separately for the ultimate determination at trial.

Plea bargaining: In criminal prosecutions, prosecutors often give defendants the option of a plea bargain, under which the defendant agrees to plead guilty in return for a lesser charge with a lower sentence. Some factors that may affect the success of the plea bargain for the defendant include:

- information disparities between the parties;
- the quality of the defendant's counsel;
- sentencing guidelines and statutes; and
- bail and detention rules.[592]

7.2 Bases for civil liability

Some of the principal liability provisions under the Securities Act and the Exchange Act are well enough known so that terms such as 'Section 11' and 'Rule 10b-5' have become part of investment banking and underwriting vernacular – both in the United States and abroad.

The common principle of US federal civil liability provisions in securities transactions is that it is unlawful to make any "untrue statement of a material fact" or to "omit to state a material fact" necessary to make other statements "not misleading". A person is generally liable for an omission only where there was a duty to disclose information arising from:

- express provisions within a statute or regulation; or

---

589 *Hendrix v Raybestos-Manhattan, Inc*, 776 F 2d 1492, 1495 (11th Circuit 1985) ("When actions involving a common question of law or fact are pending before the court, it may order a joint hearing or trial of any or all the matters in issue in the actions; it may order all the actions consolidated; and it may make such orders concerning proceedings therein as may tend to avoid unnecessary costs or delay").

590 *Hendrix v Raybestos-Manhattan, Inc*, 776 F 2d 1492, 1495 (11th Circuit 1985).

591 28 USC §1407.

592 See generally Stephanos Bibas, "Plea Bargaining Outside the Shadow of Trial", 117 *Harvard Law Review* 2463 (2004).

- the duty to disclose information so as not to render previous statements false or misleading.[593]

Civil liability for material misstatements or omissions arises under the following statutory provisions:

- Section 11 of the Securities Act applies this principle to registered public offerings under this act, imposing liability on specific classes of persons:
  - the issuer;
  - underwriters;
  - directors and principal officers of the issuer; and
  - 'experts' (eg, auditors, with regard to financial statements).
- Section 12 of the Securities Act applies the principle to 'sellers' of securities pursuant to a public offering prospectus.
- Section 10(b) of the Exchange Act (and Rule 10b-5 thereunder) applies the principle not just to securities transactions where capital is raised, but generally to "the purchase or sale of any security". (Section 17 of the Securities Act is virtually the same as Rule 10b-5, but is generally considered to afford a right of action only to the SEC and not to investors.) Unlike Sections 11 and 12, where mere negligence can give rise to liability, Section 10(b) and Rule 10b-5 require knowledge, awareness or reckless disregard of wrongdoing.

The text of Rule 10b-5, set forth below, includes the relevant components of any securities fraud claim:

> *It shall be unlawful for any person, directly or indirectly, by the use of any means or instrumentality of interstate commerce, or of the mails or of any facility of any national securities exchange,*
>
> *(a) To employ any device, scheme, or artifice to defraud,*
>
> *(b) To make any untrue statement of a material fact or to omit to state a material fact necessary in order to make the statements made, in the light of the circumstances under which they were made, not misleading, or*
>
> *(c) To engage in any act, practice, or course of business that operates or would operate as a fraud or deceit upon any person,*
>
> *in connection with the purchase or sale of any security.*[594]

There is much overlap between the various statutory provisions of securities fraud. For example, where a class action is brought against the issuer of securities alleging a defective registered offering, it is customary to allege violation of all three prongs.

Section 11 liability is confined to misstatements or omissions in the public offering registration statement and prospectus, while Section 12 liability is limited to

593 *Resnik v Swartz*, 303 F 3d 147, 151 (2d Circuit 2002); *Vladimir v Bioenvision, Inc*, No 09-3487-cv, 2010 US App LEXIS 7139, *4 (2d Circuit April 7 2010).

594 17 CFR §240.10b-5.

defects in a public offering prospectus. However, liability under Section 10(b) or Rule 10b-5 can be based upon defects in formal prospectuses, private offering memoranda, Exchange Act reports and a wide range of other materials, such as issuer press releases, website publications and oral communications. An issuer's periodic press releases and website postings, and its executives' interviews and meetings with security analysts, if used to disseminate false or misleading information about the issuer's business or finances, may be deemed by the courts to perpetrate a 'fraud on the market' that is actionable under Section 10(b) or Rule 10b-5.

7.3 Exposure of issuers and others

If an issuer disseminates false or misleading disclosure materials, the issuer as an entity will be exposed to damage claims, even if the persons actually responsible for the defective materials are individuals (ie, directors, officers and employees of the issuer, lawyers, accountants and financial advisers).

(a) Issuer liability

Under Section 11 of the Securities Act, the issuer has no defence if there has been a disclosure violation. As a practical matter, it will be difficult for the issuer as an entity to assert defences based on lack of knowledge or exercise of reasonable care under other civil liability provisions, because the knowledge and negligence of its officers and other agents are likely to be imputed to it.

The Offering Reform Rules[595] clarify that, in a registered public offering, the issuer is a 'seller' for Section 12 purposes, regardless of whether the usual structure of issuer sale to the underwriter on a firm commitment basis was used.[596]

(b) Director and officer liability

The management of an issuer should be concerned with the possibility of US federal securities law litigation from a personal as well as a corporate standpoint. This is particularly the case for the principal officers of an issuer that reports under the Exchange Act, who must certify its reports.[597] Section 11 of the Securities Act specifically imposes liability for defective disclosure on directors of the issuer and on its senior officers (the principal executive, financial and accounting officers), as well as on underwriters and 'experts'. Unlike the issuer, such persons may avoid liability by showing that, after reasonable investigation (or due diligence), they had reasonable grounds to believe and did believe that the Securities Act registration statement was not defective. In addition, outside (ie, non-employee) directors' damages may be limited by the Private Securities Litigation Reform Act.[598] Depending upon the extent of their activities in connection with marketing efforts, individual members of management may be included along with underwriters within the category of 'sellers' of the issuer's securities for purposes of liability under Section 12 of the Securities Act. There is an analogous defence if the defendant can show that it

595 Described in "Public offerings".
596 SEC Release No 33-8591, "Securities Offering Reform," IV-B (July 19 2005); Securities Act Rule 159A.
597 See the section on the Sarbanes-Oxley Act in "Periodic reporting requirements".
598 This is discussed further in this chapter below.

lacked knowledge and, in the exercise of reasonable care, could not have known of the defects in the offering materials. Individuals who make misstatements or omissions with what the courts call scienter (ie, knowledge, awareness or reckless disregard of misstatements or omissions) can be held accountable under Section 10(b) of the Exchange Act and Rule 10b-5 thereunder. A reasonable investigation that produced no cause for alarm would negate scienter.

(c) Aiding and abetting

Section 104 of the Private Securities Litigation Reform Act provides limited liability for aiders and abettors of securities fraud.[599] Under this section, an individual may be found guilty of:

- directly or indirectly controlling an issuer of securities;
- carrying out unlawful securities activity through the means of another person;
- delaying or obstructing the making or filing of a document; or
- trading in securities while in possession of non-public information.

The implied private right of action under Section 10(b) does not extend to aiders and abettors.[600] Any claim against a defendant must satisfy all six of the following elements:

- a material misrepresentation or omission;
- wrongful state of mind;
- connection with the sale or purchase of a security;
- reliance (that the plaintiff used the misinformation to its detriment);
- economic loss; and
- 'loss causation' – that is, a connection between the injury and the material misrepresentation.[601]

Therefore, an aider or abettor may be found guilty (under a private action) only if the plaintiff can satisfy all of the requisite conditions as a primary violator. Yet Congress granted express power to the SEC to bring claims against individuals that aid and abet violations of the securities laws. In practice, however, liability for aiders and abettors is limited.

Additionally, secondary actors, such as law firms and banks, may be held liable, but only where they themselves have made a material misstatement that satisfies the aforementioned conditions.[602] Even where secondary actors have substantially participated in a securities fraud scheme, plaintiffs face difficulty in proving reliance.[603]

---

599 Exchange Act §20.
600 *Stoneridge Investment Partners, LLC v Scientific-Atlanta, Inc*, 552 US 148, 158 (2008).
601 *Dura Pharms, Inc, v Broudo*, 544 US 336, 341-342 (2005).
602 *Stoneridge Investment Partners, LLC v Scientific-Atlanta, Inc*, 552 US 148, 158 (2008).
603 *Pacific Investors v Brown*, 603 F 3d 144, 144 (2d Circuit 2010).

(d) *Controlling persons*

Liability for controlling persons, which is distinguished from aiding and abetting, provides a form of secondary liability where the defendant controlled a primary violator and achieved 'culpable participation' in the fraud.[604] The Securities Act and the Exchange Act extend civil liability to persons that control an issuer of securities, unless the controlling person can show absence of knowledge of defects in the disclosure material. Under Section 15 of the Securities Act, a person that controls an issuer "by or through stock ownership, agency or otherwise" is jointly and severally liable along with the issuer for the issuer's Section 11 and Section 12 violations, unless the controlling person had no knowledge or reasonable ground to believe that the offering material was defective. Under Section 20(a) of the Exchange Act, a controlling person is jointly and severally liable along with the issuer for the issuer's Rule 10b-5 violations, unless the controlling person "acted in good faith" and did not induce the acts constituting the violation.

US federal securities laws do not define 'control' in precise terms. Whether a particular person controls an issuer of securities requires a factual determination in each case.[605] Obviously, a parent corporation will be deemed to control a majority-owned subsidiary. A few years ago, in a federal court case, the owner of a 22% interest in the European telecommunications company Deutsche Telekom AG was held not to be in control where there was a larger (43%) government ownership stake.[606]

However, on different facts, a court presented with the issue in civil liability litigation could well conclude that a 10% owner with significant managerial input was a controlling person. A court may determine that control of a widely held company rested with a group of directors and senior officers acting in concert or with particular executive officers.[607] Another federal court decision involving the audit committee members of the foreign private issuer Lernout & Hauspie lists many of the regular functions of an audit committee as demonstrating 'control' for Section 20(a) purposes.[608]

Because the question of whether an individual is a controlling person involves a guilty state of mind, it is unclear whether the heightened pleading standards of the Private Securities Litigation Reform Act, discussed below, should apply. Courts in different jurisdictions remain split on this point.[609]

There is no way of obtaining definitive advance assurance as to whether a particular person or group will be deemed to be in control of an issuer. The SEC does not provide such advance determinations.[610] Opinions of counsel must necessarily be hedged because the existence of control is a factual matter. It is advisable for an issuer's principal shareholders and for its directors and its principal officers to assume

---

604 *Suez Equity Investments, LP v Toronto-Dominion Bank*, 250 F 3d 87, 101 (2d Circuit 2001).

605 See Securities Law Techniques (Matthew Bender), § 37.01[2].

606 *In re Deutsche Telekom AG Securities Litigation*, No 00 CIV 9475, 2002 WL 244597 (SDNY February 20 2002).

607 *In re Royal Ahold NV Sec & ERISA Litigation*, 384 F Supp 2d 838 (D Md 2005).

608 *In re Lernout & Hauspie Securities Litigation*, 286 BR 33 (D Mass 2002).

609 See generally Lisbeth Freeman, "Who's Guarding the Gate? Credit-Rating Agency Liability as "Control Person" in the Subprime Credit Crisis", 33 *Vermont Law Review* 585 (2009).

610 SEC Release No 33-6253, "Provisions Utilized by the Division of Corporation Finance For Rendering Informal Advice" (October 28 1980).

that they may be treated as controlling persons in securities litigation. Their exercise of due diligence in the preparation and dissemination of disclosure materials will protect not only the issuer, but themselves as well.

(e) *Enforcement proceedings*

SEC enforcement actions can address violations of other securities law provisions besides those giving investors rights to sue for damages. Such administrative proceedings may result in monetary penalties, such as fines and disgorgement of profits, as well as non-monetary sanctions (eg, injunctions against future violations, bars on officers and directors serving in such capacities in the future, and prohibitions of accountants and attorneys from practising their professions in securities-related matters).

The following actions involving foreign private issuers and foreign individuals illustrate the scope of SEC enforcement proceedings:

- In its December 2003 settlement with Vivendi Universal, SA, the SEC cited violations not only of Rule 10b-5, but also of Section 17(a) of the Securities Act and the books and records, internal control and reporting provisions of Section 13 of the Exchange Act. It imposed a $50 million civil penalty on the issuer and monetary penalties on the former principal officers, together with a bar on their future service with any Exchange Act reporting company.[611]
- The SEC's complaint charging Parmalat Finanziaria, SpA with "one of the largest and most brazen corporate financial frauds in history", brought in December 2003, alleges violation of Section 17(a) and asks for injunctive relief and imposition of civil monetary penalties.[612]
- The Royal Dutch/Shell companies – Royal Dutch Petroleum Company and Shell Transport and Trading Company, PLC – agreed in August 2004 to pay a $120 million civil penalty in connection with overstatement of previously reported proven hydrocarbon reserves.[613]
- Although civil penalties against Royal Ahold NV were waived at the request of foreign prosecuting authorities, officers of the foreign private issuer agreed to permanent bans against future service as officers or directors of public companies as part of the October 2004 settlement of claims of accounting improprieties at the issuer's US subsidiary.[614]
- In February 2005 the SEC settled a civil action claiming misinformation and improper accounting regarding financial results against Elan Corporation, plc, an Irish pharmaceutical company. The SEC accepted $16 million in civil penalties and disgorgement and obtained a permanent injunction against future violation of Rule 10b-5 and the reporting and internal controls provisions of the Exchange Act.[615]

---

611 SEC Litigation Release No 18523, *SEC v Vivendi Universal, SA* (December 24 2003).

612 SEC Litigation Release No 18527, *SEC v Parmalat Finanziaria SpA* (December 30 2003).

613 SEC Litigation Release No 18844, *SEC v Royal Dutch Petroleum Company and The Shell Transport and Trading Company, plc* (August 24 2004).

614 SEC Litigation Release No 18929, *SEC v Koninklijke Ahold NV* (Royal Ahold) (October 13 2004).

615 SEC Litigation Release No 19066, *SEC v Elan Corporation, plc* (February 8 2005).

- In May 2007 the SEC obtained a temporary restraining order freezing assets of two Hong Kong residents held at a branch office of Merrill Lynch & Co in Hong Kong. The SEC alleged that the foreign individuals made approximately $8 million in profits by purchasing $15 million worth of Dow Jones stock in the weeks before the company's acquisition announcement.[616]
- In December 2008 the SEC brought charges against Zurich Financial Services Group for aiding and abetting a fraud by a subsidiary engaged in reinsurance transactions. The company's reinsurance business was spun off in an initial public offering and the new entity assumed the fraudulent transactions. The documents filed with the SEC in connection with the initial public offering were alleged to be materially misleading. Zurich settled with the SEC, agreeing to pay a $25 million penalty and $1 million disgorgement, and accepting a cease and desist order.

Additional cases: In January 2005 the SEC filed civil fraud charges against TV Azteca, a Mexican issuer whose ADRs traded on the New York Stock Exchange (NYSE), its parent company, Azteca Holdings and three TV Azteca officers and directors, including its controlling shareholder, Ricardo Salinas Pliego.[617] The SEC alleged that the defendants engaged in an elaborate scheme to conceal Salinas' role in a series of transactions through which he personally profited by $109 million, and that Salinas and another of the officers sold TV Azteca stock while Salinas' self-dealing remained undisclosed to the marketplace.

The SEC alleged that Salinas and others caused TV Azteca or Azteca Holdings to file periodic reports and issue public statements that did not disclose (and even falsely denied) Salinas' involvement in related-party transactions between Unefon, a subsidiary of TV Azteca, and a privately held company co-owned by Salinas, called Codisco. In the related-party transactions, Salinas purchased from a third party approximately $325 million of indebtedness owed by Unefon to the third party, at a steep discount. At the time that Salinas purchased the indebtedness, he was aware that Unefon was in negotiations with another large telecommunications company, which would provide substantial cash to Unefon, enabling it to pay off the full amount of the indebtedness that Salinas had purchased at a discount. Only three months later, when Unefon closed the deal with the other telecommunications company, Salinas profited by $109 million upon Unefon's repayment of the debt at full value.

This happened despite advice from the company's US counsel that these transactions were material, reportable transactions under US federal securities laws. TV Azteca's resistance to disclose Salinas' involvement led to the eventual resignation of its US counsel, who told the company's board of directors and management that it was resigning consistent with its obligations under Section 307 of the Sarbanes-Oxley Act. Salinas also was found to have executed and delivered false officers' certifications under the act.

---

616 SEC Litigation Release No 20106, *SEC v Wong* (May 8 2007).

617 SEC Litigation Release No 19833, *SEC v TV Azteca, SA de CV* (September 14 2006)

In September 2006 Salinas agreed to consent to:

- a final judgment imposing a permanent injunction prohibiting future violations of various securities law provisions;
- the payment of $7.5 million in penalties and compensation to settle these accusations without admitting or denying any wrongdoing; and
- an agreement not to serve as officer or director of a US publicly listed company for a period of five years, except under limited circumstances.

Another case in 2010 demonstrates both the severity of potential consequences for securities laws violations and the politics behind SEC enforcement proceedings. In April 2010, in a split panel decision (with the SEC commissioners approving by a vote of only three to two), the SEC charged Goldman Sachs with securities fraud and material misstatements in connection with the sale of mortgage-backed securities.[618] The charges concerned the hedge fund Paulson & Co, which had taken a short position on such securities, but had also played a significant role in the portfolio selection of those same securities. This dual role created a potential conflict of interest and Paulson had an economic incentive to choose poor-quality mortgage securities. Goldman failed to disclose Paulson's role in the selection of such securities to investors and those who purchased the securities ultimately lost money, while Paulson profited.[619]

The SEC originally charged Goldman with fraud in this securities offering, in violation of Rule 10b-5. However, in another split panel decision, in July 2010 the SEC authorised a settlement of $550 million under only the lesser charge of material misstatements.[620] As part of the settlement agreement, Goldman acknowledged that it had distributed marketing materials with incomplete information. In addition to the fine, Goldman agreed to:

- a permanent injunction to refrain from violating the Securities Act;
- the implementation of training seminars covering disclosure requirements under the US securities laws; and
- an expanded role for its firm-wide capital committee to ensure the creation of adequate procedures to prevent material misstatements.[621]

The Goldman case highlights a trend whereby corporations eagerly settle securities fraud cases brought by the SEC or the Department of Justice (DOJ), even where the evidence against them is weak. Some commentators have argued that the fact that the SEC dropped its fraud charges against Goldman proves that it did not have strong evidence in the case.[622] Goldman was willing to pay such a large fine to

---

618 *SEC v Goldman Sachs & Co*, 10 Civ 3229 (SDNY 2010); SEC Litigation Release No 21489, "The SEC Charges Goldman Sachs With Fraud In Connection With The Structuring And Marketing of A Synthetic CDO" (April 16 2010).

619 For more on this case, see the section on the Securities and Exchange Commission in the "Introduction".

620 *SEC v Goldman Sachs & Co*, 10 Civ 3229 (SDNY 2010); SEC Litigation Release No 21592, "Goldman Sachs to Pay Record $550 Million to Settle SEC Charges Related to Subprime Mortgage CDO" (July 15 2010).

621 *SEC v Goldman Sachs & Co and Fabrice Tourre*, Final Judgment as to Defendant Goldman Sachs & Co, 10 Civ 3229 (SDNY 2010).

622 Kara Scannell and Susanne Craig, "SEC Split over Goldman Deal", *The Wall Street Journal* (July 17 2010).

settle the case because its main concern was to eliminate the fraud charges. This is common across corporations facing securities fraud charges, where the primary concern lies in the long-term health and reputation of the corporation. The problem is that this facilitates politically motivated securities fraud charges where the evidence is thin. The SEC can bring charges to serve a political purpose and then capitalise on corporate incentives to force a settlement where the evidence is not strong enough to ensure success in court on the merits.

Recently, the SEC has created new initiatives to foster full and complete cooperation by corporations suspected of wrongdoing. The Division of Enforcement within the SEC may enter into a cooperation agreement whereby the corporation formally agrees to cooperate and receives 'credit' to be considered by the division in its punitive actions against it. In a deferred prosecution agreement, the corporation formally agrees to cooperate and to take remedial actions in return for a promise from the SEC that any prosecution will be deferred. A non-prosecution agreement is similar to a deferred prosecution agreement, except that the SEC agrees not to prosecute at all. Such agreements are used only in exceptional circumstances.

7.4 Coping with civil liability risks

US federal securities laws require materially accurate business and financial disclosure, not successful financial performance. Business failure is not a crime or even a tort. A company whose business is replete with risks may offer and sell its securities without incurring damages under the civil liability provisions of the Securities Act and the Exchange Act – even if the business ultimately winds up in bankruptcy – provided that its disclosure documents adequately apprise investors of the risks.

(a) Due diligence defence

Section 11 of the Securities Act provides a defence for defendants, other than the issuer, that have conducted due diligence. The requirements under this defence vary dramatically. The court inquires as to whether the defendant is an expert and whether the portion of the registration statement that is alleged to contain false statements is 'expertised'. When the defendant is not an expert and the statement is expertised, the individual may escape liability if he or she had no knowledge of the false statements. Other scenarios involving experts or non-expertised portions of the statement require a more thorough showing of due diligence in order to escape liability.[623]

(b) Risk factor disclosure and bespeaking caution

There is increasing emphasis on so-called 'risk factor' disclosure in securities offering materials and in reports, press releases and communications with analysts. In Securities Act registration statements both US and foreign private issuers are required to disclose prominently those significant factors that make the offering speculative or risky.[624] Even companies whose offerings would not be thought of as speculative

623 See Appendix C below for a Sample Checklist for Due Diligence Review in International Securities Offerings.

624 Form S-1 (Regulation S-K, Item 503); Form F-1 (Form 20-F, Item 3.D).

or risky may include a list of risks or uncertainties under the heading "Risk factors". The International Organisation of Securities Commissions standards that the SEC incorporated into Form 20-F[625] call for a discussion of risk factors that are specific to the foreign private issuer or its industry, under the heading "Risk factors", in both Securities Act registrations and Exchange Act registrations and annual reports. This section "is intended to be a summary of more detailed discussion contained elsewhere in the document".[626] Mandatory risk factor discussion in Exchange Act reports was extended to US issuers in 2005 in the SEC's Offering Reform Rules.[627] This formalised the practices of a growing number of established US companies. The management discussion and analysis (MD&A), which addresses "known trends, events and uncertainties", already calls for an analysis of risks not only in public offering registration statements, but also in Exchange Act registrations and reports.[628] The footnotes to financial statements prepared in accordance with US generally accepted accounting principles (GAAP) must contain certain risk factor information, much of which parallels the textual discussion in the MD&A.[629] Additionally, the 2009 amendments to the international financial reporting standards brought risk disclosure requirements closer into line with US GAAP standards.[630]

The US federal courts have also developed the 'bespeaks caution' doctrine, which denies recovery of damages from issuers that, in disseminating prospective or forward-looking information, have adequately described company-specific risks and uncertainties that may prevent the expected results from being achieved.[631] For disclosure of investment risks to afford meaningful protection in litigation, the cautionary statements should be more than simple generalisations. Merely saying that there can be no guarantee of investment reward or issuer success is not enough. Risk disclosures should be specific, clear and precise; they should not be buried or contain information concerning what the company is doing to address the risk. The risks that a reasonable management sees in the issuer's current business climate must be articulated with some degree of specificity. So too must the disclosure of trends and uncertainties in response to the MD&A requirements.

As discussed below, the availability of the statutory safe harbour for forward-looking statements that was added to the Securities Act and the Exchange Act in December 1995 may depend on the issuer having made 'meaningful cautionary statements'.

The bespeaks caution doctrine has been litigated in a number of cases. The

625 See the section on international disclosure standards in "Periodic reporting requirements", as well as Appendix A.

626 Form 20-F, Item 3.D.

627 SEC Release No 33-8591, "Securities Offering Reform," VII-A (July 19 2005).

628 See the section on other disclosure issues in "Periodic reporting requirements".

629 American Institute of Certified Public Accountants, Accounting Standards Division, Statement of Position 94-6 (December 30 1994).

630 International Accounting Standards Board, *IASB Enhances Financial Instruments Disclosures* (March 5 2009).

631 All US federal circuit courts which have considered the doctrine have adopted some form of it. See, for example, *Salzberg v TM Sterling/Austin Associates, Ltd*, 45 F3d 399 (11th Circuit 1995); *In re Worlds of Wonder Sec Litig*, 35 F3d 1407 (9th Circuit 1994), cert denied, 516 US 868 (1995); *In re Donald J Trump Casino Sec Litig*, 7 F3d 357 (3d Circuit 1993), cert denied, 510 US 1178 (1994); see also *Virginia Bankshares, Inc v Sandberg*, 501 US 1083 (1991).

following list provides examples of when courts have addressed this doctrine in securities litigation:

- In the case of *In re Worlds of Wonder* the court ruled in favour of the defendant, WOW, a toy manufacturing company, which had declared bankruptcy within six months of issuing $80 million in high-yield bonds.[632] The court of appeals agreed with the district court's findings that the prospectus "clearly bespoke caution on the serious risks WOW's liquidity crisis posed to investors… Plaintiffs are not entitled to an inference that they were misled in the face of such disclosures". The plaintiffs in the case argued that the prospectus was misleading because WOW omitted key facts, such as the reduction in size of its high-yield bond offering, but the court concluded that such facts were not reasonably foreseeable by WOW.
- In *Livid Holdings* the court reiterated the standard for dismissing a claim based on the bespeaks caution doctrine. There must be cautionary language such that reasonable minds could agree that the statements as a whole were not misleading.[633] The court also expressly denied applying the bespeaks caution doctrine to historical facts in addition to forward-looking statements.[634]
- In *Heller v Goldin* the court read the bespeaks caution doctrine as creating a "reasonable investor" standard of materiality to be applied by the court as a matter of law.[635] In other words, the court reasoned that the doctrine operates such that false or misleading statements may be rendered immaterial when taken in context with cautionary statements and risk disclosures. However, the court failed to apply the doctrine in this case because the bespeaks caution doctrine applies only to forward-looking statements.[636]
- In *Hall v Children's Place Retail Store* Inc the judge denied the defendant the bespeaks caution defence because it found that, due to the large number of material misstatements at issue in the case, it was likely that the defendants were aware that the risks they cautioned against had materialised into reality.[637] Therefore, their statements were not "mere puffery" and the bespeaks caution defence was not applicable.

(c) Plain English

Securities disclosure documents win no awards for literary merit. They are written in part with the aim of making sufficient disclosure of risks and uncertainties to avoid future lawsuits, and lawyers often craft documents that are difficult to read and understand. The SEC has been trying to get issuers and their advisers to write materials that investors can comprehend. It has called its simplification campaign "plain English". Plain English, according to the SEC, includes, among other things:

---

632 *In re Worlds of Wonder Securities Litigation*, 35 F3d 1407 (9th Circuit 1994).

633 *Livid Holdings, Ltd v Salomon Smith Barney, Inc*, 416 F3d 940, 947-948 (9th Circuit 2005).

634 *Id* ("We now expressly adopt the logic of the First and Seventh Circuits and hold that extension of the bespeaks caution doctrine to statements of historical fact is inappropriate").

635 *Heller v Goldin Restructuring Fund*, LP, 590 F Supp 2d 603, 617 (SDNY 2008).

636 *Id* ("[T]he Court notes that the 'bespeaks caution' doctrine only applies to forward-looking statements, and not to misrepresentations of present or historical fact").

637 *Hall v Children's Place Retail Stores, Inc*, 580 F Supp 2d 212, 229 (SDNY 2008).

- short sentences;
- active voice;
- no technical legal terminology; and
- tables or lists whenever possible.

Certain of the SEC rules that govern the form and content of prospectuses in Securities Act registrations were revised in January 1998 to require that the responsive material be written in accordance with the SEC's plain English principles.[638] These rule changes apply specifically to the prospectus front cover page and the summary and risk factor sections of the document, and generally to the entire prospectus.[639] Foreign private issuer registration forms are amended along with comparable forms applicable to US issuers.

The plain English rules have not yet been formally extended to Exchange Act reports (except to the extent that information is incorporated from reports to meet Securities Act risk factor requirements), although companies are urged to apply plain English principles to these materials and the SEC's December 2003 interpretive release recommends a comparable approach to drafting the MD&A.[640] Reactions to inadequate disclosure of risks and uncertainties have stressed the need for simplicity and clarity of presentation, as have the reactions of US federal courts to risk disclosures that (in the words of the Supreme Court) "would take a financial analyst" to understand.[641]

(d) *Use of competent professionals*

Perhaps the best protection for an issuer is the engagement of competent auditors, lawyers, underwriters and placement agents. This is particularly true for foreign private issuers, whose personnel may have limited familiarity with US securities laws.

Although the disclosure contained in public offering registration statements may differ quantitatively and qualitatively from that contained in private placement memoranda,[642] experienced counsel and financial advisers will recommend that private as well as public offering documents include all material financial and business information.

(e) *Indemnification*

Securities firms acting as underwriters of public offerings or as dealers or placement agents in private offerings typically extract indemnification agreements from issuers. These agreements obligate the issuer to defend securities litigation brought against the securities firm on account of misstatements or omissions by the issuer in its offering materials and to hold the firm harmless against ensuing damage awards.

---

638 SEC Release No 33-7497, "Plain English Disclosure" (January 28 1998).

639 Securities Act Rule 421.

640 SEC Release Nos 33-8350 and 34-48960, "Interpretation: Commission Guidance Regarding Management's Discussion and Analysis of Financial Condition Results of Operations", III-A (December 19 2003).

641 *Virginia Bankshares, Inc v Sandberg*, 501 US 1083 (1991).

642 As discussed in the section on disclosure in "Private placements".

Indemnification by the issuer of its directors, officers and controlling persons against securities law liabilities is another matter. The rules governing indemnification vary by state. Many states provide for indemnification of officers or directors in the event that they successfully defend against an action for wrongful conduct in their performance of duties for the corporation.[643] An issuer's certificate of incorporation may, in some cases, actually require indemnification for officers or directors.[644] Indemnification agreements may also provide for the advancement of legal fees before an action has been resolved.[645]

In some cases indemnification is available even where the director does not prevail on the merits, if the court finds that the director acted in good faith and for the benefit of the corporation.[646] Alternatively, even if claims are settled successfully, indemnification might not be available where the court determines that the officer did not act in good faith.[647] The issue of good faith is therefore central to whether an officer or director can receive indemnification. In many states, such as Delaware, the requirement of good faith for officer and director indemnification cannot be contractually altered.[648] The SEC has historically taken the position that indemnification of directors and officers for violation of US securities laws is against public policy and unenforceable, and, as a condition to granting an issuer's request for effectiveness of its registration statement in a public offering, requires the issuer to give an undertaking that, unless the director or officer successfully defends against any suit for which indemnification is sought, the issuer will submit to an appropriate court the question of whether such indemnification is against public policy and will be governed by the final adjudication of such question. Accordingly, directors and officers should not rely entirely on an issuer's indemnification provisions with respect to violations of US securities laws.[649]

(f) *Insurance*

The SEC's policy against issuer indemnification of its directors and officers (D&O) generally does not extend to insurance afforded by regular insurance companies, even though the issuer may have paid the premium. The insurance industry in the United States offers so-called 'D&O liability' policies, insuring directors and officers

643 *Sequa Corp v Gelmin*, 828 F Supp 203, 205 (SDNY 1993).

644 See, for example, *Vergopia v Shaker*, 922 A2d 1238 (NJ 2007).

645 See, for example, Delaware Code Annotated Tit 8 §145 (e) ("Expenses (including attorneys' fees) incurred by an officer or director of the corporation in defending any civil, criminal, administrative or investigative action, suit or proceeding may be paid by the corporation in advance of the final disposition of such action, suit or proceeding upon receipt of an undertaking by or on behalf of such director or officer to repay such amount if it shall ultimately be determined that such person is not entitled to be indemnified by the corporation as authorized in this section").

646 *Owens Corning v National Union Fire Ins Co*, 257 F3d 484, 494 (6th Circuit 2001) ("Mandatory indemnification for defense expenses occurs when the director is 'successful on the merits or otherwise' in defense of the action brought against him. § 145(c). Permissive indemnification may occur, if the corporation so chooses, for the costs imposed on directors who have been determined to have acted in good faith. §§ 145(a), (b)").

647 *Owens Corning v National Union Fire Ins Co*, 257 F3d 484 (6th Circuit 2001).

648 *Id* at 494 (6th Circuit 2001) ("The requirement of good faith on the part of the directors indemnified under §§ 145(a), (b) however, is statutory, and cannot be waived by attempting to extend indemnification even further").

649 Form F-1, Item 5 (Regulation S-K, Item 510).

of publicly traded corporations against a variety of risks arising out of their service as part of corporate management.

There are three types of D&O insurance schemes:

- insurance for managers against shareholders' derivative lawsuits (Side A coverage);
- insurance to cover corporate indemnification obligations (Side B coverage); and
- insurance for the corporation against lawsuits (Side C coverage).

Corporations typically purchase an insurance package with a mix of coverage, which has the overall effect of shifting the risk of litigation from the corporation to the third-party insurance provider.[650] In some states corporations are even allowed to insure against losses for which indemnification is not available.[651]

7.5 Jurisdiction of US courts

A foreign private issuer offering its securities in the United States or having its securities traded in the US capital markets is subject to suit for violations of US securities laws, just as a US issuer would be. So too are the foreign private issuer's directors, officers and controlling shareholders.

There are differences between foreign private and US issuers and their management in terms of practical exposure to securities law litigation risks. The SEC requires that these differences be summarised in the foreign private issuer's public offering prospectus under the Securities Act. Typically, they are described as set forth in Appendix G below.[652]

The US Supreme Court has determined that, in order to be liable under the Exchange Act, a corporation must either issue securities on a US exchange or engage in domestic transactions with securities in the United States.[653]

Therefore, subject-matter jurisdiction (the right of a court to hear a complaint against a person/entity) does not extend extra-territorially with respect to securities fraud claims.

In June 2010 the US Supreme Court ruled in *Morrison v National Australia Bank, Ltd* that Section 10(b) of the Exchange Act did not apply in private actions involving a foreign plaintiff, a foreign defendant and securities purchased on a foreign exchange, even if there was some domestic impact or effect. However, a few weeks later, the Dodd-Frank Act was enacted. This act provides for US jurisdiction over

650 Sean J Griffith, "Uncovering a Gatekeeper: Why the SEC Should Mandate Disclosure of Details Concerning Directors' and Officers' Liability Insurance Policies", 154 *University of Pennsylvania Law Review* 1147, 1168 (2006).

651 See, for example, Delaware Code Annotated Tit 8, §145(g) ("A corporation shall have power to purchase and maintain insurance on behalf of any person who is or was a director, officer, employee or agent of the corporation, or is or was serving at the request of the corporation as a director, officer, employee or agent of another corporation, partnership, joint venture, trust or other enterprise against any liability asserted against such person and incurred by such person in any such capacity, or arising out of such person's status as such, whether or not the corporation would have the power to indemnify such person against such liability under this section").

652 See Regulation S-K, Item 101(g). Information may appear in response to Form 20-F, Item 3D.

653 *Morrison v National Australia Bank*, 130 S Ct 2869 (2010).

actions brought by the SEC (not private litigants) under the Exchange Act's anti-fraud provisions for foreign securities transactions, where the defendant took "significant steps" in the United States to further the fraud violation or if the foreign misconduct had a "foreseeable substantial effect" in the United States.[654]

7.6 Private Securities Litigation Reform Act of 1995

The Private Securities Litigation Reform Act amended both the Securities Act and the Exchange Act[655] in response to complaints – from issuers and their managements, from investment banking firms and from auditors and other securities professionals – that the private litigation system was being abused by plaintiffs and their attorneys to the point of creating an undue hazard. The Private Securities Litigation Reform Act amendments adopted a number of procedural safeguards, placed certain limits on damages and created a safe harbour for 'forward-looking statements'[656] (defined in the same way that the SEC defines 'forward-looking information'[657]).

(a) Procedural changes

The Private Securities Litigation Reform Act introduced a number of provisions calculated to reduce the frequency of lawsuits that are brought – without a reasonable basis in law or fact – for the purpose of forcing monetary settlements with the plaintiffs in order to avoid extensive litigation costs and the unpredictability of jury verdicts.

Race to the courthouse and professional plaintiffs: Formerly, courts ceded substantial control of securities litigation to the lawyers representing plaintiffs on a first come, first served basis. This rewarded plaintiffs' lawyers who used captive nominal or 'professional' plaintiffs to file the first complaint. Now, the first plaintiff to sue must notify the affected class of securities holders. The court will apply a statutory presumption that the plaintiff with the largest financial stake in the litigation should have control of the lawsuit. This reform is intended to shift control of litigation from the plaintiffs' bar to institutional investors, at least in the absence of conflicts that would render an institutional investor unsuitable to represent the class.[658]

Pleading fraud: Under Federal Rule of Civil Procedure 9(b), plaintiffs "must state with particularity the circumstances constituting fraud". Similarly, under the Private Securities Litigation Reform Act , "the complaint shall specify each statement alleged to have been misleading, the reason or reasons why the statement is misleading, and, if an allegation regarding the statement or omission is made on information and belief, the complaint shall state with particularity all facts on which that belief is formed".[659] The heightened pleading standards are designed to winnow out unwarranted claims of fraud.

---

654 Public Law 111-203.
655 Securities Act §27; Exchange Act §21D.
656 Securities Act §27A; Exchange Act §21E.
657 See the section on other disclosure issues in "Periodic reporting requirements".
658 Securities Act §27(a)(3); Exchange Act §21D(a).

Scienter standard: Plaintiffs must allege particular facts evidencing the requisite scienter or knowledge and guilty mind element of the crime. The statute specifically requires that the complaint "state with particularity facts giving rise to a strong inference that the defendant acted with the required state of mind".[660] In the groundbreaking *Tellabs* case, the US Supreme Court interpreted the 'strong inference' standard strictly, requiring that the inference of fraudulent intent be "at least as compelling as any opposing inference of non-fraudulent intent".[661] Although various US circuit courts of appeal have interpreted the requisite guilty mind standard differently, generally, plaintiffs attempt to show scienter by pleading facts showing that a defendant consciously misbehaved or acted with recklessness.[662] It is clear that the Supreme Court's interpretation of a "strong inference" will make defending against securities litigation easier for corporations.

Loss causation: The Private Securities Litigation Reform Act holds that a private plaintiff bringing a securities action must prove that the defendant's fraudulent acts were responsible for the loss for which he or she now seeks to recover.[663] To establish loss causation, a plaintiff must plead and prove that the value of the security declined "after the truth became known".[664] Typically, this is done by pointing to a "corrective disclosure", which reveals the truth and causes a subsequent drop in the security's value. Thus, "[a]ny reliable theory of loss causation that uses corrective disclosures will have to show both that corrective information was revealed and that this revelation caused the resulting decline in price".[665]

The discovery stay: The Private Securities Litigation Reform Act curbs discovery to prevent plaintiffs' lawyers from embarking on abusive and costly fishing expeditions, which frequently forced companies to settle frivolous securities class actions. Now, whenever a defendant requests dismissal of a complaint, a court must stay all discovery except in extraordinary circumstances, such as to preserve the testimony of a terminally ill witness. Discovery may resume only if the court decides that the complaint sufficiently alleges a claim for the lawsuit to proceed.[666]

---

659 Exchange Act §21D(b)(1).

660 Exchange Act §21D(b)(2).

661 *Tellabs, Inc v Makor Issues & Rights, Ltd*, 551 US 308, 314 (2007).

662 See *ATSI Commc'ns, Inc v The Shaar Fund, Ltd*, 493 F 3d 87, 99 (2d Circuit 2007) (plaintiffs can also plead scienter by pleading facts showing motive and opportunity); *Ottmann v Hanger Orthopedic Group, Inc*, 353 F 3d 338, 343-44 (4th Circuit 2003) (plaintiffs must show that the defendant actually had the "intent to deceive, manipulate, or defraud" or acted with "severe recklessness", which in the context of a securities fraud case means "an act so highly unreasonable and such an extreme departure from the standard of ordinary care as to present a danger of misleading the plaintiff to the extent that the danger was either known to the defendant or so obvious that the defendant must have been aware of it"); *In re Silicon Graphics Litig v McCracken*, 183 F 3d 970, 974 (9th Circuit 1999) ("We hold that a private securities plaintiff proceeding under the [Private Securities Litigation Reform Act] must plead, in great detail, facts that constitute strong circumstantial evidence of deliberately reckless or conscious misconduct"); *Bryant v Avado Brands, Inc*, 187 F 3d 1271, 1287 (11th Circuit 1999) ("[w]e hold that a complaint alleging with particularity that a defendant acted with a severely reckless state of mind still suffices to state a claim for civil liability under §10(b) and Rule 10b-5").

663 Exchange Act §21D(b)(4).

664 *Dura Pharms, Inc v Broudo*, 544 US 336, 347 (2005).

665 *In re Williams Securities Litigation*, 558 F 3d 1130, 1140 (10th Circuit 2009).

666 Securities Act §§27(b), 27A(f); Exchange Act §§21D(b), 21E(f).

Fee shifting: The Private Securities Litigation Reform Act requires courts to scrutinise closely filings at the conclusion of securities class actions and provides that sanctions, including costs and attorneys' fees, may be awarded against parties making improper, unwarranted or frivolous filings.[667]

Fee caps: Plaintiff attorneys' fee awards are limited to a reasonable percentage of the amount paid to the class.[668]

(b) ***Damage awards***

The Private Securities Litigation Reform Act amendments place certain limitations on the damages that can be awarded in securities lawsuits.

Proportionate liability: Under the prior rule of joint and several liability, a defendant that was only 1% liable could be responsible for paying 100% of the damages with no recourse against insolvent co-defendants that were 99% at fault. Such liability created coercive pressure to settle even wholly meritless claims and discouraged people from serving on corporation boards. The act's fair share rule limits a defendant's liability to the defendant's proportionate share of the damages in a claim under the Exchange Act.[669] It also extends to outside directors in a claim under Section 11 arising from a registered public offering.[670]

Exception: The fair share rule cannot be invoked by persons that knowingly violate the securities laws, or against smaller investors (with a net worth of less than $200,000) that suffer significant damages (more than 10% of their net worth).[671]

(c) ***Safe harbour provisions***

The discussion of other disclosure issues in "Periodic reporting requirements" highlights some of the circumstances in which issuers may find it necessary or expedient to disclose prospective or forward-looking information. Whether prospective disclosure is mandatory or optional, issuers can be exposed to claims that their predictions of future developments were fraudulent or reckless if actual results turn out to be materially different from those forecasted.

The safe harbour provisions that the Private Securities Litigation Reform Act added to the Securities Act and the Exchange Act afford protection from liability under those acts where either of the following tests is satisfied:

- Test 1 – the challenged statement:
  - is a forward-looking statement that is identified as such when made; and
  - is accompanied by "meaningful cautionary statements identifying important factors that could cause actual results to differ materially from those in the forward-looking statement" (or, in the case of oral forward-

---

667 Securities Act §27(c); Exchange Act §21D(c).
668 Exchange Act §21D(a)(6).
669 Exchange Act §21D(f).
670 Securities Act §11(f)(2).
671 Exchange Act §21D(f)(4).

looking statements, states that actual results may differ materially and identifies a "readily available" document that contains such "meaningful cautionary statements").

In order to meet the test of meaningful cautionary statements, the forward-looking statements may not be vague, boilerplate or generic from disclosure to disclosure.[672]

- Test 2 – the challenged statement is a forward-looking statement and the plaintiff fails to prove that it was made with actual knowledge that it was false or misleading (or, in the case of a business entity, that it was made by or with the approval of an executive officer of the entity with such actual knowledge).

Some courts have ruled that the safe harbour defence applies where either of the two tests is satisfied.[673] Other courts find that the actual knowledge component is relevant even where the first test has been satisfied; that is, if cautionary statements are made with knowledge that the statements were misleading, they are not immune under the safe harbour defence.[674] Another unsettled question is whether courts may grant motions to dismiss based on the first test of the safe harbour defence at the pleading stage before discovery.[675]

The statutory safe harbour is available only where the issuer is subject to the ongoing reporting requirements of the Exchange Act. In other words, a foreign private issuer availing itself of Rule 12g3-2(b)[676] would be unable to use it. There are several other exceptions to the coverage of the safe harbour, two of which are particularly significant:

- It does not apply to forward-looking statements made in connection with initial public offerings that are registered under the Securities Act; and
- It does not apply to forward-looking statements included in financial statements prepared in accordance with US GAAP.

It has become common for issuers reporting under the Exchange Act to include language in their registrations and reports that is designed to satisfy the first of these two tests. Consequently, the safe harbour defence has become a frequent point of contention in securities fraud cases.[677] Early cautionary statements tended to be brief

---

672 *Slayton v American Express Co*, 604 F 3d 758 (2nd Circuit 2010).

673 *Beaver County Ret Bd v LCA-Vision Inc*, No 1:07-CV-750, 2009 WL 806714, at 14 (SD Ohio March 25 2009); *Miller v Champion Enters, Inc*, 346 F 3d 660, 672 (6th Circuit 2003); see also Allan Horwich, "Cleaning the Murky Safe Harbor for Forward-Looking Statements: An Inquiry into Whether Actual Knowledge of Falsity Precludes the Meaningful Cautionary Statement Defense", 35 *Iowa Journal of Corporate Law* 519, 539-546 (2010).

674 *Freeland v Iridium World Communications, Ltd*, 545 F Supp 2d 59 (DDC 2008); In *re Seebeyond Techs Corp* Sec Litig, 266 F Supp 2d 1150, 1164-65 (CD Cal 2003).

675 Compare *Harris v Ivax Corp*, 182 F 3d 799 (11th Circuit 1999) with *Asher v Baxter Int'l Inc*, 377 F 3d 727 (7th Circuit 2004).

676 See "Periodic reporting requirements" for discussion of Rule 12g3-2(b).

677 Wendy Gerwick Couture, "White Collar Crime's Gray Area: The Anomaly of Criminalizing Conduct not Civilly Actionable", 72 *Albany Law Review* 1, 13-14 (2009) ("For instance, out of a set of 248 civil securities fraud opinions issued by federal district courts in 2006 and 2007, the safe harbor was analyzed at least sixty-seven times. In other words, the court addressed the safe harbor in twenty-seven percent of the opinions.").

and uninformative. Increasingly, the corporate community has been giving more detailed descriptions of company-specific risks in order to provide meaningful caution.

The Private Securities Litigation Reform Act safe harbour is not intended to replace the bespeaks caution doctrine that has been developed by the courts and is discussed above.[678] That doctrine may be pleaded as a defence not only by issuers that are subject to Exchange Act reporting requirements, but also by issuers such as those using Rule 12g3-2(b) or seeking protection for forward-looking statements that are statutorily excluded from the safe harbour.

Since the Private Securities Litigation Reform Act was enacted in 1995, the number of securities class actions has decreased.[679] Some commentators attribute this to the success of the safe harbour provision at protecting issuers against liability.

7.7 State law risks

The Private Securities Litigation Reform Act did not address the various civil liability statutes and rules of the individual states. These civil liability laws are potentially more of a concern than the state regulatory or 'blue-sky' laws mentioned in the "Introduction" above, although historically the federal civil liability laws have presented by far the more serious litigation problem. There are state liability provisions that parallel such federal provisions as Rule 10b-5, and there are others that purport to create liability for conduct ranging from recklessness to negligence. State courts have traditionally been less receptive than federal courts to securities class actions. Nevertheless, the plaintiffs' bar has attempted to avoid the application of the Private Securities Litigation Reform Act by filing suits in state courts instead of federal courts or, in some instances, by filing parallel proceedings in state and federal courts.

The Securities Litigation Uniform Standards Act of 1998 was designed to curtail this use of state courts as a forum for litigation alleging securities fraud. Any such claims involving 50 or more investors must now be brought in US federal court if they relate to nationally traded securities. The Supreme Court has given this act a broad interpretation in view of Congress's intention to stop avoidance of the Private Securities Litigation Reform Act.[680]

7.8 Bases for criminal liability

Foreign private issuers of securities in the United States should be aware that, in addition to civil liability risks, they also face potential criminal liability. Corporate criminal law is expansive and includes both state and federal penalties. Additionally, under US law both the corporation itself and employees face the threat of criminal sanction.

(a) Exposure to criminal liability

Corporate entity: Where officers or agents within the corporation engage in

---

678 Conference Committee Rep No 104-369, 104th Cong, 1st Sess (1995).
679 Cornerstone Research, *Securities Class Action Case Filings, 2007: A Year in Review 20* (2007).
680 *Merrill Lynch, Pierce, Fenner & Smith, Inc v Dabit*, 547 US 71 (2006).

criminal behaviour, they may create liability for the corporation itself. Under the *respondeat superior* doctrine, courts generally hold the corporation liable where the officer's or agent's conduct falls within the scope of his or her employment and is performed, at least in part, for the benefit of the corporation.[681]

In practice, prosecutors do not always choose to charge corporations with criminal conduct, even when it is within their power to do so. Prosecutors sometimes threaten to prosecute a corporation in order to obtain cooperation in investigations against key offenders.[682] In 1999 the DOJ issued a memorandum to prosecutors, known as the Holder memorandum, outlining the factors that should be taken into account when determining whether to charge a corporation with criminal activity.[683] Since that time these factors have evolved and have been codified in the US Attorneys' Manual.[684] The nine factors prosecutors are instructed to consider are:

- the nature and seriousness of the offence, including the risk of harm to the public, and applicable policies and priorities, if any, governing the prosecution of corporations for particular categories of crime;
- the pervasiveness of wrongdoing within the corporation, including complicity in, or the condoning of, the wrongdoing by corporate management;
- the corporation's history of similar misconduct, including prior criminal, civil and regulatory enforcement actions against it;
- the corporation's timely and voluntary disclosure of wrongdoing and its willingness to cooperate in the investigation of its agents;
- the existence and effectiveness of the corporation's pre-existing compliance programme;
- the corporation's remedial actions, including any efforts to implement an effective corporate compliance programme or to improve an existing one, to replace responsible management, to discipline or terminate wrongdoers, to pay restitution and to cooperate with the relevant government agencies;
- collateral consequences, including whether there is disproportionate harm to shareholders, pension holders, employees and others not proven personally culpable, as well as the impact of the prosecutions on the public;
- the adequacy of the prosecution of individuals responsible for the corporation's malfeasance; and
- the adequacy of remedies such as civil or regulatory enforcement actions.[685]

The DOJ has consistently noted that a corporation's willingness to cooperate with the government should factor into the decision over whether to charge it.[686] The DOJ may no longer request corporations to waive their attorney-client privilege or

681 *NY Central & Hudson River RR Co v US*, 212 US 481 (1909).

682 Daniel Richman, "Decisions About Coercion: The Corporate Attorney-Client Privilege Waiver Problem", 57 *DePaul Law Review* 295, 322–23 (2008).

683 Memorandum from Eric Holder, Deputy US Attorney General, to All Component Heads and United States Attorneys (June 16 1999).

684 United States Attorneys' Manual, "Principles of Federal Prosecution of Business Organizations" (2008).

685 *Id.*

work-product protection as a precondition to cooperation. Nevertheless, the corporation may waive its right to advance legal fees to its employees under investigation; the prosecution is free to consider this when evaluating the corporation's cooperation.[687] This may create pressure on the corporation to sell out its employees in order to avoid prosecution.

Compliance programmes and good-faith defences: Many corporations attempt to cope with liability risks by adopting codes of conduct, which instruct their employees how to stay within the boundaries of the law. However, these codes do not necessarily mitigate a corporation's risk of liability. Moreover, a corporation may be found liable even where the guilty employee's conduct violates corporate policy.[688] Yet courts do routinely take such programmes into account when making a determination on the good-faith defence under the controlling-persons provisions of the Securities Act and the Exchange Act.[689] The ability of a compliance programme to meet the good-faith defence depends in part on the adequacy of the compliance programme in place and the diligence of those in charge of implementing its procedures.[690] In general, it is always good business practice to maintain a thorough compliance programme and to ensure that employees understand their obligations under the law.

On November 1 2010 the US Sentencing Guidelines Manual, which provides guidance on sentencing in US federal courts, was amended. Among the amendments are reduced sentences for corporations that can demonstrate the existence of a compliance and ethics programme at the time of the criminal conduct, despite the participation or knowledge of high-level personnel in the offence.[691] Corporations must also meet four additional criteria for this reduced sentence:

- The individuals responsible for the compliance and ethics programme have direct reporting obligations to the corporation's governing board of directors or an appropriate sub-committee;
- The offence was discovered by the compliance and ethics programme before it could be discovered outside the corporation;
- The corporation properly reported the offensive conduct to appropriate government authorities; and

---

686 Memorandum from Eric Holder, Deputy Attorney General, to All Component Heads and United States Attorneys (June 16 1999); Memorandum from Larry D Thompson, Deputy Attorney General, to All Component Heads and Unites States Attorneys, Principles of Federal Prosecution of Business Organizations (January 23 2003); Memorandum from Paul J McNulty, Deputy Attorney General, to Heads of Department Components (December 12 2006).

687 Philip Kushner, "Internal Investigations: What is at Stake for Employers and Employees?" 34 Champion 38, 39 (April 2010).

688 *Kravitz v Pressman, Frohlich & Frost, Inc*, 447 F Supp 203, 213 (D Massachusetts 1978) (despite accountability mechanisms in place, the employee's conduct should have attracted the attention of managers).

689 See, for example, *Carpenter v Harris, Upham & Co*, 594 F 2d 388, 394-95 (4th Circuit 1987).

690 See *Haynes v Anderson & Strudwick, Inc*, 508 F Supp 1303 (D Virginia 1981) ("Of course, the courts will also want to take other circumstances into account, such as the egregiousness of the violation, its duration, the agent's experience with the company, evidence of lax applications of safeguards and the like").

691 See 2010 Federal Sentencing Guidelines Manual & Supplement, United States Sentencing Commission, §8c2.5(f).

- No individual with operational responsibility for the compliance and ethics programme was a participant in, condoned or was wilfully ignorant of the offence.

This amendment provides further incentive for corporations to establish compliance programmes.

Personal liability: Individuals within a corporation may be held personally and severally liable for crimes directly or indirectly committed in the course of their employment. An individual is liable for any direct participation in a criminal act, regardless of whether it was done for the benefit of the corporation.[692] There is no difference under the law for a criminal act committed for a corporation and one committed outside the scope of employment.[693] Individuals are also liable for crimes in which they aid and abet.[694]

Corporate officers are generally not liable for the criminal actions of the corporation. However, this is subject to important limitations and exceptions. For certain strict liability public welfare crimes, corporate officers and directors may be held liable for crimes committed by others within the corporation, even when they had no knowledge of wrongdoing.[695] This is known as the 'responsible corporate officer doctrine', whereby criminal liability for corporate officers is imposed merely because the officer had control over the department in which the criminal conduct occurred. This doctrine is usually applied only to public welfare offences. However, some state legislators have codified this doctrine into law and some judges have applied it with respect to civil law claims.[696]

In response to the threat of personal liability, many corporations include provisions in their certificate of incorporation that explicitly limit liability for corporate officers and directors. Most states allow for the enforcement of such provisions, with certain limitations. For example, Delaware, the most common state of incorporation, does not allow any limitation of liability for a breach of fiduciary duty, any acts or omissions not performed in good faith and transactions that involve a personal benefit for the director. Corporations may also provide for insurance or indemnification.[697]

Current trends in criminal enforcement: In response to the global credit crisis since 2007, the US government has acted more aggressively with respect to corporate criminal

---

692 *Commissioner v RLG, Inc*, 755 NE 2d 556, 560 (Indiana 2001).

693 *Butts v Com*, 581 SW 2d 565 (Kentucky 1979).

694 See 18 USC §2 (this general statute provides liability for aiding and abetting for all crimes unless otherwise indicated by statute).

695 See, for example, *US v Park*, 421 US 658 (1975) ("Moreover, the principle had been recognized that a corporate agent, through whose act, default, or omission the corporation committed a crime, was himself guilty individually of that crime. The principle had been applied whether or not the crime required 'consciousness of wrongdoing' and it had been applied not only to those corporate agents who themselves committed the criminal act, but also to those who by virtue of their managerial positions or similar relation to the actor could be deemed responsible for its commission").

696 *Commissioner v RLG, Inc*, 755 NE 2d 556, 560 (Indiana 2001).

697 See the section on coping with civil liability risks in this chapter above.

prosecution. In November 2009 President Obama created an interagency taskforce to combat corporate fraud.[698] This agency is headed by the DOJ, which works in conjunction with a number of other agencies, including the SEC and the US Treasury. Criminal enforcement of securities fraud is likely to increase under the taskforce.[699]

(b) *Liability under the Exchange Act and Securities Act*

The penalties provision of the Exchange Act provide for criminal sanctions against anyone that wilfully violates any provision of this act or any rule or regulation therein.[700] Notably, it sanctions the conduct of one that "willfully and knowingly makes, or causes to be made, any statement in any application, report, or document…[which is] false or misleading with respect to any material fact". This act authorises punishment of up to $5 million in fines or 20 years in prison, or both, and $25 million in fines for the corporate entity.

Similarly, the Securities Act also criminalises the making of "an untrue statement of a material fact" or omission. This act provides penalties of up to $10,000 in fines, five years in prison or both.[701]

Unlike civil lawsuits under the Exchange Act and the Securities Act, there is no safe harbour defence for criminal prosecutions. Further, unlike civil complaints, a criminal indictment need not state facts with particularity according to the Private Securities Litigation Reform Act's pleading standards. This means that there is a range of conduct for which a corporation could incur criminal, but not civil liability.

(c) *Mail and wire fraud*

The mail and wire fraud statutes, including Section 10(b) of the Exchange Act, are federal criminal provisions that are broad enough to ensnare a host of unsuspecting activity, including securities fraud. These statutes generally criminalise conduct involving:

- the existence of a scheme to defraud;
- using or causing the use of the mail or wires to execute the scheme; and
- with a specific intent to defraud.[702]

Charging securities fraud under the mail and wire fraud statutes is particularly appealing to prosecutors, because the materiality requirement for a false statement is significantly less stringent than the requirement under securities laws.

Additionally, actions that traditionally fall under the definition of 'insider trading' can be prosecuted under the mail and wire fraud statutes under the theory that the defrauded property was the right to exclusive use of confidential information.[703]

---

698 Exec Order 13519, "Establishment of the Financial Fraud Enforcement Task Force" (2009).

699 Eric Holder, US attorney general, address at the Financial Fraud Enforcement Task Force Press Conference (November 17 2009) ("We will be relentless in our investigation of corporate and financial wrongdoing, and will not hesitate to bring charges, where appropriate, for criminal misconduct on the part of businesses and business executives").

700 Exchange Act §32(a).

701 Securities Act §24.

702 18 USC §1341; 18 USC §1343.

(d) Insider trading

Section 10(b) of the Exchange Act and Rule 10b-5 thereunder have been interpreted to create a prohibition on trading on material non-public information. Corporate insiders are under an affirmative obligation to disclose information concerning their trading in securities,[704] and are also prohibited from giving tips to others concerning inside information, even in vague terms. Additionally, even non-corporate insiders are obligated either to disclose material non-public information before trading in securities or to refrain from trading on the information altogether. In order to prosecute an individual for insider trading, the information must be non-public and material.

The duty to disclose or abstain from trading is contingent on a fiduciary relationship between the source of the information and the individual trading on it.[705] The person receiving the inside information (the tippee) may be held liable even in the absence of a fiduciary duty, if he or she knew or should have known that the person providing the information (the tipper) had breached his or her fiduciary duty.[706] Moreover, courts have expanded the concept of insider trading under the misappropriation theory, holding that even temporary insiders are guilty of insider trading insofar as their actions breached a duty to the source of the information.[707]

To avoid prosecution for insider trading, some corporations have chosen to develop internal codes of conduct, as described below:

- Chinese walls are designed to prevent information access within a firm.
- 'Restricted lists' are lists of securities that corporate employees are prohibited from trading because the corporation may be in possession of non-public information.
- 'Watch lists' are monitoring devices alerting the corporation that a certain security may need to be placed soon on a restricted list.
- 'Rumour lists' are functionally similar to watch lists, but are not limited to the issuers that the corporation is doing business with and include potential business partners.

Although rigorous compliance programmes are desirable to prevent employee misconduct, they do not provide a shield for corporate criminal liability.

The Insider Trading and Securities Fraud Enforcement Act of 1988 requires public corporations to create programmes and mechanisms to prevent employee insider trading.[708] Every public corporation must put in place policies and procedures to prevent the misuse of material, non-public information, and these policies must be updated and enforced regularly.

The SEC is also authorised to seek injunctive relief when it has reason to believe that an individual is engaged or about to engage in insider trading. The SEC is vested with the power to change personnel, bar guilty persons from serving as an officer,

---

703 *Carpenter v US*, 484 US 19 (1987).
704 *In re Cady, Roberts & Co*, 40 SEC 907, 911 (1961).
705 *Chiarella v US*, 445 US 227, 235 (1980).
706 *Dirks v SEC*, 463 US 646, 659-660 (1983).
707 *United States v O'Hagan*, 521 US 642 (1997).
708 Exchange Act §20A-21A and Investment Advisers Act §204A.

director or investment adviser, or seek the disgorgement of profits gained as a result of insider trading.

An interesting example of insider trading by foreign individuals is one in which a partner in a prominent Mexico City law firm representing Prodigy Communications Corporation's owner (Telmex, ultimately owned by Carlos Slim Helú, who topped the 2010 Forbes list of world billionaires) in the SBC Communications Inc acquisition of a large interest in Prodigy back in November 22 1999. This partner tipped his best friend, a banker, and his brother-in-law, a securities law author, about the transaction. The two tippees purchased Prodigy shares using offshore funds and sold these shares for substantial profits following the announcement of the Prodigy-SBC transaction. They then transferred $148,300 to the partner's offshore trust as a kickback.

In December 2002 the US District Court for the Southern District of New York entered final judgments against the lawyer and the author for insider trading. The defendants consented to the judgments without admitting or denying the allegations and were permanently barred from violating Section 10(b) of the Exchange Act and Rule 10b-5 thereunder. In addition, the court ordered the partner to pay $182,895 in disgorgement and pre-judgment interest and a $57,105 civil penalty, and the author to pay $25,375 in disgorgement and pre-judgment interest and a $7,925 civil penalty.[709]

The SEC and the DOJ have become increasingly concerned with prosecuting violations of insider trading. Consequences for violations are substantial. Not only may an individual be found guilty of securities fraud, but he or she may also be found guilty under the mail and wire fraud statutes, as well as under the Insider Trading and Securities Fraud Enforcement Act of 1988. Corporations whose employees are under investigation for insider trading may be forced to make early disclosure of non-public information and the corporation's stock price may also be affected.

(e) *Sarbanes-Oxley Act*

The Sarbanes-Oxley Act added various civil and criminal liability provisions:

- Section 302 and Section 906 of the act, known as the certification provisions, require officers of the corporation to certify that all regulatory filings with the SEC are accurate.[710] The purpose of these provisions is to create a tie between the SEC filings and the executives who oversee them, to reduce the likelihood that corporations will release false or misleading statements. These provisions also make it difficult for executives to deny that they were aware of false or misleading information that was submitted to the SEC, and provide direct criminal penalties for executive violations. Knowing violations can result in up to 10 years in prison and $1 million in fines.[711] Wilful violations can result in up to 20 years in prison and $5 million in fines.[712] However, Sections 302 and 906 do not apply to the interim reports filed by foreign private issuers,

709 SEC Litigation Release No 17903, "Mexican Traders in Prodigy Insider Trading Case To Pay $273,300 in Settlement With SEC" (December 19 2002).
710 15 USC §7201 *et seq.*
711 18 USC §1350(c)(1).
712 18 USC §1350(c)(1).

such as Form 6-K.[713]

- Section 802 creates criminal liability for obstructing or impeding a federal court, agency or congressional proceeding by altering or destroying documents or records in any way with the specific intent to obstruct.[714] Penalties include a fine and/or imprisonment for up to 20 years. This provision is very broad and reaches individuals who direct others to alter documents, as well as those that make the physical alterations. Companies should be extremely careful about maintaining their documents, particularly when they are under investigation.
- Section 807 of the act amended the mail fraud statute criminalising th obtaining, by false or fraudulent purposes, of money or property in connection with the sale or purchase of a security.[715] Penalties under this provision, include a fine or a prison sentence of up to 25 years. Under this provision prosecutors have slightly more flexibility because they need not prove that the fraud was conducted wilfully.[716]
- Section 902 creates new crimes for those that attempt or conspire to commit fraud (including securities fraud).[717] The punishment for those found guilty of conspiracy or attempt is the same as that for the underlying offence.
- Section 1102 creates liability for those that obstruct by threatening, coercing or killing an individual.[718]
- Sarbanes-Oxley includes protection for whistleblowers, employees who provide the government with truthful company information concerning a possible violation of the law. Under Section 1107 it is a felony to take harmful action towards a whistleblower.[719] This crime carries a penalty of up to 10 years in prison.

(f) Foreign Corrupt Practices Act

The Foreign Corrupt Practices Act[720] was enacted in 1977 to combat bribery of foreign officials by US businesses, which was considered widespread and systemic in the 1970s.[721] The act has two fundamental components: the anti-bribery provisions[722] and the accounting provisions.[723]

---

713 SEC Release No 33-8124, "Certification of Disclosure in Companies' Quarterly and Annual Reports" (August 29 2002).

714 18 USC §1519.

715 18 USC §1348.

716 James K Robinson and Scott T Lashway, *The Sarbanes-Oxley Act of 2002: A Brief Summary of the New Professional Responsibility Obligations for Securities Attorneys, New Criminal Provisions, & Reforms to the Sentencing Guidelines, American Bar Association, Committee on Criminal Litigation 7-8* (2003).

717 18 USC §1349.

718 18 USC §1512.

719 18 USC §1513(e).

720 See Kevin Abikoff, *Corporate Governance: Avoiding and Responding to Misconduct*, New York: Law Journal Press (2009).

721 *Ibid*, §§18.01-02 (2009).

722 See Exchange Act §30A and Foreign Corrupt Practices Act §104, §104A (codified at 15 USC §78dd-1(a) §78dd-2(a), §78dd-3(a)).

723 See Exchange Act §13(b)(2)(A) (codified at 15 USC §78m(b)(2)(A) (the books and records provisions) and Exchange Act §13(b)(2)(B) (codified at 15 USC §78m(b)(2)(B) (the internal accounting control provisions).

Anti-bribery provisions: In general, the act's anti-bribery provisions criminalise the direct or indirect payment or promise of bribes to foreign officials that are intended to assist the person or entity that pays or promises any such bribe in obtaining or retaining business. Specifically, the anti-bribery provisions prohibit a person or entity from:

- making a payment, gift, offer or promise to pay, or authorising a payment;
- of money or anything of value;
- with corrupt intent;
- to a foreign government official,[724] a foreign political party, a candidate for a foreign political office or to any person while knowing that such person will provide the money or thing of value to any of these persons;
- for the purpose of:
  - influencing an official act or decision;
  - inducing a person to do or omit an act in violation of his or her official duty;
  - inducing a foreign official to use his or her influence with a foreign government to affect or influence any government decision or action; or
  - securing an improper advantage;
- to assist the person or entity in obtaining or retaining business.[725]

Under the Foreign Corrupt Practices Act, "a person's state of mind is 'knowing' with respect to conduct, a circumstance, or result" if he or she has actual knowledge of the conduct, circumstance or result or "a firm belief that such circumstance exists or that such result is substantially certain to occur".[726] In addition, knowledge of a circumstance can be found when there is a "high probability" of the existence of such circumstance.[727]

Since the 1977 enactment of the Foreign Corrupt Practices Act, the anti-bribery provisions have applied to US and foreign private issuers of securities that registered their securities with or reported to the SEC and to domestic concerns such as US citizens and companies organised under US law or with a principal place of business in the United States, if the US mail or a means or instrumentalities of US interstate commerce (eg, an interstate wire transfer) were used in furtherance of the anti-bribery violation.[728]

In 1998 amendments to the anti-bribery provisions generally extended US jurisdiction to cover:

- acts outside US territory in furtherance of an anti-bribery violation by US issuers and domestic concerns; and
- acts inside US territory in furtherance of an anti-bribery violation by other persons, such as foreign non-issuers and foreign nationals, that were not previously subject to the Foreign Corrupt Practices Act.[729]

---

724 This term has been construed by US federal prosecutors to include employees – even relatively low-level employees – of state-owned institutions.
725 See Exchange Act §30A, Foreign Corrupt Practices Act §104.
726 *Id.*
727 See Exchange Act §30A(f)(2)(B).
728 Exchange Act §30A(a), Foreign Corrupt Practices Act §104(a).
729 Exchange Act §30A(g), Foreign Corrupt Practices Act §104(i), §104A(a).

Such extended jurisdiction is not dependent upon the use of US mail or means or instrumentalities of US interstate commerce.[730]

The Foreign Corrupt Practices Act also applies to officers, directors, employees or agents of any organisation subject to the act and to stockholders acting on behalf of any such organisation.[731]

Exceptions and defences to anti-bribery violations: Under the Foreign Corrupt Practices Act, 'grease payments' – that is, facilitating payments "to expedite or to secure the performance of a routine governmental action" – are excepted from the anti-bribery provisions.[732] This is a narrow exception that applies only to non-discretionary acts, such as obtaining official documents or securing utility service, and not to any decision to award or continue business with a particular party.[733] Note that many other jurisdictions and international conventions do not permit these types of facilitation payments. Counsel should be consulted if there is a question as to whether a particular activity falls under this exception.

Additionally, there are two affirmative defences to the Foreign Corrupt Practices Act's anti-bribery provisions:

- The payment, gift, offer or promise of anything of value that is at issue was lawful under the written laws and regulations of the recipient's country;[734] or
- The payment, gift, offer or promise of anything of value was a reasonable, *bona fide* expenditure directly related either to the promotion, demonstration or explanation of products or services, or to the execution or performance of a contract with a foreign government or agency.[735]

These defences are narrow in practice and the defendant has the burden of proving their applicability in the face of a Foreign Corrupt Practices Act prosecution.

Accounting provisions: The Foreign Corrupt Practice Act's accounting provisions apply to issuers that have securities registered with the SEC or that file reports with the SEC.[736] A foreign private issuer that qualifies for a Rule 12g3-2(b) exemption and is not otherwise a reporting company is not subject to the Foreign Corrupt Practice Act's accounting provisions because it does not have any class of securities listed on a US securities exchange.[737]

The books and records provisions compel such issuers to make and keep books,

---

730 *Id.*
731 Exchange Act §30A(a), (g), Foreign Corrupt Practices Act §104(a), (i), §104A(a).
732 Exchange Act §30A(b), Foreign Corrupt Practices Act §104(b), §104A(b).
733 Exchange Act §30A(f)(3)(B), Foreign Corrupt Practices Act §104(h)(4)(B), §104A(f)(4)(B).
734 Exchange Act §30A(c)(1), Foreign Corrupt Practices Act §104(c)(1), §104A(c)(1).
735 Exchange Act §30A(c)(2), Foreign Corrupt Practices Act §104(c)(2), §104A(c)(2).
736 Exchange Act §13(b)(2). The accounting provisions were passed in 1977 as part of the original Foreign Corrupt Practices Act legislation out of concern over companies improperly recording payments on their books and records and failing fully to account for illicit 'slush' funds, from which improper payments could be made. However, these provisions have broader application than simply within the context of the Foreign Corrupt Practices Act. For purposes of this book, when violations of these provisions are alleged in the context of improper payments to foreign officials or similar conduct, they are referred to as violations of the Foreign Corrupt Practices Act's accounting provisions.
737 See also Abikoff above, Chapters 14 and 18.

records and accounts, which accurately and fairly reflect the transactions and dispositions of the assets of the issuer in reasonable detail.[738]

The internal accounting controls provisions require such issuers to devise and maintain a system of internal accounting controls regarding accounting for assets, enabling the preparation of financial statements and providing reasonable assurances that management authorises transactions and controls access to assets.[739]

As used in the accounting provisions, 'reasonable detail' and 'reasonable assurances' mean a level of detail and degree of assurance as would satisfy prudent officials in the conduct of their own affairs.[740]

Penalties: The Foreign Corrupt Practices Act imposes substantial criminal and civil penalties. The DOJ has exclusive jurisdiction to prosecute criminal violations of the Foreign Corrupt Practices Act, while the DOJ and the SEC share jurisdiction over civil enforcement actions. The penalties for Foreign Corrupt Practices Act violations depend on the type of provision that is violated.

Wilful violations of the anti-bribery provisions carry maximum criminal fines of $2 million for organisations and $250,000 for individuals, per violation.[741] Under US criminal law, alternative fines of up to twice the pecuniary gain from the offence apply instead, if the alternative fine exceeds the maximum fine under the Foreign Corrupt Practices Act.[742] Individuals also face up to five years' imprisonment for wilful violations of the anti-bribery violations.[743] In addition, anti-bribery violations carry civil penalties of up to $10,000 for organisations or individuals, per violation.[744] These fines are not indemnifiable by a person's employer or principal.[745]

Wilful violations of the accounting provisions carry maximum criminal fines of $25 million for organisations and $5 million for individuals or, if greater, the alternative fine of twice the pecuniary gain.[746] Individuals face up to 20 years' imprisonment for wilful violations of the accounting provisions.[747] Civil penalties include disgorgement of any ill-gotten gains and penalties of up to $500,000 for organisations and $100,000 for individuals, per violation, in actions brought by the SEC.[748]

Enforcement: Over the last 15 years an increasing number of enforcement actions have been brought for Foreign Corrupt Practices Act violations. The Sarbanes-Oxley Act's focus on the adequacy of internal control procedures helped to invigorate enforcement by both the SEC and the DOJ. Since 2002, there has been a dramatic escalation in the SEC's efforts to enforce the Foreign Corrupt Practices Act.

The DOJ recently stated that is pursuing more than 120 Foreign Corrupt Practices

738 Exchange Act §13(b)(2)(A).
739 Exchange Act §13(b)(2)(B).
740 Exchange Act §13(b)(7).
741 Exchange Act §32(c), Foreign Corrupt Practices Act §104(g), §104A(e); 18 USC §3571(b)(3), (e).
742 18 USC §3571(d), (e).
743 Exchange Act §32 (c)(2)(A), Foreign Corrupt Practices Act §104(g)(2)(A), §104A(e)(2)(A).
744 Exchange Act §32 (c), Foreign Corrupt Practices Act §104(g), §104A(e).
745 Exchange Act §32 (c)(3), Foreign Corrupt Practices Act §104(g)(3), §104A(e)(3).
746 Exchange Act §32(a); 18 USC §3571(d), (e).
747 Exchange Act §32(a).
748 Exchange Act §21(d)(3), (5).

Act investigations. In addition, the Dodd-Frank Act could lead to increased Foreign Corrupt Practices Act enforcement activity by increasing employee whistleblowing, given that this act contains a provision that the SEC must pay a reward of between 10% and 30% of the total sanctions to whistleblowers in certain securities enforcement actions.

These developments make it essential that US and foreign private issuers maintain compliance programmes that satisfy all of the jurisdictions where they do business, since failure to do so often results in harsh consequences, including large corporate fines and prison time for individual executives.

Some examples of representative enforcement actions include the following:

- In December 2002 the SEC announced a $500,000 civil penalty against Syncor International Corp, based on:
  - bribes paid by international subsidiaries of Syncor with some alleged knowledge by Syncor's chairman; and
  - Syncor's failure to ensure that its international subsidiaries implemented the Foreign Corrupt Practices Act's accounting requirements, thereby facilitating illegal bribes.

  Separately, the DOJ obtained a $2 million criminal fine against Syncor's Taiwanese subsidiary for violation of the anti-bribery provisions. The case against the Taiwanese subsidiary was the first in which DOJ used its authority to prosecute foreign persons for actions taken in the United States in furtherance of a foreign bribe.
- In July 2004 the SEC and the DOJ announced a settlement of Foreign Corrupt Practices Act charges against ABB Ltd, a Swiss corporation, for payments made by US and foreign subsidiaries doing business in Nigeria. ABB Ltd was subject to the Foreign Corrupt Practices Act 's books and records provisions as an issuer. Its subsidiaries were charged with bribery counts, while ABB itself was charged with maintaining inadequate internal controls. The settlement required that ABB pay a civil penalty of $5.9 million and that two of its subsidiaries pay a criminal penalty of $10.5 million.
- In December 2008 Siemens AG, Europe's largest engineering conglomerate, settled a Foreign Corrupt Practices Act investigation in connection with the violation of the anti-bribery provisions (at least 4,200 allegedly corrupt payments in various countries) and violations of the accounting provisions, resulting in combined penalties of $800 million to the DOJ and the SEC which, together with penalties imposed in Germany, added up to a record-setting $1.6 billion.
- In January 2010 the DOJ announced that it had conducted, along with the Federal Bureau of Investigation (FBI), a multi-year undercover sting operation and netted indictments of 22 individuals from 16 different companies in the military and law enforcement products industry. This action represents the single largest prosecution against individuals in the history of Foreign Corrupt Practices Act enforcement and is further evidence that international bribery is a top priority for the DOJ. The case also demonstrated that the DOJ and the FBI will devote increased attention to individual prosecutions and

the use of traditional law enforcement methods, such as sting operations – both agencies suggested that further undercover operations would be forthcoming.

- In July 2010 the SEC reached a $23.4 million settlement with General Electric Company for charges that it violated the Foreign Corrupt Practices Act, allegedly making certain illegal kickback payments totalling $3.6 million to the Iraqi government in order to obtain contracts under the UN Oil for Food Programme. This was the 15th Foreign Corrupt Practices Act case brought by the SEC against companies involved in this programme, resulting in a recovery of more than $204 million.
- In September 2010 ABB Ltd settled a civil action in which the SEC alleged that ABB, through its subsidiaries, paid bribes to government officials in Mexico (including a $1.8 million yacht, a $300,000 Ferrari and more than $160,000 in credit card charges) to obtain business with government-owned power companies, and paid kickbacks to the former regime in Iraq to obtain contracts under the UN Oil for Food Programme. The complaint alleges that ABB's subsidiaries made at least $2.7 million in illicit payments in these schemes to obtain contracts that generated more than $100 million in revenues for ABB. The settlement in this case includes $22.8 million in disgorgement of profits and a civil fine of $16.5 million. ABB also reached a settlement with the DOJ in related criminal proceedings and agreed to pay a $19 million criminal penalty.

Trends: These and other recent enforcement actions reveal the following trends in the practices of the SEC and the DOJ with respect to the Foreign Corrupt Practices Act and related anti-corruption matters:

- Foreign Corrupt Practices Act enforcement continues to grow – with each year, the resources and efforts being devoted to enforce the Foreign Corrupt Practices Act are growing. In 2009 the SEC and the DOJ brought 44 enforcement actions, the most ever filed in one year. In February 2010 the DOJ's top anti-corruption prosecutor stated that the department's fraud section could grow by as much as 50% in 2010 and 2011, even after several years in which the enforcement activities of the DOJ and SEC have set a new record each year in terms of investigations, settlements and fines.
- The evolving philosophy of Foreign Corrupt Practices Act enforcement – until now, efforts have focused on pursuing companies that have violated the law. The 2010 undercover sting operation shows the DOJ's willingness to seek out individuals who are willing to violate the law. The use of undercover agents in this manner exhibits the DOJ's desire to deter foreign bribery actively. These forward-looking approaches not only show a full commitment to ensuring compliance with the act in the coming years, but also represent a shift to a more aggressive philosophy.
- Larger corporate penalties – the civil and criminal fines resulting from Foreign Corrupt Practices Act prosecutions and settlements continue to rise. The combined $1.6 billion in penalties levied against Siemens, far exceeding

all previous Foreign Corrupt Practices Act-related sanctions, was quickly followed by the KBR/Halliburton settlement totalling $579 million. Combined fines and disgorgement amounts in the hundreds of millions of dollars, while once thought improbable, now appear almost commonplace, with the BAE ($400 million), Daimler ($185 million) and Alcatel-Lucent ($137 million) settlements following this trend.

- Prosecutions of individuals – the SEC and DOJ remain willing to pursue charges against individuals when the facts warrant such action. The DOJ recently obtained its most severe sentence for an individual's Foreign Corrupt Practices Act violation to date – the 87-month prison term handed to Charles Paul Jumet for his involvement in a bribery scheme in Panama.
- Trials on corruption charges – with the now completed trials of Connecticut businessman Frederic Bourke, Congressman William Jefferson and film executives Gerald and Patricia Green, it is now clear that the DOJ is willing to try corruption charges before a jury when it is unable to reach a satisfactory settlement agreement. The convictions in whole or in part of each of these individuals make clear that such prosecutions can be successful.

Lessons: In view of the above, there are some lessons that can be learned by US and foreign private issuers alike:

- Appropriate due diligence – although the Foreign Corrupt Practices Act does not have an express due diligence requirement or an explicit defence based on due diligence, conducting appropriate due diligence remains one of the best ways to prevent Foreign Corrupt Practices Act violations or prosecutions. Failure to conduct due diligence leaves a company in a position where it cannot rationally form a basis to conclude that no illegal payment was made and, therefore, can subject the company to liability under the Foreign Corrupt Practices Act.
- Foreign Corrupt Practices Act opinion procedures – these provide a mechanism by which the DOJ reviews proposed business conduct, per request, and states whether it would pursue enforcement under the given set of facts. As of mid-2010, the DOJ had issued 53 opinion procedure releases. While the releases each caution that they have no binding application to any party that did not join in the request, they nevertheless serve as a significant body of guidance as to the DOJ's position on numerous factual circumstances and interpretations of the statute. This provides companies with a mechanism by which to screen the legality of future business conduct. Although this procedure is open only to US companies, the releases are available on the DOJ's website. These opinions are informative, but not binding as precedent for future cases.
- Paper procedures – company procedures that require due diligence, anti-corruption covenants, other contractual provisions and certifications or appropriate accounting practices provide no protection (and may prove harmful) when they are not followed.
- Appropriate employee and third-party training – companies that fail to

conduct appropriate employee or third-party training may face liability if the conduct of those parties ends up violating anti-corruption laws. Employees overseeing high-risk transactions should receive frequent training, which may also serve to expose any improper activity so that it may be effectively acted upon.

- 'Anything of value' – the Foreign Corrupt Practices Act prohibits far more than mere cash payments and can be violated by the provision of such diverse benefits as travel, entertainment, scholarships, vehicles, property, shoes, watches, electronics, office furniture, stock and share of profits.
- Commonality of practice – the fact that a practice is common in a region or industry is not a defence, despite common misperceptions to this end. Further, even in extreme circumstances, such as extortion by foreign officials, prosecutors are unlikely to excuse illegal conduct.
- Experienced anti-bribery counsel – while the mere use of outside counsel will not completely insulate a company from Foreign Corrupt Practices Act liability, the selection of experienced anti-corruption counsel gives the greatest chance of compliance with the expectations and requirements of enforcement agencies.

Other anti-bribery laws: In addition to the Foreign Corrupt Practices Act, there are other federal laws that prohibit bribery or corrupt payments. The mail and wire fraud statutes (discussed above), as well as the Travel Act,[749] allow for federal prosecution of violations of state bribery laws.

(g) State law

Issuers should be aware that they may also face criminal liability under the law of the state in which they have registered their securities. For example, the Martin Act in the State of New York criminalises false statements[750] and has a lower scienter requirement than the federal civil securities fraud provisions. The territoriality of the statute likely extends to every security that has a transaction through the NYSE, NASDAQ or another national securities exchange.

7.9 Defensive actions

Once a criminal or civil suit has commenced, the defendant (company or individual) should quickly develop a strategy for coping with that litigation. Below are some considerations to keep in mind when defending a securities lawsuit in the US legal system.

(a) Document retention

Once a company learns that it has been sued or that a lawsuit against it is about to be commenced, it must take immediate action to preserve anything that could potentially be evidence. If evidence is destroyed after a company knows of a suit, the

---

749 18 USC §1952.
750 NY General Business Law §359-c(1)(c) (1996).

court can impose serious sanctions on the company, even if the destruction was not intentional. These sanctions include monetary penalties, instructions to the jury that they can infer that the destroyed evidence would have supported the plaintiff's case, or even a verdict in favour of the plaintiff.

It is essential that the defendant identify everyone in the company who may have any relevant documents and all of the collections of relevant documents that may exist, and inform the employees who control those documents not to destroy them.

(b) Internal investigation

The defendant should retain counsel and begin an internal investigation of the claims as soon as practicable. Identifying key witnesses and key documents as early as possible is crucial. However, the company should bear in mind that, with respect to a criminal case, the government will likely ask for the results of the internal investigation. If it decides to turn over the results of this investigation to the government in order to cooperate and decrease the chances of facing prosecution, this could have serious consequences for its employees, who may not have realised that statements that they made during the course of the company's internal investigation might later be used against them in a criminal prosecution. Inaccurate statements could be considered an obstruction of justice. Therefore, corporations seeking to conduct an internal investigation should adequately prepare their employees, preferably with the assistance of counsel.

(c) Venue

The potential cost of litigation in the United States often depends greatly on where the case will be tried. Therefore, a crucial early step in developing a litigation strategy is to determine what can be done to move the litigation into more favourable venues. Motions to dismiss for *forum non conveniens*, motions for removal and motions to change venue are the principal means to deal with this issue.

(d) Discovery process

As discussed above, discovery can add tremendous cost to the litigation. It will be crucial to develop a strategy that addresses questions that will make the discovery process manageable:

- What documents should be offered?
- How should trade secrets and confidential documents be protected?
- How should the collection and production of documents be managed?

In securities class actions, the cost of discovery is usually higher for the defendant than the plaintiff. Some defendants opt for settlement in an effort to avoid the high cost of discovery and settlement is usually reached within the insurance limits.[751]

---

751 Tom Baker and Sean J Griffith, "How the Merits Matter: Directors' and Officers' Insurance and Securities Settlements", 157 *University of Pennsylvania Law Review* 755, 777–778 (2009).

(e) Settlement

Most companies find that settling a securities class action case is more favourable than risking litigation. Securities class actions nearly always settle.[752] The likelihood of settlement usually increases substantially after a complaint has survived a motion to dismiss. It is crucial to decide on a settlement strategy as soon as possible. Some cases are more appropriate for settlement than others.

When a decision to settle has been made, typically, the value that a defendant should be willing to pay to settle a case is determined as follows. The defendant should determine how much plaintiff could possibly win and discount that amount by the likelihood that plaintiff will lose. That amount, plus the cost to the defendant of litigating the case, is an appropriate value for settlement. Likewise, a defendant company must take into account other potential costs from continued litigation, such as exposing the company to unfavourable media attention or revealing other areas where the company may have potential legal difficulties. Such downsides to litigating may raise the value of settlement.

The government generally has an incentive to settle cases, so companies should take that into account when making their calculations.

752 Stephanie Plancich and Svetlana Starykh, "Recent Trends in Securities Class Action Litigation: 2009 Mid-Year Update", National Economics Research Associates (2009) ("As mentioned above, very few securities class action cases result in a verdict at trial – the vast majority are settled or dismissed. Since the passage of the [Private Securities Litigation Reform Act], only 22 cases have gone to trial").

Appendix A
Commentary on Form 20-F: disclosure requirements for foreign private issuers

Form 20-F contains a number of items of disclosure instructions. Items 1 through 16G call for various textual presentations. Numbers 17 and 18 require financial statements. These are followed by signatures and exhibit requirements, including certifications. The following brief commentary makes reference to corresponding informational requirements of Regulation S-K for US issuers.

General instructions to Form 20-F

[Applicable to Securities Act and Exchange Act registrations and Exchange Act annual reports.]

The second page of the form requires the issuer to indicate whether it is a "well-known seasoned issuer" or an "accelerated filer".[753]

General Instruction C(e) references Item 10 of Regulation S-K. The language implements provisions of Section 401(b) of the Sarbanes-Oxley Act and the SEC's responsive January 22 2003 rules. In addition to noting the SEC's policy on projections of future economic performance, foreign private issuers should consider the SEC's policy on the use of non-US generally accepted accounting principles (GAAP) financial measures.[754]

General Instruction G implements the Security and Exchange Commission's (SEC) "one-time accommodation" for issuers switching to international financial reporting standards (IFRS).

Item 1. Identity of directors, senior management and advisers

[Applicable to Securities Act and Exchange Act registrations. Inapplicable to Exchange Act annual reports.]

"Senior management" includes members of the company's "administrative, supervisory or management bodies" as determined by US standards.

The item asks for the identity of the issuer's "principal bankers and legal advisers" only if such disclosure is required in a jurisdiction outside the United States.

Item 2. Offer statistics and expected timetable

[Applicable only to Securities Act registrations.]

753 See "Public offerings" and "Periodic reporting requirements".
754 See "Periodic reporting requirements".

The SEC expects that timetable information in the typical offering "would be very brief and would likely focus more on the sequence of events than on precise dates".

Item 3. Key information
[3A and 3D are applicable generally. 3B is inapplicable to Exchange Act annual reports. 3C is applicable only to Securities Act registrations.]

A. Selected financial data
Item 3A is comparable to Item 301 of Regulation S-K. It calls generally for a five-year columnar presentation of major line items from the financial statements. If the foreign private issuer's financials are prepared using home country GAAP, rather than IFRS as issued by the International Accounting Standards Board (IASB), a reconciliation to US GAAP is required.

Selected data for the earliest two years of the five-year period may be omitted if the issuer represents that the information cannot be provided "without unreasonable effort or expense".

The 3A instructions do not include the invitation in the instructions to S-K 301 to discuss material uncertainties that might cause the selected financial data not to be indicative of future performance. US issuers almost universally confine such discussion to the management discussion and analysis (MD&A).

B. Capitalisation and indebtedness

C. Reasons for the offer and use of proceeds
Item 3C calls for the same type of information that Item 504 of Regulation S-K asks of US issuers in Securities Act registration statements.

D. Risk factors
See the discussion of risk factor disclosure in "Securities litigation risks".

Item 4. Information on the company
[Applicable to Securities Act and Exchange Act registrations and Exchange Act annual reports.]

A. History and development of the company
Item 4A requires information as to "important events in the development of the company's business", such as material reclassifications, business combinations or dispositions, insolvency proceedings and changes in types of products or services, except that an Exchange Act annual report only has to give information for the period since the beginning of the last fiscal year (paralleling the Form 10-K instruction for US issuers).

The item also calls for information on past and planned capital expenditures and on any takeover offers – by or directed against the issuer – that have occurred since the beginning of the last fiscal year.

B. Business overview

Item 4B and Item 4A cover much of the information that Item 101 of Regulation S-K requests US issuers to provide.

Any segment information that is provided under Item 4B can be presented on the same basis that is followed for accounting purposes under home country GAAP. Item 4B specifically calls for revenue information by segments and geographic markets for the last three years.

Although there are numerous differences between 4B and the requirements for a narrative description in S-K 101, in substance they both call for a comprehensive textual business description.

C. Organisational structure

D. Property, plants and equipment

Item 4D is somewhat more expansive than the comparable requirement for a description of physical properties in Item 102 of Regulation S-K. Foreign private issuers need to discuss material construction plans (in greater detail than they otherwise might in discussing commitments for capital expenditures in the MD&A) and any environmental issues that may affect utilisation of their tangible properties (a subject that is addressed by S-K Items 101 and 103 rather than S-K Item 102). Foreign private issuers should be aware that disclosure of environmental problems faced by issuers has been a particular concern of the SEC, reflecting governmental and social movements that often impose significant expense burdens and liabilities upon industrial corporations.

Item 4A. Unresolved staff comments

[Applicable to Exchange Act annual reports.]

Well-known seasoned issuers and accelerated filers must disclose the substance of any written comments from the SEC staff regarding their Exchange Act reports that are received not less than 180 days before the end of the annual report fiscal year, if such comments remain unresolved.

Item 5. Operating and financial review and prospects

[Applicable to Securities Act and Exchange Act registrations and Exchange Act annual reports.]

Item 5 is the MD&A, under a different caption.[755] The MD&A provisions of Item 303 of Regulation S-K cover the same matters as Item 5 of Form 20-F, but are arranged and worded differently. The instructions to Item 5 refer to the guidance given by the SEC's 1989 MD&A interpretive release. Footnote 1 of the SEC's December 19 2003 MD&A interpretive release says that the guidance in that release is also intended to apply to Item 5 of Form 20-F. The two interpretive releases are the SEC's most useful explanations of its MD&A requirements.

Under Item 5, the responsive information "shall relate to all separate segments of

755 See the section on other disclosure issues in "Periodic reporting requirements".

the company". In contrast, Item 303 calls for segment information in the MD&A where it would be appropriate in the issuer's judgement; in practice, US issuers treat this instruction as requiring segment analysis.

Management's analysis must focus on liquidity, capital resources and results of operations of the issuer, discussing not only factors that had a historical effect, but also factors and trends that are anticipated to have a material effect in future periods.

A. Operating results

Among the specific matters to be considered by a foreign private issuer are the impact of foreign currency fluctuations and governmental economic, fiscal, monetary or political policies or factors. [An example (set out in a May 8 2001 letter from the SEC chairman to a congressional committee) is any material impact of likely US government sanctions for carrying on business in countries where US companies are prohibited from doing business.]

B. Liquidity and capital resources

Liquidity is to be addressed on both a short and long-term basis, evaluating the sources and amounts of the issuer's cash flows. The analysis of commitments for capital expenditures should be accompanied by an indication of sources of funds to fulfil such commitments.

[Foreign private issuers should consult the 1989 and December 19 2003 interpretive releases and the December 19 2003 interpretive release No 33-8350[756] for the SEC's views on liquidity discussion in the MD&A.]

C. Research and development, patents and licences, etc

US issuers provide this information in the description of business.

D. Trend information

The instructions emphasise the difference between forward-looking information that a foreign private issuer can elect to provide – and that is protectable under the Private Securities Litigation Reform Act's safe harbour[757] if the issuer is an Exchange Act reporting company – and known trends, uncertainties, demands, commitments or events that are similarly protectable, but that are required to be disclosed.

E. Off-balance sheet arrangements

F. Tabular disclosure of contractual obligations

If home country GAAP is followed and this does not distinguish between capital and operating leases, then all leases may be presented under one category.

---

756 Discussed in the subsection on management's commentary on financial statements in "Periodic reporting requirements".

757 Discussed in "Securities litigation risks".

Item 6. Directors, senior management and employees

[Applicable to Securities Act and Exchange Act registrations and Exchange Act annual reports.]

A. Directors and senior management

B. Compensation

C. Board practices

D. Employees

E. Share ownership

Much of the information called for by Item 6 would appear in the annual meeting proxy statement of a US issuer (foreign private issuers are exempt from complying with the SEC's proxy rules).[758]

Item 7. Major shareholders and related party transactions

A. Major shareholders

B. Related party transactions

C. Interests of experts and counsel

Much of the information requested by Items 7A and 7B would also appear annually in the proxy statement of a US issuer.[759]

Item 8. Financial information

[Applicable to Securities Act and Exchange Act registrations and, except for interim period information, to Exchange Act reports.]

A. Consolidated statements and other financial information

Item 8A sets out the general requirements for financial statements (principally, balance sheets at the end of the last two fiscal years and three years' income and cash-flow statements, audited in accordance with US generally accepted auditing standards by auditors meeting US independence standards). Items 17 and 18 of Form 20-F contain rules for reconciliation to US GAAP. Regulation S-X continues to govern the form and content of financial statements and prescribes additional financial statement requirements for special situations.

Information is required on legal proceedings "which may have, or have had in the recent past", significant effects on financial position or profitability. Instructions for providing information on insolvency proceedings and proceedings in which any

758 See "Periodic reporting requirements".
759 See "Periodic reporting requirements".

director, senior officer or affiliate of such a person has an interest adverse to the foreign private issuer correspond to those in Item 103 of Regulation S-K for US issuers. An Exchange Act annual report must also describe the disposition during the last fiscal year of any previously reported litigation.

B. Significant changes

The registration statement or report must disclose "whether or not any significant change has occurred" since the date of the most recent financial statements included in the document. This suggests an MD&A-type analysis by management. As discussed in "Periodic reporting requirements" above, unannounced declines in financial performance can prompt lawsuits.

Item 9. The offer and listing

[Applicable to Securities Act registrations. Only 9C and portions of 9A are applicable to Exchange Act registrations and annual reports.]

This is basically for securities offerings. It is essentially the same information that Item 505 of Regulation S-K requires of US issuers.

A. Offer and listing details

B. Plan of distribution

C. Markets

D. Selling shareholders

E. Dilution

F. Expenses of the issue

Item 10. Additional information

[Applicable to Securities Act and Exchange Act registrations and Exchange Act annual reports, with various exceptions.]

A. Share capital

B. Memorandum and articles of association

C. Material contracts

Item 10C requests "a summary of each material contract, other than contracts entered into in the ordinary course of business" for the past two years. For Exchange Act registrations and reports, the instructions as to exhibits at the end of Form 20-F prescribe the sorts of contracts that are considered material and must be filed.

D. Exchange controls
Foreign private issuers must describe any governmental laws and regulations of the home country that may affect the import or export of capital or the remittance of dividend or interest payments to non-residents.

E. Taxation
Foreign private issuers are required to provide information on taxes (including withholding taxes) to which US shareholders may be subject.

F. Dividends and paying agents

G. Statement by experts

H. Documents on display
Documents that may be inspected and exhibits "generally should be translated" into English.

I. Subsidiary information

Item 11. Quantitative and qualitative disclosures about market risk
[Applicable to Securities Act and Exchange Act registrations and Exchange Act annual reports.]

Since 1997, the SEC has required the disclosure of market risks inherent in derivative financial and commodity instruments (eg, futures, forwards, swaps and options) and other financial instruments, such as structured notes, mortgage-backed securities and indexed debt instruments – reflecting the SEC's concern over the market risks that arise from adverse changes in interest rates, foreign currency exchange rates, commodity prices and other market rates and prices. Both US and foreign private issuers are subject to these requirements and must disclose quantitative and qualitative market risk information in their MD&A or elsewhere.

The Item 11 instructions are virtually identical to those of Item 305 of Regulation S-K that govern US issuers.

Quantitative information must distinguish between market risk sensitive instruments entered into for trading purposes and such instruments entered into for other purposes (eg, to hedge against fluctuations), to the extent that material, information must be presented for each market risk exposure category (ie, interest rate risks, foreign currency exchange rate risks, commodity price risks and other relevant market risks). One of three alternative presentations may be used:

- a tabular presentation (a format is suggested in Item 11);
- a sensitivity analysis of potential losses in future earnings, fair values or cash flows; or
- value-at-risk disclosures of such potential losses.

Qualitative information should describe the issuer's primary market risk exposures and how the exposures are managed – with separate presentations for instruments entered into for trading purposes and those entered into for other purposes.

Item 12. Description of securities other than equity securities
[Applicable to Securities Act and Exchange Act registrations and Exchange Act annual reports, with various exceptions]

A. Debt securities

B. Warrants and rights

C. Other securities

D. American depositary shares
As a result of 2008 amendments to Form 20-F, the SEC requires disclosure of American depositary receipt (ADR) fees on an annual basis, including any fee for general depositary services. Additionally, issuers are required to disclose all direct and indirect payments made by the depositary to the foreign private issuer whose securities underlie the ADRs.

[Items 13-14 of Form 20-F covers: defaults, dividend arrearages and delinquencies; material modifications to the rights of security holders and use of proceeds.]

Item 15. Controls and procedures
[Applicable to Exchange Act annual reports.]

The issuer must disclose:

- the conclusions of its principal executive and principal financial officers about the effectiveness of its disclosure controls and procedures; and
- whether there were significant changes in internal controls since the last evaluation.

Additionally, a foreign private issuer must satisfy the "internal control report" requirement of Section 404 of the Sarbanes-Oxley Act, pursuant to which its management must provide a year-end assessment of the effectiveness of its internal control structure that is accompanied by an auditor's "attestation".

There are parallel statements in the officer certifications.[760] The certifications are called for by General Instruction B(e) of Form 20-F.

Item 16A. Audit committee financial expert
[Applicable to Exchange Act annual reports.]

If the issuer says that it has an audit committee financial expert, the expert must be named. If it says that it has no such expert, it must explain why. The instructions

760 Discussed in the subsection on officer certifications in "Periodic reporting requirements".

to Item 16A list the attributes that an expert must possess and specify the ways in which the expert can have acquired such attributes.

In the case of a foreign private issuer with a two-tier board of directors, the determination of whether there is an audit committee financial expert should be made by the supervisory or non-management board.

Item 16B. Code of ethics

[Applicable to Exchange Act annual reports.]

The issuer must disclose whether it has adopted a code of ethics that applies to its principal executive, financial and accounting officers (and if not, why not). A code of ethics must have specified minimum written standards and must be available either as an exhibit to Form 20-F, on the issuer's internet website or upon request (without charge). Amendments or waivers applicable to any such officer must be disclosed in the 20-F or, alternatively, on the issuer's website.

Item 16C. Principal accountant fees and services

[Applicable to Exchange Act annual reports.]

Disclosure of aggregate fees billed in each of the last two fiscal years is required under the following separate captions: "audit fees"; "audit-related fees"; "tax fees"; and "all other fees". In all but the first category, issuers shall describe the nature of the services comprising the fees. The audit committee's pre-approval policies and procedures must be disclosed.

Item 16D. Exemption from the listing standards for audit committees

[Applicable to Exchange Act annual reports.]

There are certain limited exemptions from the independence requirements for the audit committee of a foreign private issuer.[761] If an issuer avails itself of such an exemption, it must make certain disclosures.

Item 16E. Purchases of equity securities by the issuer and affiliated purchasers

[Applicable to Exchange Act annual reports.]

This item calls for a tabular presentation of information with respect to recent repurchases by the issuer (or an "affiliated purchaser") of its equity securities.

Item 16F. Change in registrant's certifying accountant

[Applicable to Securities Act and Exchange Act registrations and Exchange Act annual reports.]

In 2008 the SEC amended Form 20-F to require that foreign private issuers report changes in and disagreements with their certifying accountants.

Item 16G. Corporate governance

[Applicable to Exchange Act annual reports.]

761 See the section on the Sarbanes-Oxley Act in "Periodic reporting requirements".

Foreign issuers must provide in their annual reports a concise summary of the significant ways in which their corporate governance practices differ from the corporate governance practices of US companies listed on the same exchange.

Item 17. Financial statements

[Applicable to Exchange Act registrations and Exchange Act annual reports.]

Foreign issuers must provide financial statements according to US GAAP or IFRS as issued by the IASB. If financial statements are prepared in accordance with another basis of accounting, they must be reconciled to US GAAP.

Item 18. Financial statements

Registration of securities under Form F-1, F-3 or F4 sometimes require Item 18 disclosure. Financial statements that are not prepared under IFRS or US GAAP must be fully reconciled to US GAAP and additionally provide all of the information required by Regulation S-X.

Appendix B Comparison of private placements and public offerings by foreign private issuers

	Private placements	Registered public offerings
Advantages of private placements	No specific disclosure is required by SEC rules in an offering memorandum sent to prospective accredited investors, although it must include information required to comply with the SEC's general standards of disclosure (ie, no material misstatement or omission) and to market the securities. As a result of these general disclosure standards, the offering memorandum may resemble a public offering prospectus.	The SEC requires extensive disclosure in the prospectus distributed to prospective purchasers, including: • audited three-year financial statements prepared in accordance with US GAAP, IFRS or with a reconciliation to US GAAP if home country GAAP are used; • segment reporting; • information on acquisitions; • an MD&A containing prospective information; and • "risk factor" disclosure. (See Appendix A above).
	Although preparation of the offering memorandum is time consuming, it typically takes less time to prepare than a public offering prospectus.	Preparation of the registration statement can take two months or more.

continued overleaf

	Private placements	Registered public offerings
	Printing, legal, accounting and other offering expenses will be sizeable, but less than the comparable expenses in a registered public offering.	The complexity of registration procedures adds to offering expenses. An SEC filing fee is payable.
	Following the offering, the issuer will have no ongoing Exchange Act reporting obligations unless and until it registers a Securities Act offering, lists on a national securities exchange or develops a sizeable US shareholder base, unless it falls under the Rule 12g3-2(b) exemption.	Following the offering, the issuer must file with the SEC annual reports on Form 20-F (see Appendix A), which will include audited financial statements following US GAAP, with a reconciliation to US GAAP or that follow IFRS, and interim reports.
	The liability provisions of Rule 10b-5 will apply.	In addition to Rule 10b-5, the liability provisions of Sections 11 and 12 will apply.
B. Disadvantages of private placements	Securities can be sold by the issuer only to persons such as "accredited investors" (including qualified institutional buyers (QIBs).	Securities can be sold by the issuer to anyone in the United States.
	After the issuer's private placement, the securities are "restricted securities" that can be resold only pursuant to SEC registration, pursuant to Rule 144 or 144A or another Section 4(1) exemption such as Section "4(1½)," or under Regulation S. This may result in a discount from the price a public offering would command.	After the public offering, the securities are freely tradable in the US public markets (assuming that the reselling holder is not an affiliate of the issuer).

continued overleaf

	Private placements	Registered public offerings
	There is less visibility for the foreign private issuer in the United States. Financial and business information is not publicly available at the SEC, except possibly under Rule 12g3-2(b).	The combination of registration disclosure and ongoing Exchange Act reporting creates a body of reasonably current public information regarding the foreign private issuer.

Appendix C
Sample checklist for due diligence review in international securities offerings

1. Timing

Due diligence is an ongoing process that is carried out from the beginning to the end of a transaction. In an international securities offering registered with the SEC, most of the due diligence is conducted before the first filing of the registration statement. In a Rule 144A/Regulation S offering, most of the due diligence is completed before the distribution of the preliminary offering memorandum.

It is important to update the due diligence between the time that the initial registration statement is filed and the time that it becomes effective. Specifically, business results from the end of the most recently reported quarter must be carefully reviewed because they are not typically disclosed in the offering memorandum or prospectus.

2. Due diligence components

2.1 Background due diligence

- Review public sources of information about the issuer and its industry.
- Carry out general internet searches of newspaper and magazine articles about the issuer.
- Review analyst or rating agency reports on the issuer and relevant industry.
- Review the issuer's website.
- Review the issuer's SEC, statutory and stock exchange filings.
- Review the prospectuses, SEC filings, offering memoranda and Rule 12g3-2(b) website postings for companies in the same industry.
- Review press releases regarding the issuer and its industry.
- Become familiar with the issuer's home country and other countries where the issuer frequently conducts business.

2.2 Business due diligence

- Investigate the integrity of the issuer's management.
- Interview the issuer's senior management.
- Conduct a background check of management.
- Interview the issuer's middle management (ie, officers in charge of

marketing, sales, human resources, production, manufacturing, legal compliance and other similar core areas).

- Conduct site tours of the issuer's principal facilities or retail locations.
- Interview the issuer's principal customers, suppliers or other business partners – without the issuer's presence – to get a realistic understanding of the issuer's business relationships.

2.3 Financial due diligence

- Review the issuer's projections and business model in conjunction with the issuer's chief financial officer and financial management:
- Analyse the assumptions behind the issuer's projections to determine their accuracy.
- Evaluate whether the business model is realistic, looking at the business's key drivers and risk factors and reviewing capital expenditure plans (for maintenance and for growth), considering when large cash outlays are needed.
- Compare the issuer's key financial statistics with those of competitors, to verify whether the issuer's credit facilities or other debt instruments need to be amended in order to allow the issuer to achieve its business plan.
- Calculate whether offerings will cause the issuer to violate financial covenants in its financing documents:
    - focus on off-balance sheet or under-recorded liabilities such as unfunded pension plans and worker's compensation liabilities; and
    - focus on large items on the income statement that affect the quality of the issuer's earnings, such as unusual or non-recurring items, related party transactions, acquisitions and divestitures, potential compensation charges as a result of cheap stock issues and reversal of accrued liabilities.
- Focus on differences between US and non-US GAAP or IFRS, depending upon whichever is used by the issuer (ie, revenue recognition, goodwill, pension accounting and accounting for stock options).

2.4 MD&A due diligence

The MD&A of the issuer's financial condition and results of operations is an increasingly important focus of the issuer's disclosure. SEC rules and guidance call for enhanced disclosures of off-balance sheet liabilities, contractual obligations, liquidity, capital resources and related party transactions.

- Review segment, divisional, operating unit and product line data to determine trends that may not be disclosed in the draft MD&A.
- Scrutinise the issuer's financial performance since the most recent period included in the MD&A. Even though the latest month or interim period will not be described in the MD&A, any material trend that appears in the financial performance for the most recent period should be described in the MD&A's overview section. This is particularly important as the new period may show that an uncertain blip in the most recent quarter is actually becoming a trend.
- Review cost items as a percentage of sales, rather than on a total basis, in

order to determine the trends in costs.

- Hold discussions with appropriate personnel regarding future, anticipated or possible cost increases, such as labour costs due to a tight labour market or supply costs due to a new supply contract.
- Focus on changes in margins, comparing profit margins over the years to see the issuer's growth in profitability or decline. Year-to-year comparisons are of less value in acquisitive companies or companies in the process of increasing their number of stores or outlets; in these cases, review the base business or same store sales to determine what is really happening.
- Compare the issuer's profit margins with those of other companies in the industry, as increases in profits and sales as well as acquisitions can mask margin difficulties.
- Margin issues can sometimes be detected by focusing on product mix.

2.5 Legal due diligence

For legal due diligence, attorneys submit a due diligence request list and review a variety of documents, including the following:

- issuer's and principal subsidiaries' board of director minutes and any documents delivered to board members in advance of any board meetings, such as agendas and financial reports;
- attorney letters to accountants;
- reports to management from accountants;
- charter, bylaws, stockholder agreements, registration rights agreements, warrants and preferred stock;
- documents relating to the issuer's outstanding equity securities, including offering documents, indentures, loan agreements and credit facilities, employment agreements, stock option plans and stock purchase plans; and
- correspondence with the SEC and other regulators.

Special attention should be paid in particular to the minutes of board of directors meetings, as these can be enlightening when assessing, for example, the issuer's view of its litigation exposure. Lawyers should review the issuer's outstanding litigation and interview the outside counsel handling the principal litigation. Often, however, reports to the board on litigation or government proceedings are far more informative than generalised comments by the issuer's counsel in terms of the issuer's ability to carry on with its business plan.

Lawyers also provide expertise in matters involving tax diligence, intellectual property and a review of the issuer's licensing agreements, employee benefit plans and stock option plans. Attorneys might need to look into special regulatory issues, involving telecommunications or other areas and antitrust, SEC or other governmental investigations of the issuer's business.

2.6 Accounting due diligence

Interview the issuer's principal accountants and, where material, the accountants of acquired entities. Principal topics of discussion may include:

- the issuer's accounting policies;
- the issuer's revenue recognition and capital expenditures;
- the consistency of the issuer's accounting policies with industry norms;
- issues discussed or raised in the accountants' management letters;
- off-balance sheet liabilities;
- the issuer's liquidity position;
- significant write-offs and proposed changes in the accounting rules or accounting literature that could impact on the issuer's financial statements;
- differences between the issuer's financial statements and US GAAP or IFRS; and
- any off-balance sheet transactions and any non-US GAAP financial information in its Exchange Act reports or press releases.

The issuer's accountants should verify whether the issuer's financial statements will be affected by cheap stock, beneficial conversion features or share-based payment issues, and should attend drafting sessions or participate in drafting conference calls, as they often know the issuer extremely well and can be very helpful in crafting accurate disclosure.

2.7 Corporate governance due diligence

In light of the Sarbanes-Oxley Act and the SEC rules thereunder, it may be important to engage in a due diligence review of the issuer's corporate governance policies. Special attention should be paid to:

- the filing of chief executive officer/chief financial officer certifications under the Sarbanes-Oxley Act;
- the issuer's disclosure controls and procedures, and internal controls;
- the issuer's code of ethics and any exemptions from this code;
- the issuer's whistleblowing procedures;
- loans from the issuer to management that would violate the Sarbanes-Oxley Act;
- the composition of the audit committee, particularly as to independence, financial knowledge and whether there is a financial expert on the audit committee;
- the composition of a nominating committee, if any;
- the composition of a compensation committee, if any;
- the issuer's internal audit function;
- the issuer's document retention policy;
- any non-audit services provided by the issuer's independent auditors; and
- any restatements of the issuer's financial statements or any unresolved comments from the SEC or the applicable local regulator in connection with any filing.

2.8 Audit committee due diligence

There should be discussions with the chairman or a member of the audit committee relating to the structure of the committee, its meeting process, any significant issues encountered by the committee and the line of communication with the issuer, noting the level of communication between the management and the audit team.

Particular attention should be paid to the audit committee's review process, such as:

- the audit committee's review process for periodic reports and monthly statements, noting any significant accounting issues that have arisen in connection with the most recent periodic reports;
- the committee's review of internal controls, taxes and tax reserves;
- the committee's review of any off-balance sheet liabilities and contingencies; and
- the audit committee's understanding of key choices made with respect to assumptions and accounting principles as used in the financial statements.

It is also important to be aware of issues such as the mechanism used to select auditors, any process for meeting with auditors without management, the issuer's critical accounting policies, related party transactions, the impact of any new accounting or SEC pronouncements on the issuer's financial statements and any goodwill amortisation. Attention should also be paid to any material issues discussed at the most recent meetings and any significant disagreements between the audit committee and the auditors, or between the audit committee and management.

2.9 Due diligence considerations specifically for debt offerings

When dealing with debt offerings, it is important to focus on issues such as the effects of transactions on the issuer's debt rating, and the effects of transactions on the issuer's cash flow. It is useful to look at the issuer's debt repayment schedule, the issuer's worst case/downside scenario, the use of proceeds of the debt offering and the necessity of raising additional cash in order to allow the issuer to complete its business plan.[762]

762 The information used in this appendix is based on the material published by one of the authors as Chapter 22, "Due Diligence in Securities Offerings by International Issuers", from the book *International Business Transactions with Brazil* published in 2008 by Juris Publishing, Inc, Huntington, New York, and is used with the permission of that publisher.

Appendix D
Sample publicity guidelines for private placements by foreign private issuers

A foreign private issuer conducting a Rule 144A or other private offering in the United States must avoid engaging in "general solicitation" before and during its offering so as not to invalidate the private placement exemption. This also includes the foreign issuer's agents, such as its management, personnel, placement agents, attorneys, accountants, underwriters, public relations firm and other representatives. These parties must not make statements to the general public, individually or as a whole, or generate publicity regarding the offering.

If an issuer or its affiliates or agents make statements that could be viewed as general solicitation, the SEC could impose a cooling-off period with respect to US investors (typically a cessation of all fundraising and a moratorium on closings for several months or more, depending on the nature and extent of the publicity). However, there is also a duty to disclose material developments to shareholders and to the markets.

Rule 135c under the Securities Act permits a reporting issuer, including a foreign private issuer or a foreign private issuer that is exempt from registration pursuant to Rule 12(g)3-2(b), to give notice of an unregistered offering without that notice being considered an offer for sale in the United States. The notice must not be intended to condition the US market, and must specify that the securities have not been registered in the United States and that they may not be offered or sold in the United States without being registered or having an exemption from registration. The notice may contain only certain limited information, such as the issuer's name, the title, amount and basic terms of the securities offered, the time and manner of the offering, and a brief statement of the manner and purpose of the offering without the name of the underwriters.

In addition to Rule 135c notice, a foreign private issuer conducting an offering both inside and outside the United States can take advantage of Rule 135e, which permits press releases so long as they occur outside the United States.

Some basic rules are as follows:

- No public statement or comment should be made about the offering or the financial or commercial position or prospects of the issuer, except as approved by counsel and managing underwriter (collectively, the 'advisers').
- All media inquiries about the offering or future developments in relation to the issuer or the issuer's country or industry should be referred to a specific

point person who will consult with the advisers.
- No material information about the issuer that has not already been published should be disclosed unless it has been cleared by the advisers.
- Except as discussed below, marketing materials and corporate communications, such as corporate brochures, press releases and employee communications (whether internal or external and in whatever form), must be vetted in advance by the advisers.
- Normal product advertising that is unrelated to the offering need not be vetted unless it is a significant new campaign or otherwise unusual.
- Normal communications with customers and suppliers are not restricted.
- Any announcement by or for the account of the issuer in respect of the offering should include appropriate legends, set forth below.

The restrictions and procedures discussed in this appendix apply irrespective of the media through which the materials or information are published (ie, press releases, websites, emails, speeches, newsletters, marketing initiatives or communications not in the ordinary course of business), and cover even those materials in the public domain.

1. Offering publicity

All relevant offering publicity must first be reviewed by the designated point person. It should comply with the internal controls normally in place to ensure accuracy. The designated point person should circulate a draft to the advisers to review as soon as possible.

2. Information requests

An issuer is likely to receive oral and written inquiries for information about the offering from the public and institutions as potential investors and also from members of the press. No offering publicity may be provided in response to any inquiries unless it has already been made public in the prospectus, a press release or other formal means. Unsolicited inquiries from journalists in the United States relating to the offering should not be answered and instead should be dealt with on a 'no comment' basis. Unsolicited inquiries from journalists in the United States relating solely to the issuer's business activities must first be discussed with the advisers before any response to ensure that:

- it does not mention the offering;
- no other information other than a direct response is given;
- it does not contain any misstatements about the issuer; and
- only factual information is communicated.

3. General restrictions

No press releases or conferences, publicity or other advertising, communications or presentations about the offering or the financial/commercial position or prospects of the issuer are permitted, except as approved by the advisers. Any publicity and responses to requests for information concerning the offering should be reviewed by the advisers to ensure that it does not contain anything which is material and which will not or could not be repeated in the prospectus.

Accordingly:

- all information must be true and accurate and not misleading (whether by omission of information, inclusion of misleading information or misleading presentation of information);
- under no circumstances should any predictions, projections, forecasts or opinions with respect to the value or to the financial situation of the issuer be published or discussed;
- nothing should be published that contradicts or may contradict anything to be included in the prospectus (eg, information about the issuer, its business, its securities, its country or its markets); and
- no information should be disclosed which could be viewed as specific information concerning the issuer or concerning the trade in the securities that has not been made public if disclosure of such information could reasonably be expected to have a significant effect on the price of the securities, irrespective of the direction of the securities price.

No publicity should contain information in relation to the management (including its track record), operations, financial position, strategy, product portfolio, product pipeline or prospects of the issuer, its investment portfolio or investment pipeline that has not already been made publicly available and verified. No comment should be made as to the relative merits or otherwise of investing in the securities or attributing any value to them. Additionally, the offering (including the anticipated use of proceeds) should not be discussed, except at approved press conferences as described below. References to forecasts or projections regarding the issuer's performance should not be made.

No information should be provided on the regulatory process relating to the offering and no mention should be made of the position of any regulatory authority involved in the offering. Care should be taken to ensure that no information issued prior to the prospectus is capable of being construed as an offer of, or an invitation to acquire, the securities, and that it does not form the basis of, and will not be relied upon in connection with, the contract under which the securities are acquired. It should be clear that the securities will be offered by and on the basis only of information contained in the final prospectus. No references to the US portion of the offering should be made.

4. Press conferences, interviews and press releases

Press conferences and interviews should not be given without being cleared in advance by the advisers and should not include any offering publicity. Press conferences and interviews relating to the issuer or the offering may not be held within the United States. This includes any publicity relating to the offering conducted by conference call where one of the participants is in the United States.

Press conferences and interviews outside of the United States can be held in accordance with local market practice, provided that the information made public at those events are reviewed and verified as described in sections 1 and 2 above of this appendix, and that the advisers have been consulted as to the content of the events. The issuer should also prepare a script of questions and answers likely to be asked, which script must be approved by the advisers.

US reporters may be admitted to press conferences or interviews about the offering, so long as:

- the press conference is open to the press generally and not only to the US media;
- there are no follow-up press contacts with the journalists located in the United States (whether they are US or foreign);
- one-on-one interviews are not given exclusively to members of the US press and are given to non-US press as well; and
- the content of all information communicated in the press conference or interview is verified for accuracy and consistent with the information in the prospectus.

It is helpful to compile a set of pre-approved information that may be freely disclosed, such as data and statistics concerning the issuer and certain aspects of the offering.

Press releases and other written press materials about the issuer or the offering may be released to journalists outside the United States (including US journalists), provided that:

- the materials are available to non-US journalists as well;
- all journalists receiving the materials do so at physical locations and addresses outside the United States;
- the content of the materials is verified for accuracy prior to publication;
- the materials do not include any purchase order or coupon that could be returned indicating interest in the offering; and
- all distributed materials state that they are "not for publication or distribution in or into the United States" and contain a prominent legend substantially as follows:

  > "These materials are not an offer of securities for sale in the United States. The securities of the Issuer have not been and will not be registered under the United States Securities Act of 1933, as amended (the 'Securities Act'), and may not be offered or sold in the United States unless registered under the Securities Act or pursuant to an exemption from such registration. There will be no public offering of the securities in the United States."

Announcements and press releases about the offering should be reviewed in advance by the advisers. They should mention the existence of the prospectus and when it will be published and made available in accordance with the applicable rules, and should include a legend, as approved by the advisers, stating that the announcement does not constitute a prospectus.

5. The Internet

An issuer should avoid posting information on its website concerning a US private offering because websites are considered generally available in the United States and may be found to constitute a general solicitation, even if published by a foreign private issuer from outside the United States. Any information that goes beyond the publication of ordinary-course information relating to factual business developments, advertising, product and marketing information should not be posted on any website, as it may be deemed to be conditioning the market for securities in violation of US law. No mention should be made of the offering and information on the website should be reviewed to make sure it is not outdated (and if so, updated with the old information moved to a separate 'archives' section), conflicts with the information in the prospectus or contains statements that might be viewed as conditioning the US market for the securities.

Particular care should be taken with respect to any hyperlinks on the issuer's website, particularly to websites of any brokers that cover the issuer. Where used, hyperlinks should be accompanied by an express disclaimer that the issuer is not responsible for the information on the hyperlinked site.

6. Permitted publicity

Despite the guidelines above, the issuer should still carry on its normal business activities. The issuer may:

- continue to send out normal reports to shareholders as required by its home country law or regulation;
- continue to publish press releases concerning factual business and historical financial developments, such as a new product or annual or interim financial reports; and
- answer unsolicited telephone inquiries concerning factual information relating to its business, other than concerning the offering.

Ordinary-course advertising of products and services need not be vetted by the advisers, provided that:

- it does not contain any reference to the offering or the securities;
- it does not contain any reference to the financial or other operational performance, investment strategy or affairs or commercial success of the issuer or track record of the issuer;
- the only references to the issuer are to the products and services provided by the issuer (to the extent applicable); and
- it is distributed only through the issuer's normal marketing channels.

Appendix E
Sample timeline for international securities offerings registered with the SEC

A practical consideration for first-time foreign private issuers is that it may take several months to prepare the required financial statements and substantial amounts of non-accounting information needed for the required SEC disclosures, depending on the availability of the information and the management resources available to help prepare it.

It is advisable to first take the steps necessary to:

- prepare the necessary financial statements, including reconciliation of home country financial statements with US GAAP or preparation under IFRS;
- undertake 'corporate cleaning' to make sure the governance procedures in place comply with Sarbanes-Oxley and applicable listing standards;
- translate any exhibits that will be filed with the registration statement; and
- decide whether confidential treatment will be requested for any of the exhibits.

continued overleaf

Pre-filing period 'quiet period' Issuer is prohibited from making offers or sales of the securities to be registered	Stage 1 Weeks 1-3	• Issuer selects counsel and underwriter. • Issuer organises necessary financial statements and other corporate documents. • Organisational meetings are held with issuer, issuer counsel and underwriter, underwriter's counsel and auditors to discuss timing and size of offering, responsibility for tasks, financial statements, anticipated issues with respect to stockholders with registration rights and disclosure and corporate clean-up issues. • Underwriter and counsel conduct due diligence (review material contracts, litigation, financial statements and presentations by management). • Commence drafting initial registration statement. • Commence drafting underwriting agreement. • Select stock exchange, reserve trading symbols and prepare listing application.
	Stage 2 Weeks 4-8	• Compile exhibits to registration statement. • Determine which exhibits, if any, require confidential treatment and prepare request for confidential treatment. • Select co-underwriters and finalise underwriting agreement. • Commence drafting comfort letter. • Complete registration statement. • Finalise audited financial statements.

continued overleaf

Waiting period SEC reviews and comments on registration statement. Oral offers are permissible. Written offers can be made through a preliminary prospectus. No sales allowed.	Stage 3 Weeks 9-13	• File registration statement and exhibits with SEC via its EDGAR database. • Submit request for confidential treatment to SEC, if necessary. • File stock exchange application, including copy of registration statement. • Begin preparing road show marketing materials.
	Stage 4 Weeks 14-16	• Receive comments from SEC. • Resolve any issues with stock exchange. • Prepare and file amendments to registration statement as necessary until SEC staff has no further comments. • Print preliminary (or 'red herring') prospectus. • Commence road shows (two to three weeks). • Receive stock exchange listing approval. • Begin preparing closing documents such as closing memorandum, legal opinions and certificates. • Finalise comfort letter.
Effective period Both offers and sales can be made to public.	Stage 5 Week 16	• Submit a request to the SEC to declare the registration effective. • Registration statement is declared effective by SEC. • Hold pricing call day before offering. • Sign all underwriting documents such as underwriting agreement and agreement among underwriters. • Deliver comfort letter. • Issue press release announcing offering. • Finalise and print final prospectus. • Begin market-making activities. • File final prospectus with SEC via EDGAR and deliver final prospectus to stock exchange.
Closing	Stage 6 Week 17	• Closing – no later than three business days after pricing. • Sign closing documents. • Distribute the securities.

Appendix F
Sample legend for Regulation S, Regulation D and Rule 144A offerings

Transactions in the securities offered hereby have not been registered under the US Securities Act of 1933 and they may not be offered or sold within the United States or to US persons except pursuant to an exemption from the registration requirements of such Securities Act. Accordingly, the securities are being offered hereby in US only to a limited number of 'accredited investors' (as defined in Regulation D) who execute a letter containing certain representations and agreements that the securities may be resold without registration only (1) to the issuer, (2) to persons reasonably believed to be qualified institutional buyers (as defined in Rule 144A), (3) in accordance with Regulation S or Rule 144, or (4) pursuant to another exemption from the Securities Act's registration requirements that is confirmed to be applicable by an opinion of counsel.

Appendix G
Sample jurisdictional warning for foreign private issuers

[Issuer] is organised under the laws of [foreign country]. Most of its directors and officers and certain of the experts named herein are residents of [foreign country], and all or a substantial portion of the assets of most of such persons and of [issuer] are located in [foreign country]. As a result, it may not be possible for investors to effect service of process in the United States upon such persons or to enforce against them or against [issuer] in United States courts judgments predicated upon the civil liability provisions of the federal securities laws of the US. [Issuer] has been advised by [foreign country] counsel that there is doubt as to the enforceability, in original actions in [foreign country] courts, of liabilities predicated solely on the US federal securities laws and as to the enforceability in [foreign country] courts of judgments of US courts obtained in actions predicated upon the civil liability provisions of the US federal securities laws.

Appendix H
Sample legend for exchange offers by foreign private issuers

This exchange offer or business combination is made for the securities of a foreign private issuer. The offer is subject to disclosure requirements of a foreign country that are different from those of the United States. Financial statements included in the document, if any, have been prepared in accordance with foreign accounting standards that may not be comparable to the financial statements of US companies.

It may be difficult for you to enforce your rights and any claim you may have arising under US securities laws, given that the issuer is located in a foreign country, and some or all of its officers and directors may be residents of a foreign country. You may not be able to sue a foreign private issuer or its officers or directors in a foreign court for violations of the US securities laws. It may be difficult to compel a foreign private issuer and its affiliates to subject themselves to a US court's judgment.

You should be aware that the issuer may purchase securities otherwise than under the exchange offer, such as in an open market or privately negotiated purchases.

Appendix I Listing standards on US national securities exchanges for international companies

NYSE

The NYSE offers two standards that foreign private issuers may use to qualify for listing: worldwide and domestic. An issuer must qualify for both the distribution and financial criteria within that particular standard.

	Worldwide	Domestic
Distribution	5,000 round-lot holders/total shareholders.	• 400 US round-lot shareholders; • 2,200 total shareholders and 100,000 shares monthly trading volume; or • 500 total shareholders and 1 million shares monthly trading volume.
	2.5 million public shares.	1.1 million public shares.
	$100 million public market value.	$40 million initial public offerings, carve-outs and spin-offs. $100 million all other listings.
Financials	$100 million aggregate pre-tax income for the last three years.	$10 million aggregate pre-tax income for the last three years (or $12 million with different minimum pre-tax income requirements).
	$25 million minimum pre-tax income in each of the two preceding years.	$2 million minimum pre-tax income in each of the two preceding years.
	Must also satisfy the requirements of either the valuation with cash-flow test or the pure valuation test. Affiliates newly registering must have a global market capitalisation of $500 million under either standard.	

NASDAQ

Global select market: initial listing

For initial listing, companies must meet one of the four financial standards set forth below and the applicable liquidity requirement.

Financial and qualitative requirements

Requirement	Standard 1	Standard 2	Standard 3	Standard 4
Pre-tax earnings (income from continuing operations before income taxes)	Aggregate in prior three fiscal years greater than $11 million; in each of the two most recent fiscal years greater than $2 million; and in each of the prior three fiscal years greater than $0.	Not applicable.	Not applicable.	Not applicable.
Cash flows	Not applicable.	Aggregate in prior three fiscal years greater than $27.5 million, and in each of the prior three fiscal years greater than $0.	Not applicable.	Not applicable.
Market capitalisation	Not applicable.	Average greater than $550 million over prior 12 months.	Average greater than $850 million over prior 12 months.	$160 million.

continued overleaf

Requirement	Standard 1	Standard 2	Standard 3	Standard 4
Revenue	Not applicable.	Previous fiscal year greater than $110 million.	Previous fiscal year greater than $90 million.	
Total assets	Not applicable.	Not applicable.	Not applicable.	$80 million in the most recently completed fiscal year.
Stockholders' equity	Not applicable.	Not applicable.	Not applicable.	$55 million.
Bid price	$4.	$4.	$4.	$4.
Market makers	3 or 4.	3 or 4.	3 or 4.	3 or 4.
Corporate governance	Yes.	Yes.	Yes.	Yes.

continued overleaf

Liquidity requirements

Requirements	Initial pubic offerings and spin-off companies	Seasoned companies: currently trading common stock of equivalents	Affiliated companies
Number of round-lot shareholders or total shareholders or total shareholders and average monthly trading volume over the past 12 months.	450 or 2,200 or 550 and 1.1. million	450 or 2,200 or 550 and 1.1 million.	4450 or 2,200 or 550 and 1.1 million.
Publicly held shares.	1.25 million.	1.25 million.	1.25 million.
Market value of publicly held shares or market value of publicly held shares and stockholders' equity.	$45 million.	$110 million or $100 million and $110 million.	$45 million.

Global select market: continued listing

Requirements	Equity standard	Market value standard	Total assets/total revenue standard.
Stockholders' equity	$10 million.	Not applicable.	Not applicable.
Market value of listed securities	Not applicable.	$50 million.	Not applicable.
Total assets and total revenue (in latest fiscal year or in two of the last three fiscal years)	Not applicable.	Not applicable.	$50 million and $50 million.
Publicly held shares	750,000.	1.1 million.	1.1 million.
Market value of publicly held shares	$5 million.	$15 million.	$15 million.
Bid price	$1.	$1.	$1.
Total shareholders	400.	400.	400.
Market makers	2.	4.	4.
Corporate governance	Yes.	Yes.	Yes.

For more on listing on the NYSE and NASDAQ, see the section on listing on national securities exchanges in "Public offerings".

List of certain defined terms

ADRs: American depositary receipts.
CEO: Chief executive officer.
CFO: Chief financial officer.
CLO: Chief legal officer.
D&O: Directors and officers.
Dodd-Frank Act: Dodd-Frank Wall Street Reform and Consumer Protection Act of 2010.
DOJ: US Department of Justice.
EDGAR: Electronic Data Gathering, Analysis and Retrieval system.
Exchange Act: Securities Exchange Act of 1934.
FASB: Financial Accounting Standards Board.
Federal Reserve: US Federal Reserve Board.
GAAP: Generally accepted accounting principles.
IASB: International Accounting Standards Board.
IFRS: International Financial Reporting Standards.
IPO: Initial public offering.
MD&A: Management's discussion and analysis of financial condition and results of operations.
NASD: National Association of Securities Dealers.
NASDAQ: NASDAQ Stock Market.
NYSE: New York Stock Exchange.
PCAOB: Public Company Accounting Oversight Board.
QIB: Qualified institutional buyer.
Sarbanes-Oxley Act: Sarbanes-Oxley Act of 2002.
SEC: US Securities and Exchange Commission.
Securities Act: Securities Act of 1933.
US GAAP: Generally accepted accounting principles in the United States.

About the authors

Eduardo Vidal
Partner, Hughes Hubbard & Reed LLP
vidal@hugheshubbard.com

Eduardo Vidal is co-chairman of the Latin America practice group at the law firm of Hughes Hubbard & Reed LLP in New York. He has extensive experience in international corporate transactions, including capital markets offerings, cross-border mergers and acquisitions, syndicated loan financings, private equity investments and financial restructurings. Mr Vidal has advised local companies, multinational corporations and international financial institutions throughout Latin America.

He received his BA in 1978 and JD in 1981 from the University of Chicago. He is fluent in Spanish and has a reading knowledge of Portuguese. He is listed in Euromoney's *Expert Guide to the World's Leading Capital Markets Lawyers* and in *Chambers* as a leading lawyer in Latin America investments. He is a frequent guest commentator on *CNN en Español* and *Desde Wall Street.*

Jan JH Joosten
Partner, Hughes Hubbard & Reed LLP
joosten@hugheshubbard.com

Jan Joosten is a corporate partner in the New York office of Hughes Hubbard & Reed LLP. His practice includes securities transactions, mergers and acquisitions and joint ventures, especially involving Dutch and other European companies. Mr Joosten received a master of civil law degree and a master of tax law degree in 1991 from the University of Leiden, the Netherlands, and an LLM in 1992 from Harvard Law School. He is a member of the New York Bar. Mr Joosten is fluent in Dutch and has a working knowledge of French and German. He lectures frequently on various aspects of US law, including securities regulation.

Index